Data for Business Performance

The Goal-Question-Metric (GQM) Model to Transform Business Data into an Enterprise Asset

Prashanth H Southekal, PhD

Foreword by Dr. Thomas C Redman

Published by:

2 Lindsley Road
Basking Ridge, NJ 07920 USA

https://www.TechnicsPub.com

Cover design by John Fiorentino
Edited by Lauren McCafferty

ISBN, print ed.   9781634621847
ISBN, Kindle ed.   9781634621854
ISBN, ePub ed.   9781634621861
ISBN, PDF ed.   9781634621878

First Printing 2017

Library of Congress Control Number: 2016961223

Endorsements

This book is absolutely timely and relevant in today's data-driven world. Most of the books on data available in the market today focus on Data Quality, Governance, and Analytics. This book from Dr. Prashanth Southekal is brilliant as it puts the business stakeholder at the center by addressing the key value propositions of the business user. This book is holistic and I strongly believe it will help to bridge the gaps we have today.

Mario Faria
Managing Vice President, Gartner, US

In today's era of Digital Transformation, Data and Information are more important than ever. But deep understanding of how to manage data and information properly is in short supply. That is what I love about this book by Dr. Southekal. He tangibly closes that gap for the reader. If you are using Digital Transformation to improve your Business Performance, this book and its discussion of Data's role in improving Business Performance is for you.

Michael Fulton
President, Americas Division, CC and C Solutions, US

Packed with insights and leveraging a process oriented approach, this book covers a unique combination of the science, the art and the strategy of unlocking the potential of Data for enterprises in a real life context. The author has managed to provide a clear action plan for creating data analytics and its management a key function in a modern enterprise.

Ashish Sonal (Vir Chakra)
CEO, Orkash, India

This book is one of the most practical sources for how companies can greatly improve their bottom line by improved data management and becoming a data-centric company. It combines leading data management theory with step-by-step implementation and real-life examples, and is a must-read for those wanting to derive more value from their corporate data.

Lance Calleberg
Application Architect, Husky Energy, Canada

Certainly, an engaging read for both information management practitioners and business unit managers alike. The tools, models and frameworks prescribed are valuable, relevant and lucidly blend inputs from the real-world to address numerous data management glitches at organizations. Overall, a compelling read with several practical takeaways. Refreshing!

Sriram Kannan
Digital & Analytics Practice Leader, IBM, India

Prashanth has given a very practical guide to implement data culture in an organization. The book **Data for Business Performance** talks about building the organization of the future and the role of data. Prashanth rightly believes and demonstrates that data is not an asset of the IT team and is an organization-wide asset. He proposes the need for the chief data officer (CDO) as a role that should anchor data and report to the CEO, and manage the stakeholders' data needs.

Harshajith Umapathy
Senior Vice President, Hansa Cequity, India

Dr. Southekal provides valuable insights on data and information management in mostly short and clearly written sections. Anyone interested in the data-driven company should read this book and learn about the hurdles on the road to be data-driven and his valuable suggestions on how to overcome them. His wisdom may prevent some of the failures that helped him learn.

Erik van der Voorden
Domain Architect, Independent Consultant, Netherlands

Data can tell us important stories when we process it by proven and structured approaches. Dr. Southekal's book presents such an approach based on the GQM method for transforming business data into an enterprise asset. This book is a valuable resource for organizations willing to become a real data-driven organization.

Ahmet Dikici, PhD
Project Manager, Tubitak Bilgem Software Technologies, Turkey

Acknowledgements

This book is a reflection of over two decades of my industry experience; there are many people who have positively impacted this project. Writing this book was a unique learning and collaborative experience and it has definitely been one of my best "investments" to date. During the entire book writing project, I had the privilege of having discussions with top researchers and industry practitioners world over who were instrumental in giving a better shape to this book.

First and foremost, I thank renowned analytics and data quality expert Dr. Thomas Redman for writing the foreword for the book. When the thought of writing the book came to me in the summer of 2015, Dr. Redman was the one who encouraged me to take up this project and provided me with the right support and guidance. I would like to express my sincere gratitude to Steve Hoberman, publisher of Technics for publishing this book, Lauren McCafferty for her patience and commitment in doing a fantastic job in editing this book, and John Fiorentino for the excellent cover design. I am also thankful to the following business and IT leaders for sharing their experiences as interviews in the book. Their interviews are covered in Appendix A.

1. Mario Faria, Managing Vice President, Gartner, US
2. Bob Pollock, CIO, Cenovus Energy, Canada
3. Rohit Girdhar, VP, Infineon Technologies, Singapore
4. Ram Kumar, SVP, QBE Insurance, Hong Kong
5. Dr. Brandon Rohrer, Senior Data Scientist, Researcher and Author, US
6. Tobias Eckert, CIO, Leapple AG, Germany
7. Melanie Mecca, Director, CMMI Institute, Carnegie Melon University, US
8. Paul Zikopoulos, Vice President, Big Data and Analytics, IBM, Canada
9. Vibhav Agarwal, SVP, Reliance Power, India

Special thanks to Lance Calleberg and Marc Nolte for taking time to proofread the book and give valuable feedback. I am extremely grateful to my former employers and clients for providing me opportunities to learn and understand the nuances of managing digital transformation initiatives.

Finally, writing a book while running my own IT advisory companies **DBP-Institute** (DBP stands for Data for Business Performance) and **Catyeus** included many hours away from my family. It took me about two years to write this book. My wife Shruthi and my two wonderful kids Pranathi "Panna" and Prathik "Peeku" understood how important this book is for me and bestowed me with terrific support.

Contents at a Glance

Contents

Foreword

As I write these words, the technology and data landscapes are confused messes.

Technology is advancing at a rapid clip: machine learning is rushing into areas previously untouched by automation; cloud computing is unleashing vast new capabilities AND driving down cost; and the Internet of Things is putting devices everywhere, promising unprecedented productivity gains. It is easy to become equally intoxicated and threatened by the likelihood that all one's dreams may be answered, that technologies on the horizon will "change everything." And indeed, there are plenty of "points of light" that demonstrate the promises may be real!

The reality for most is far more humble: most applications are mediocre and expensive, systems "don't talk," and the failure rate of Tech projects is well north of fifty percent. It is easy to become disenchanted!

Similarly, big data, advanced analytics, and data-driven decision-making are all the rage. And again, there are many points of light. Many have gotten in front of data quality issues and made enormous gains, saving themselves millions in the process. Others have gained fresh insights into buying patterns, ways to streamline logistics, and otherwise further their businesses by diving into their data. Indeed, Google and Uber have made enormous businesses by helping people find the data they need and simply connecting, "I need a ride" with "I'm looking for a fare."

Of course, the reality for most is far more mundane: People don't trust data, analysts waste enormous amounts of time dealing with basic quality issues, decision-makers still rely on their intuition alone, and far too many big data/analytics projects fail. It is easy to grow frustrated and decide to merely wait until others sort out how these ideas will work in practice.

The problem is not simply that so many tech and data initiatives fail — they can fail spectacularly. The notion of slicing and dicing mortgages into Collateralized Debt Obligations (essentially tranches) that better meet the risk/reward tradeoffs sought by different investors was brilliant! It satisfied investors, made billions for those who packaged them, and helped people buy homes who otherwise couldn't. Until, of course, the whole scheme was laid low by bad data, on mortgage applications, in ratings, and on balance sheets. The ensuing chaos caused the financial crisis. While all were hurt, those who lost their homes and livelihoods were devastated.

Unfortunately, it gets even worse. As Cathy O'Neil so eloquently describes in *Weapons of Math Destruction*, even apparently successful efforts can have negative consequences. She cites example after example of people who've lost their jobs, couldn't get new ones, paid more for credit, and on and on. It is easy to conclude it is time to run — not walk — away!

But growing disenchanted, waiting around, or running away hardly seem like ways forward! A better response includes surveying the landscape, developing a deeper understanding of the potential and the risk, and conducting a series of "experiments" to gain some experience and sort out "what's best for us." Indeed, for most, it is too soon to set a strategy — they simply don't know enough to do so. But it is past time to start gaining that knowledge.

This advice stems from my inherent skepticism of "this changes everything" claims, my read of how progress really happens, and my experiences working with those trying to get in front of data. All of these lead me to the following conclusions:

First, you can't stop progress. The technologies I noted above, plus plenty more, will weave their way into your personal and professional lives, whether you like it or not.

Second, I believe the "winners" will be those with the best data. My rationale is simple — everyone has the same access to technology, but your data are uniquely your own. It is the data that will allow you to distinguish yourself!

Third, "getting there" is going to prove far more challenging than you can imagine. You'll need to make enormous quality improvements, sort out your strategy for competing with data, and build new organizational capabilities. There will be plenty of resistance, lots of failures, and many re-dos.

Finally, "data provocateurs" and leaders, from all levels, will prove decisive! Overcoming the resistance, learning from failures, and trying again and again are not for the faint of heart!

A good first step is to read Prashanth Southekal's new book, *Data for Business Performance*. You'll particularly benefit from three features:

First, Prashanth sorts out the confused language that makes the space so frustrating. Ever wonder about the distinctions between "metadata," "reference data," and "master data" (or why you should care)? You'll find them here.

Second, it provides a way of thinking through the issues: "goals" first, "questions" second, and "metrics" third. Sorting out what's right for your organization is your job; providing a structured way to do so is Prashanth's.

Third, Prashanth recognizes that while there are plenty of good insights, there is far more blather. He skillfully synthesizes insights from Bain, Davenport, Laney, McKinsey, Porter, myself, and others into a cohesive whole. Not everything here will prove useful in your specific circumstances, but it forms a great place to start!

Now get on with it!

Thomas C. Redman
"the Data Doc"
Data Quality Solutions, Rumson, NJ 07760
January 2017

Today, digital transformation is considered the fourth industrial revolution after steam engines, electricity, and information technology. This digital transformation is facilitated primarily by data, and it is seen as a key strategic asset that can enable companies to acquire and sustain a competitive edge. A Forrester Consulting research study found that the key drivers of digital transformation are profitability, customer satisfaction, and increased speed-to-market. These and other benefits have driven many organizations to increasingly undertake efforts to improve data quality, leading to positive impacts on the overall performance of the business. McKinsey Global Institute estimates data to be a 300 billion dollar-a-year industry today.

However, while many companies are investing their resources in improved data and information management, only a few have achieved results that boost business performance. This is primarily due to two main reasons. First, much of today's thinking on managing data originates from an Information Technology (IT)-centric view with emphasis on technology like hardware, applications, and databases. While there exist many resources on data quality, databases, data science, and data governance, what is missing is a comprehensive book devoted to data and information from the usage perspective of the business stakeholder. The business stakeholder is an important player in digital transformation, as he or she is the one who derives value from data. Second, there are numerous insightful reports available from research, analysis, and advisory firms that indicate the high cost of poor data quality and poor utilization of data. But there is very little practical guidance to help business enterprises to move their data up the value chain and leverage it for business performance.

ABOUT THE BOOK

To address these two gaps, this book provides readers with practical guidance and proven solutions to derive value from data in the business context. Specifically, the book has five key elements that will make it unique in the marketplace:

1. This book is **holistic**. Today, deriving value from data is almost synonymous with insight. But insights aren't the only reason enterprises use data. They use data for compliance, and to facilitate better customer service. Hence this book looks at all three of these important purposes of data and its management, using ten key data and information lifecycle functions.

2. This book is for **practitioners,** by practitioners. It is based on my experience in data, information management, and business transformation projects in companies such as GE, SAP, P&G, Accenture, and Deloitte, to name a few. Along with my experience, business and IT leaders from companies such as Gartner, Infineon Technologies, QBE, IBM, and many more have shared their experiences in the book as interviews. This book also includes real world case studies of data and information management initiatives across diverse industry sectors.

3. This book is **relevant.** Organizations operate under stiff competition, expanded business networks, and emerging technologies such as cloud computing, social media, NoSQL, big data, in-memory computing, machine learning, and many more. Businesses are looking to technology to connect people and machines with each other, or with data and information. This book caters to this current business and IT landscape.

4. This book is **novel**. I have used GQM (Goal-Question-Metric), a proven performance management framework, and derived a ten-step data management model that can help practitioners to harness the value of

business data. Essentially, this book looks at the GQM framework as the core mechanism to monetize data for the organization.

5. This book is **technologically agnostic**. Many books available in the market are IT product-centric. Unfortunately, system integrators and management consulting companies are usually influenced by their partnerships with IT product vendors. This book looks at the technical concepts without any reference to proprietary vendor technologies. Any business leader who is keen to derive value from data can use this book, regardless of which IT products they utilize.

ORGANIZATION OF THE BOOK

This book is organized into three parts — **Define, Analyze,** and **Realize** — with nine chapters among them. Chapter 10 provides a summary of all nine chapters.

Part 1 builds for readers a common foundational understanding by **defining** key terms and concepts pertaining to digital transformation. It looks at the different processes needed to transform data into a business asset, and the role of technology in this digital transformation journey. But data per se is of little value to the business. What businesses need is quality data from which to draw information, gain knowledge about the current business situation, and glean wisdom to make decisions on the future course of action. Moving up the data value chain to derive value has been challenging for most companies.

Hence part 2 of this book focuses on **analyzing** the key challenges that prevent enterprises from moving up the data value chain. This section also looks at solutions that are practical and actionable. Once the analysis is performed, the next phase is implementation; this is where most digital transformation initiatives fail.

Part 3 provides some practical **realization** strategies needed to transform business data into an enterprise asset. While it is important to implement a good data and management initiative, it is also critical to sustain the initiative so that enterprises can continue to derive value from data. As such, part 3 also looks at aspects such as frameworks, standards, procedures, guidelines, and change management to effectively and efficiently sustain the investments made on data management. The organization of this book and the purpose of each chapter are as shown below.

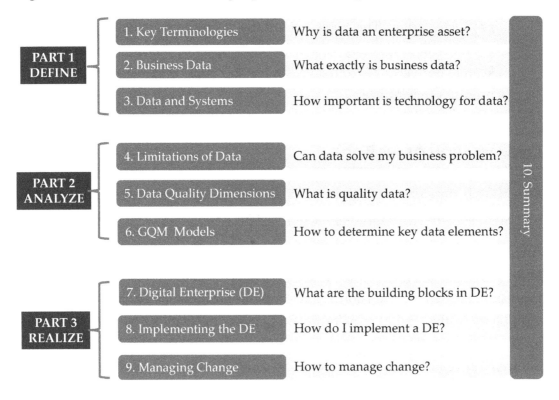

Book chapters

To further support these ten chapters, appendix A includes the results of interviews with key business and IT leaders on the role of data and information in digital transformation. Appendix B contains references, appendix C a list of abbreviations, and appendix D the glossary.

Below is a simple flow chart to help the reader make the decision.

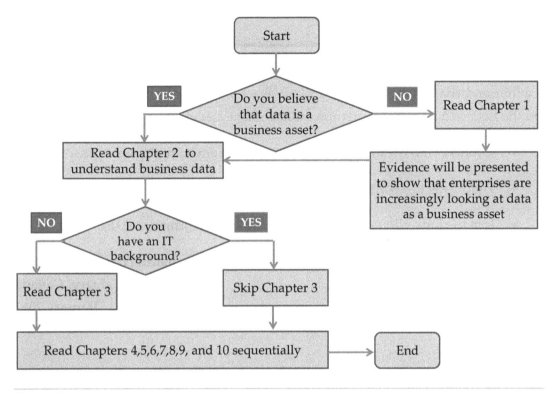

Chapter flow chart

WHO SHOULD READ THIS BOOK?

This book will explain in simple terms the core concepts of data management, with emphasis on those relevant to a business enterprise. It will also provide enterprises a step-by-step methodology to derive value from data. However, there are no perquisites needed to read and apply the concepts mentioned in this book. The book is intended for anyone who has a stake and interest in harnessing the value of business data. The audience could be the Business President, Chief Data Officer, Chief Information Officer, Procurement Director, Accounting Analyst, Data Scientist, HR Manager, Enterprise Architect, a Business Analytics student, or even an IT Database Administrator. In a line, this book is for anyone who wants to derive **more value** from business data (provided the initiative is driven with senior management support).

Stay in Touch

Let us keep the conversation going. You can get in touch with me on LinkedIn or Twitter and share your thoughts and feedback not only about the book, but also on the field of data and information management. Let us learn from each other.

- Connect with me in LinkedIn at www.linkedin.com/in/prashanthsouthekal

- Follow me in Twitter at https://twitter.com/prash_sh

- Join the LinkedIn group **Data for Business Performance (DBP)**

Prashanth H Southekal, PhD
Calgary, Canada
January 2017

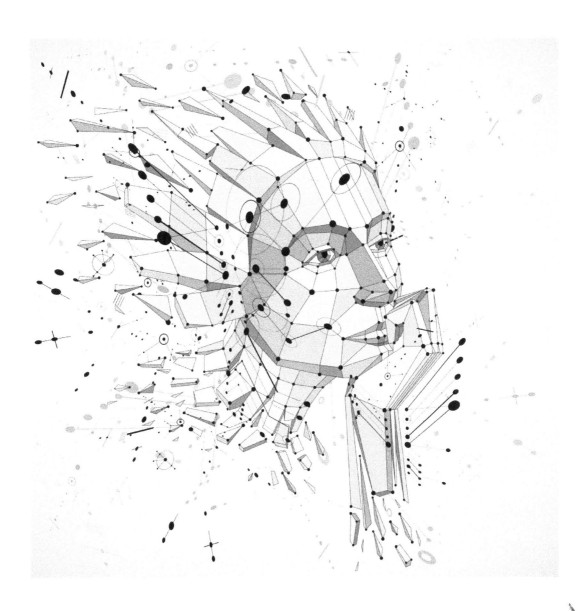

Chapter 1: Establishing the Terminology

In God we trust. All others must bring data.

Edwards Deming, American Scientist

Information Technology (IT) is one of the key strategic functions in most organizations, because data in IT systems enables organizations in almost every industry sector to work more efficiently, improve decision making, and maximize productivity. For example, the CEO of the multinational investment firm Goldman Sachs, Lloyd Blankfein, referred to his firm as a "tech company" to emphasize the key role of IT and data in investment. In 2016, logistics company UPS decided to invest $1 billion to leverage data in logistics. General Electric has clearly declared its intent to reinvent itself as a data company. Oil field services company Schlumburger captures drilling data from simulators and sensors to improve drilling performance in oil wells. Nestle, a global food and beverage company, leverages social media data to analyze sentiments of over 2000 brands in near real-time.

It is not just business enterprises that are gaining from the digital wave. Consumers are also reaping significant benefits from improved digitization happening within the business enterprises. Today homeowners can get a real-time report of their electricity consumption. It is estimated that over 50 percent of air travel tickets are now purchased online after comparing prices from different airlines. Life insurance companies are increasingly looking at data and analytics to simplify business processes, trim the amount of time to get insurance, and cut back expenses. These changes not only save insurance companies money, but also cater to consumer's desire for less invasive and time consuming medical tests.

IT, through digitization, is fundamentally changing the business landscape by providing more opportunities for delivering business strategies. While the data managed in IT systems brings tangible business benefits, lack of data results in adverse consequences. In 2016, the total cost for just a five-hour IT outage for Delta Airlines was $150 million, due to delays in data processing. A data glitch in HSBC's IT systems resulted in over 275,000 delayed payments in UK in 2015.

To harness potential benefits (and avoid potential losses) of data managed in IT systems, organizations are investing in improved IT infrastructure. According to PricewaterhouseCoopers (PwC), a "big four" consultancy firm, in most companies today IT expenses find a place in the five largest general ledger (GL) expenses; in some industries the annual IT spend is as high as 10 percent of total operating costs.

Where is this IT investment specifically going? Fundamentally, the IT investments from the business perspective are primarily for data management activities. The businesses do not care much about server configuration, operating system versions, or even the latest software patches. Businesses are concerned with data held within the IT systems and the competitive advantage gleaned from that data.

In the last ten years, data has gradually replaced hardware and software as the key tool for deriving competitive advantage. This is partly because both hardware and software have become much more commoditized and optimized. For example, VMware's server virtualization platform vSphere and SAP's Ariba cloud solution for procurement can be deployed as standard out-of-the box solutions for any organization in the world. Though hardware and software bring repeatability, consistency, scalability, integration, security and visibility to the business processes, most enterprises have optimized them; there isn't much more room for improvement. If these enterprises want to move forward, they must look to new avenues for advancement; data provides these opportunities to derive business performance.

For example, Netflix has publicly released much of its custom infrastructure and monitoring software, but has not shared its data. Netflix has massive amounts of data about its users' viewing habits, and can break it down by region, time of day, watching hours, and more. This has put Netflix in the unique position of being able to accurately predict what viewers want and create customized offerings, thereby gaining an edge over competitors. It is not just Netflix that has leveraged data for business performance. Many enterprises such as GE, Amazon, and Monsanto have leveraged data to differentiate themselves in the marketplace.

One of the key differentiating elements for businesses today is effective and efficient management of data and information. Forrester says "Data is a source of business innovation. We are seeing firms innovating with data." Overall, digitization is dramatically changing the business landscape; many organizations have started to treat data as a real and measureable business asset for business performance. The data economy (i.e. the ecosystem that enables exchange of digitized information for business performance) is becoming increasingly embraced worldwide. But many organizations that embark on digital transformation journeys struggle to get value even from high-quality data. There are many reasons for this, from strategy to planning to execution to sustainment.

But before we go any further, let us first look at the title of this book — Data for Business Performance: The Goal-Question-Metric (GQM) Model to Transform Business Data into an Enterprise Asset —and understand the key elements that make up this title. We will start by introducing the GQM Model, defining data, enterprise, asset, and transformation — all in relation to data and business performance.

UNDERSTANDING THE GQM MODEL

The Goal-Question-Metric (GQM) method was formulated by Victor Basili, Emeritus Professor of Computer Science at the University of Maryland, to provide a methodology for defining goals, refining them into questions, and formulating metrics for data collection, analysis and decision making. Fundamentally, GQM is a measurement model based on a goal, a question, and metrics. A **goal** is a desired result that a person or a system envisions, plans, and commits to achieve within a finite time. **Questions** characterize the assessment or achievement of the specific goal. Finally **metrics** are objective measurements associated with every question, to track performance toward answering the question. The GQM method will be covered in detail in chapters 6 and 8.

UNDERSTANDING DATA

Data is the representation of real world entities and events as text, numbers, images, sound or video; this representation allows for better encapsulation, analysis, processing, and usage. Generally, data is a gathered body of facts in an unorganized format to represent, conditions, ideas, categories or objects. The key characteristics of data are:

- Data is captured with a purpose

- Data is stored in a medium

- Data is repetitive, reproducible, and renewable in nature

- Data is always encoded in a specific format

Technically the word "data" is plural while "datum" is singular. However, in the business world, "data" is often considered singular; so it will be throughout the book.

Furthermore, there is a clear difference between data and information. When data is processed, structured or presented in a given context so as to make it useful, it is known as information. The context is typically provided by the consumer of data. Basically, data becomes information when it is applied for a purpose and brings value to the consumer. Once the information is available, knowledge is derived, and knowledge gives rise to wisdom. The journey or progression from data to information, to knowledge, and finally to wisdom is known DIKW Model, or the "data value chain." Chapter 9 covers the DIKW model in detail.

UNDERSTANDING THE ENTERPRISE

Businesses are managed at different organizational levels such as enterprise, company, lines of business (LoB), and geographic units. However, the word "enterprise" is often associated with terms like entrepreneur, enterprise class, enterprise solutions, enterprise architecture, and digital enterprise. So what really is meant by "enterprise," and what differentiates the "enterprise" from a company or a LoB or even a business function?

The Oxford dictionary defines an enterprise as a business, but it's much more than that. An enterprise is a sector-level grouping of organizational entities with similar economic characteristics. According to Canadian computer scientists Mark Fox and Michael Gruninger, an enterprise encompasses structure, activities, processes, information, resources, people, behavior, goals, and constraints [Fox and Gruninger, 1998]. An enterprise can even have multiple companies, organizational levels, locations, divisions or departments that collaborate to leverage economies of scale. An enterprise is governed by the frequency, risk profile, jurisdiction, and value of the business transactions it has with its suppliers, customers, government, employees, regulators, competitors, and other business partners.

In his book *Reimagine Business Excellence in an Age of Disruption*, renowned management strategist Tom Peters said "An enterprise at its best is an emotional, vital, innovative, joyful, creative, entrepreneurial endeavor that elicits maximum concerted human potential in pursuit of excellence and the wholehearted provision of service to others." Hence, an enterprise is a multidimensional organizational entity that reflects, among other dimensions, a defined purpose, sense of action, complexity, and value for the stakeholders — both internal and external.

How, then, is an enterprise associated with an industry sector and other business entities (such as company, LoB, or business function)? An industry sector is a close grouping of similar businesses, and the businesses within the industry sector are managed as enterprises. Within an enterprise there can be many companies. A company is fundamentally a legal entity at a specific jurisdiction that is set up for generating profits by trading goods, services, or both. In its simplest form, a company has defined purpose and accountability as per the legal terms and conditions of the particular jurisdiction. Jurisdiction in the business context refers to the geographic area where the business is incorporated. Typically the company can be set up as a sole trader, partnership, limited liability company (LLC), or even as a corporation. A company can have multiple lines of business (LoB), which are revenue generating entities associated with growth and profitability. According to the research and advisory firm Gartner, a LoB is a corporate subdivision focused on a single product or family of products or services. Finally, within a LoB there could be multiple business functions, such as procurement, marketing, human resources, and engineering, among others.

To summarize, an enterprise is a broad aggregation of companies at the sector level, typically in multiple industries. A company is an aggregation based on products, services, and other characteristics operating at a specific jurisdiction. A company typically has multiple business units called LoBs, which are each aligned to products or services or geographic segmentation to drive focus and profitability. A LoB includes many business functions or departments that routinely carry out the mission of the LoB, company, and enterprise. The relationship between enterprise, company, LoB, and business function is shown in the figure below.

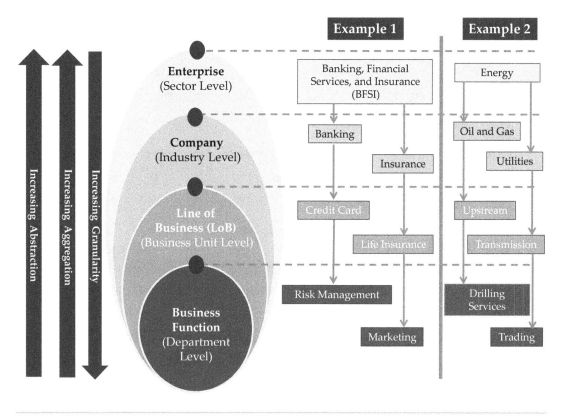

Organizational structure

ASSOCIATING ENTERPRISE AND DATA

So why should the data be associated with the enterprise? Why can't data be linked to the company or LoB or even to the business function? Some of the major changes in the business landscape over the past two decades include increased globalization, stringent laws and regulations, and improved internet connectivity. While this trend is enabling businesses to operate in new markets, it is also exposing the businesses to increased risks.

To minimize risk, businesses or enterprises are no longer focused on working in one jurisdiction; businesses are consolidating their functions, collaborating with external partners, and operating as single entities by consolidating different business units. When operating as a single business entity, visibility across operations provides competitive advantage. This visibility can be seen only when the organization is managed at the highest level — that of the enterprise. When it comes to digitization, data that is specific to the enterprise brings the right levels of abstraction and aggregation to empower business performance.

- **Abstraction.** Complexity is a major reason for increased cost, schedule overruns, and poor quality in business. From the digitization perspective, one approach to reduce complexity is "abstracting," also known as "information hiding." In the enterprise context, abstraction of the data reduces complexity by providing only those details that are common to every organizational entity. Following this idea, a fundamental rule of data governance is "collect once and use many." This refers to the practicality of collecting data just once at the enterprise level, and then sharing it across the organization. For example, different geographic legal entities of Walmart transact with different geographic legal entities of P&G. If data elements are managed locally across these legal entities in both P&G and Walmart, the data management would be chaotic and inefficient in both P&G and Walmart. The efficiency can only be achieved if the collaboration between P&G and Walmart is at the highest level, i.e. the enterprise level.

- **Aggregation**. Aggregation is the process of drawing patterns on the current or future needs, and normalizing those patterns. Aggregation in the data context helps in standardizing different data sets, from different systems and formats, into a common enterprise data model. For example, aggregating product data across the enterprise can provide new opportunities for cross-selling across companies and LoBs. Sophisticated analysis of sales data sets can allow precise segmentation of customers in order to tailor products and services. If there is no effort to aggregate data at the enterprise level, efforts at lower levels will result in poor data model structure, poor accessibility, and untrustworthy data.

Fundamentally managing data at the enterprise level enables a high degree of abstraction and aggregation, thereby facilitating efficient and effective management of data across the entire business value chain and the data lifecycle – from origination to purging or archival. Hence, from cost, quality, and schedule perspectives, data management is most effective and efficient when managed at enterprise level. Data management at the enterprise level with the right level of abstraction and aggregation helps in the optimization of the end-to-end business value chain.

UNDERSTANDING THE ASSET

In today's data economy, the valuations of many enterprises such as Google, Amazon, and Facebook are typically based on two things: their potential to generate profits from their user base, and the amount of data they manage. For example, in 2015 Facebook was worth about $250 billion. Air Canada, a company that actually owns tangible assets like airplanes and has licenses to use airport facilities and operate world over, was worth only $34 billion in the same year. In 2013, Johnson & Johnson purchased Synthesis, a medical device manufacturer, for $19 billion; this was significantly cheaper than Microsoft's acquisition of LinkedIn for $26 billion in 2016. But in 2015, LinkedIn's profit was only $166 million, while Synthesis' profit stood at $966 million. In 2015, IBM acquired the Weather Company, which provides weather content from over 195,000 weather stations, for $2 billion. While many analysts were surprised at this acquisition of a weather company by a technology company which was in a completely different industry sector, a year later, IBM used the data from the Weather Company and addressed retailers' concerns of bad weather with a global forecasting model that worked at 0.2 mile resolution. These are some examples reflecting the shift in enterprise valuation, accounting, and business strategy from tangible to intangible assets such as data.

In the world of financial accounting, a business asset is typically an economic resource that can be owned or controlled such that it has monetary value. According to the International Accounting Standards Board (IASB), an asset is a resource controlled by the enterprise as a result of past events, and from which future economic benefit is expected to flow to the enterprise. In simple words, assets represent value that can be easily converted into cash or legal tender. Against this backdrop, enterprises have traditionally reported both tangible and intangible assets such as cash, machinery, land, buildings, brands, inventory, intellectual property, copyrights, and even employees as current and fixed assets in their balance sheets.

While tangible resources such as money, machinery, land, and buildings have been considered business assets for quite some time, treating an intangible commodity like data as an enterprise asset is a recent trend. Prior to this, data was considered to be an enabler or supporter of other businesses processes; the real benefits of effective data management were intertwined within the business processes. Mark Weinberger, Global Chairman & CEO of Ernst & Young, recently reported, "In 1975, 83 percent of the average firm's value was counted on the balance sheet. Today, it is only 16 percent. We need to find a new and a standardized way of reporting the full value of a company beyond the basic financials."[Weinberger, 2016]. Adding data to the mix of business assets has proven a way to help achieve this.

Furthermore, data not only provides competitive advantage, but is also considered a business in itself. For enterprises such as Amazon and Expedia, data is the core of their business. For example, Amazon's history of purchasing transaction data helps them to determine the amount of inventory to carry and to devise product pricing strategies. Companies like Bloomberg, Equifax, and ACNielsen have financial, consumer credit, and marketing datasets, respectively, that they monetize as data products. Businesses such as Apple, Monsanto, and New York Times are offering data products (i.e. digital information) that can be purchased by customers. Monsanto sells precision planting data products to farmers. The impact of data on business is so profound that General Electric (GE) has started an industrial internet platform company called GE Digital, and GE's CEO Jeff Immelt is aiming to make GE Digital a top ten data-driven company by 2020 [Fehrenbacher, 2016].

At the same time, while data can help create new products or service lines, it can even serve as a barrier to entry for new enterprises facing well-established competition. For example, if someone were to build a new professional social networking service tomorrow, it would be impossible to compete with LinkedIn. LinkedIn has so much data about its professional users that the new player, with no such data, will find it extremely difficult to even enter the market.

Clearly, data has become as real a business asset as inventory or employees. If data is a business asset, can it be subject to valuation? Doug Laney, Gartner's Distinguished Analyst covering big data and analytics, believes asset valuation of any kind boils down to three things [Woodie, 2016]:

1. An asset is a thing that can be owned and controlled

2. An asset is something that's exchangeable for cash

3. An asset is something that generates probable future economic benefits

According to Laney, information and data meet these requirements; as such, organizations should treat data and information just like any other physical or financial asset, or human capital. Laney believes data can be monetized using methods such as measurable business performance improvements, beneficial terms or conditions from business partners, information bartering, productizing information, "informationalizing" products (i.e. including information as a value-add component of an existing offering), or selling data outright via a data broker or independently.

UNDERSTANDING TRANSFORMATION

Given the rise of data as an important asset, enterprises are seeking to implement lasting, positive, and integrated change for long-term competitive advantage. Important drivers behind this data-focused business transformation include improved technologies, increased competition, product and service obsolescence, need for faster time to market, change in customer preferences, new government regulations, and the need to act on emerging new opportunities.

By definition, transformation is a whole-scale change to the foundational components of a business: from its operating model to its infrastructure. What it sells, to whom, and how it goes to market. A transformation initiative touches every function of a business, from purchasing, finance, and human resources, to operations and technology, sales, and marketing. Essentially, businesses undertake transformation initiatives to be more relevant in the market. According to John Kotter, an expert on leadership and change, business transformation is essentially making fundamental changes in how business is conducted, in order keep up with the shifting market environment.

Currently, most business transformation initiatives invariably include technology or digitization components. The SMAC (**s**ocial media, **m**obile, **a**nalytics and **c**loud) technologies have created an ecosystem that really empowers a business to improve its operations and get closer to its markets. Social media has provided businesses with new ways to reach and interact with customers, while mobile technologies have changed the way people communicate, shop, and work. Analytics allow businesses to understand how, what, when, and where people consume certain goods and services, and cloud computing provides new ways to access technology and the data. In former BlackBerry CEO Jim Balsillie's assessment, "every industry is shaped by technology now; everything is a technology game" [Balsillie, 2016]. The transition from desktop, to laptop, to mobile devices, and now to wearable devices has forced businesses to make sweeping strategic change to adapt to the new technical landscape.

While digital and SMAC technologies are now key levers for business operations, poor data quality is hindering effective business transformation, including data-driven decision making. According to Bernard Marr, one of the world's most highly respected voices on business performance and data in business, "the reality is that most businesses are already data rich, but insight is poor" [Marr, 2015]. As such, unlocking the value of data should be seen as a transformation exercise that aligns the organization's resources and capabilities with its business strategy and vision.

DATA AND BUSINESS VALUE

Businesses collect, process, and report on massive volumes of data. However, it is not the quantity of data itself that matters. Data are "raw facts," and without context they hold little value. In her 2007 book, "Successful Business Intelligence", Cindi Howson suggests that an average manager spends two hours per day hunting for data. What is the reason for this effort? What is the exact role data plays in enterprise operations? Fundamentally, that two-hour daily hunt for data is fueled by one (or more) of three main reasons: decision making, compliance, or customer service.

DECISION MAKING

Business categories, entities, and events are captured in an appropriate data structure so that insights can be derived and decisions can be made. Prior to making any important business decision, three key questions must be asked:

- What is the current level of performance?

- What are the causes affecting the current outcome?

- What needs to be done to manage the business into the future?

The answers to these questions are not simple or straightforward. They cannot just be based on somebody's intuition or opinion. This is where data can help answer the above questions and provide the support needed to make informed decisions. Enterprise performance expert Bernard Marr says, "Data should be at the heart of strategic decision making. Data leads to insights and business can turn those insights into decisions and actions that improve business performance. This is the power of data" [Marr, 2015].

COMPLIANCE

Data is also required for compliance with government regulations, internal security policies, and industry standards. In general, compliance means conforming to a rule, such as a specification, policy, standard or law. Regulatory compliance is ensuring that organizations comply with relevant government laws and regulations. Examples of regulatory compliance laws include data privacy laws such as:

- PIPEDA (Personal Information Protection and Electronic Documents Act) in Canada

- ECHR (European Court of Human Rights) in the European Union

- Payment Card Industry Data Security Standard (PCI DSS) in the US

- Health Insurance Portability and Accountability Act (HIPAA) in the US

- Anti-Money Laundering and Counter-Terrorism Financing Act 2006 (AML/CTF Act) in Australia

- Sarbanes-Oxley Act (SOX) in the US

Compliance with these regulations is critical for managing risk in every organization. Take for example Nexen, an oil company based in Alberta, Canada. When Nexen spilt over 31,500 barrels of crude oil in July of 2015, the Alberta

Energy Regulator (AER) ordered immediate suspension of 15 pipeline licenses issued to Nexen due to lack of maintenance data records.

When business enterprises talk about compliance, though, they are not just concerned about government laws and regulations. Compliance also covers adherence to industry standards and internal security policies. For instance, within the supply chain business area many businesses need their suppliers to comply with DUNS number (Data Universal Numbering System) and GTIN numbers (Global Trade Item Number) while conducting business transactions. In accounting, global businesses need to comply with IFRS (International Financial Reporting Standards) and GAPP (Generally Accepted Privacy Principles) standards. The third area of compliance is adherence to internal security policies and complying with certifications such as ISO 27001, ISO 27002, and SSAE16/SOC1.

CUSTOMER SERVICE

Businesses also generate and capture data merely by running their daily business operations, in order to efficiently serve its internal and external customers. For instance, within some company, the finance department might ask the marketing department for a list of all sales orders issued against specific general ledger accounts for budgetary allocations. Meanwhile, the procurement department might want purchase orders to be issued only against contracts for traceability and efficiency.

At the same time, stakeholders outside the company might also need some data. For example, a car owner might ask AIG, a multinational insurance corporation, for insurance and claims details during a car accident. The self-service tools found in internet banking are more instances where external customers demand data wherever and whenever they want it. In 2016, CloverLeaf Seafoods announced a unique traceability program called "Trace My Catch" to help customers trace CloverLeaf tuna and salmon products from the ocean to their plates. This means every CloverLeaf tuna and salmon product features a unique code that, when entered online, provides detailed information about that individual product, including the species of fish, fishing method, ocean of catch, vessel name(s) and flag(s), fishing trip dates, and the location the fish was processed. Ron Schindler, President of CloverLeaf Seafoods, says that "Trace My Catch provides the level of transparency in its service to the customers. All these examples have nothing to do with compliance or insights per-se; but they help to serve the customers better and run the business efficiently" [Robertson, 2016].

To summarize, data has three main purposes: to derive business insights, to ensure compliance with industry standards, security policies, and government laws and regulations, and finally to provide the desired level of service for internal and external customers of the enterprise. In the words of David Loshin, a thought leader in data quality, "most enterprises use data in two ways: transactional use i.e. running the business and analytical use i.e. improving the business." So while compliance and customer service are integral to "running the business," decision making pertains to "improving the business" [Loshin, 2010].

WHAT HAS CHANGED?

Businesses have captured, processed, distributed, retrieved, and analyzed data for decades. Way back in the 18th century, French emperor Napoleon Bonaparte said that "war is 90 percent information." Benjamin Disraeli, a British Prime Minister in the 19th century, said "the most successful man in life is the man who has the best information." In 1985, Michael Porter and Victor Miller of Harvard Business School detailed this observation in a seminal business systems article called "How Information Gives You Competitive Advantage" [Porter and Miller, 1985]. Clearly the belief that data and information can provide value has existed for a very long time. So why is data receiving such heightened attention today? What are the drivers that are forcing enterprises to unlock the value of data? Here are some of the key reasons:

- **Changing business landscape.** The business landscape has grown more complex. The pace of change is accelerating due to globalization, growth of new economies, and increased relevance of technology in business operations. Revenue and profit are shifting from tangible goods such as oil, gas, retail, and mining to intangible goods that revolve around information, brands, patents, software, copyrights, and more. According to McKinsey consulting, while sectors such as finance, information technology, media, and pharmaceuticals remain profitable, margins are being squeezed in capital-intensive industries such as energy, mining, airlines, and telecom.

- **Increased competition.** Businesses today face vigorous competition and are continually pressed to become more efficient and more productive. The competition comes not only from incumbent and established players, but also from technology enabled start-ups that derive value from data by leveraging data-driven strategies. While data can potentially create barriers to entry for new players, technology and the internet have created low entry barriers for new entrants to take on established players. According to research by McKinsey, analyzing large datasets (known as "big data") will become a key basis of competition, underpinning new waves of productivity growth, innovation, and consumer surplus.

- **More regulatory compliance.** Due to an increasing need for operational transparency, businesses today are more regulated than ever. Heavily regulated industry sectors such as government, financial services, healthcare, insurance, retail, and energy are mandated to ensure compliance of data — especially on privacy, security, retention, environment, and intellectual property. Data breaches in large enterprises like banks and retail chains have made data privacy and protection a critical part of business operations, and have consequentially necessitated the creation of stringent and complex laws around data privacy and protection. Noted European Union (EU) politician, Meglena Kuneva says that "personal data is the new oil of the Internet and the new currency of the digital world."

- **New data models for increased collaboration.** Until the year 2000, most enterprises primarily ran their business transactions in on-premises ERP systems — the software was run on computers on the premises (in the data center) of the organization. These systems were based on highly structured data, and were used primarily to keep track of operations or to forecast needs. However, today's technologies such as Blockchain and IoT (Internet of Things) leverage distributed databases and device networks that grow continuously. For many companies like Uber and Netflix, their business models are primarily based around the internet. Most businesses interact with their customers and partners via mobile apps and social media. Most of the data coming from social media is unstructured, resides outside the enterprise, and exposes the enterprise to new volumes, velocities, and varieties of data. The changed data ecosystem, with its new data models and business networks, promises better integration and collaboration ultimately resulting in big business opportunities. According to Jim Fowler, CIO of GE Water & Power, by integrating external weather data with the terabyte of data per day from each of its sensor-equipped turbines, GE is helping customers with a small 1 percent improvement in output that translates to $2 to $5 million in savings per turbine per year [Henschen, 2014].

- **New technologies.** We also have new computing technologies such as virtualization, in-memory computing, computing platforms, artificial intelligence (including cognitive computing and machine learning), communications, and security protocols, to extract value from data effectively. While databases are getting bigger, the computing costs to process data are getting lower. In 1985, the Intel 386 microprocessor was capable of processing 9.9 million instructions per second (MIPS). By 2013, Intel core i7 4770k microprocessor was capable of processing 128,000 MIPS.

Basically, storing and processing data has become much cheaper and more robust [Lake and Drake, 2015].

Overall, today there is a strong push to leverage the value of data in businesses, governments, and communities. In a recent survey conducted by NewVantage Partners, Fortune 1000 executives believe that reducing time-to-insight enables their firms to act faster by analyzing data, gaining insights, making critical decisions, and bringing new capabilities to market. A 2016 study released by the Economist Intelligence Unit reported that 60 percent of the professionals they quizzed feel that data is generating revenue within their organizations; 83 percent say it is making existing services and products more profitable.

Governments are leveraging digital technologies to enhance service delivery quality, increase citizen engagement and satisfaction, and to improve public sector productivity. Private equity firms are investing in initiatives on analytics and business intelligence. Many top universities including MIT, Stanford, and Berkeley are offering programs on Business Analytics. There are numerous conferences and more research papers published on data than ever before. Top ERP, business intelligence (BI) and analytics vendors are regularly releasing new software versions with improved features. McKinsey reports that by 2018, there will be 140,000 to 190,000 Data Science job postings that will not be filled; research firm IDC (International Data Corporation) predicts that the market for big data and analytics will hit $187 billion in 2019 [Davis, 2016].

CONCLUSION

The enterprise data landscape is changing, from both within and outside the enterprise. Many organizations have started to use data in transforming their businesses to gain competitive advantage. Hence why data is seen as the fuel on which modern enterprises run.

Though data can be managed at different organizational levels (such as enterprise, company, LoB, and function), data governed at an enterprise level brings increased quality, economies of scale, and reduced cost in the long run.

Data, per se, is of little value to the business; data must be leveraged appropriately for business performance. In short, data is useful only if the business has the capability to respond to the data. The first step in this journey is to define business data clearly. Though this chapter provided an introduction to business data, the next chapter covers business data in more detail.

Chapter 2: Demystifying Business Data

The price of light is less than the cost of darkness.

Arthur Nielsen
Founder of ACNielsen

The competitive edge to be gained from improved data management is no longer limited to a few technology companies or data-intensive industries. For an increasing number of businesses, data collection, analysis, and distribution have become critical to their business operations. Brian Hopkins, Principal Analyst at Forrester, says "Data is a source of business innovation. Firms are innovating with data. In all industries, everyone is taking a look at what they know better than anyone else in the world" [Saran, 2013]. According to Dr. Thomas Redman, renowned expert on data quality and author of the popular book *Data Driven*, "Data permeates every element of an organization; it does not follow vertical structure. Unlike other assets, data does not deplete as it gets used, on the contrary it grows, creating new data all the time. If your organization is not managing and using data, it is missing a huge opportunity." Given these insights, this chapter critically examines the role of business data, including the relationships that business data has with other elements in the enterprise.

BUSINESS DATA IN THE ENTERPRISE VALUE CHAIN

In Chapter 1, the term "business enterprise" was defined. But what exactly does a business enterprise *do*? A business enterprise is usually involved in the trade of goods, services, or both to consumers, suppliers, and other business partners. In the management of this economic activity, the enterprise is subject to an increasing number of statutory, regulatory, and business constraints for operating and moving the business forward.

A business is a continuous process; it is conducted regularly to grow and gain regular returns. To run the business, the business' characteristics, entities, assets, rules, events, and organizational elements are captured as business data. In other words, business data is any data associated with the operation of the business, throughout the entire business value chain, where "business value chain" refers to a set of activities the business performs to deliver a valuable product or service.

So what are the typical activities or operations within this business value chain? Renowned business strategist Michael Porter grouped the business activities within an enterprise into two classes: primary activities and support activities [Porter, 1998]. He embedded these activities in the value chain with focus on systems and customers instead of departments or accounting cost types.

PRIMARY ACTIVITIES

Primary activities are the operational activities that the business performs to add value to its products and services. Primary activities are further classified into product-related and market-related activities. The product-related activities pertain to the products and services, and the market-related activities deal with the transfer of finished products or services to the market.

Here are the five main primary activities:

1. **Inbound logistics.** Inbound logistics refers to all the activities related to receiving goods from the suppliers, transportation scheduling, inventory, management, or any activities pertaining to goods or inputs received for the production of end products.

2. **Operations.** These include the production process, development activities, testing, packaging, maintenance, and all other activities that transform the inputs into finished products.

3. **Services.** Business will continue to offer services after the initial products and services have been sold. These service activities include sales guarantees, warranties, spare parts management, repair services, installation, trainings, and others.

4. **Outbound logistics.** These include activities that are required to move the finished products to the customers via warehousing, order fulfillment, transportation, and distribution management.

5. **Marketing and sales.** These activities include the advertising, channel selection, product promotion, selling, product pricing, retail management and other activities for targeted customer groups.

SUPPORT ACTIVITIES

Activities performed by an enterprise to assist the primary activities can be classified as support (or "secondary") activities. These activities are key enablers to an organization's success, but they are often considered "overhead." As such, these activities need to be aligned to support the efficient and effective delivery of primary activities. The activities include:

1. **Procurement.** Procurement activities include acquisition of quality goods and services at the best price, at the right time, and in the desired place.

2. **Technology management.** Technology management includes research and development, IT, and other related activities.

3. **Human resource management (HRM).** Key HRM activities are hiring, recognition, reward, appraisal systems, carrier planning, and employee development.

4. **Infrastructure.** This includes the planning management, legal framework, financing, accounting, public affairs, quality management, general management, and other functions.

The figure below shows the nine value chain activities in a business enterprise.

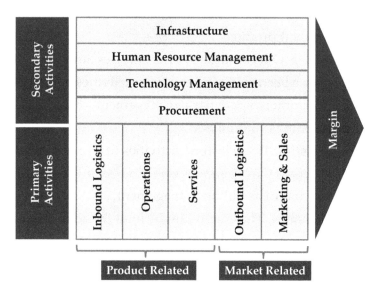

Porter's value chain activities

Of course, the specifics of any business value chain depend on the industry sector the enterprise is operating within. Below is a simple value chain model for a financial institution.

Value chain activities for a financial institution

While executing these nine primary and support business activities, the enterprise interacts with a variety of business entities (such as employees, suppliers, and general ledger accounts), events (purchasing, selling, and contracting), and business categories (product groups, plants, and sales offices), among others. Information about these business entities is generated and captured as business data within the business process. According to Howard Smith and Peter Fingar, authors of *Business Process Management — The Third Wave*, "A business process is the complete and dynamically coordinated set of collaborative and transactional activities that deliver value to customers."

How does data enable companies to improve business performance? Data is integral to business performance, as it provides good visibility of the activities within the business process performed in the enterprise. Visibility is essential for the business to monitor the performance of business processes. According to Thomas Davenport, one of the best-known thinkers on data management, "business processes are among the last remaining points of differentiation." For this reason, Davenport suggests that businesses that create a sustainable right to use data to "bring every last drop of value from their processes" [Davenport, 2006].

In addition, effectively managing business data within the business process can potentially create a data economy, data ecosystem, and data products. It is these data infrastructures that have enabled companies such as Amazon, GE, and Expedia to efficiently run their business processes. Their systems can tell valuable information about top customers (marketing and sales business activity in the value chain), how much they spend on different categories (procurement business activity in the value chain), what prompts demand and supply (inbound and outbound logistics business activity in the value chain), and many more.

BUSINESS DATA VERSUS NON-BUSINESS DATA

How is the data pertaining to the nine key business activities different from data coming from business processes in non-business organizations? While there are many kinds of data, "business data" refers specifically to data associated with a business entity whose primary purpose is to generate profit. Other types of data associated with legal entities could include research or academic databases such as PubMed, data issued by government agencies such as Statistics Canada and International Energy Agency (IEA), or even databases of non-profit organizations such as Red Cross and Ford Foundation.

These are organizations whose purpose is more than making just a profit. Allan Fogwill is the CEO of the Canadian Energy Research Institute (CERI), an independent, non-profit Canadian research institute formed to analyze energy economics. According to Fogwill, "Data in non-business organizations such as CERI is broader and foundational. The data CERI deals with pertains to macroeconomic and environment aspects. The context is around policies that need to be formulated for the energy businesses to thrive. Compared to CERI, the data within the energy companies is insular and specific as they deal with situational or project level contexts." While some of the concepts pertaining to enterprise business data might be applicable to non-business data and vice-versa, the key factors that differentiate business data from non-business data are:

- **Homogeneity.** Enterprise business data is typically homogenous, where different organizational units within the enterprise can potentially rely on a common data model for context and point of reference. This means the structural and descriptive details of business data (such as purpose, definition, taxonomy, and relationship) are assumed to be consistently understood by stakeholders within the enterprise. For example, if the product code is defined as integer type with 18 characters in length, this means every stakeholder within the enterprise accepts this definition for the product code as part of the enterprise data model.

- **Competitive advantage.** Enterprise business data is specific and exclusive to the enterprise. It has the potential to help devise business strategies, retain customers, reduce costs, and develop new markets to the enterprise. Amazon's inventory management and Uber's automatic dispatching are based on curated data that supports these companies' leadership positions in their respective industry segments. Today data (or content) is enabling the companies' growth as well. IBM acquiring the Weather Company in 2015 for $2 billion was mainly for the data Weather Company held.

- **Data origination.** An enterprise's business data is normally originated, created, and owned by the enterprise. Even if the data is purchased from external agencies, such as IEA (International Energy Agency) for energy data, Bloomberg for finance data, or Nielsen for marketing data, those data elements are licensed or owned by the purchasing enterprise for appropriate consumption. Overall the enterprise's business data is normally originated either by systems (machines and applications) or by people within the enterprise; exceptions include some cases of cloud computing where systems are hosted outside the enterprise environment.

- **Data authenticity and integrity**. Technically data can be assumed to be authentic if it is not corrupted or changed after its origination. But with non-business data, the data authenticity and integrity is typically tied to the publisher of data rather than the originator of data. The publisher in most cases is not the originator of data. For example, when Statistics Canada, the agency which provides data on Canada's economy, society, and environment, publishes data sets on agricultural farms, the actual source of data is aggregation from the CALF (Census of Agriculture Longitudinal File) database. This means it is difficult to trace the origin of data and one takes the data publisher's word regarding data authenticity and integrity. But the data origin and change of values pertaining to the data element in business is typically traceable.

TYPES OF ENTERPRISE BUSINESS DATA

To review, in operating these nine primary and secondary business activities, business processes are executed as activities resulting in the capture of data as business entities, events, and business categories. These business data elements can be of four main types: reference data, master data, transactional data, and metadata.

REFERENCE DATA

Reference data is a set of permissible values that businesses use to categorize master data and transactional data. Reference data consists of sets of values, statuses, or classification schema, and has two key characteristics:

- The first key characteristic of reference data is that it is defined by standards. For example, country codes are defined in ISO 3166 and UoM codes are in ISO 2022. Other types of reference data such as plant codes, purchasing organizations, sales offices, and employee positions are internal to the enterprise and follow standards specific to the organization.
- The second important characteristic of reference data is its impact on the business process. For example, introducing a new product category will invariably result in change to the business process.

MASTER DATA

Master data are business entities to be used across multiple systems, LoB, business functions, and business processes in the enterprise. Master data is considered the backbone of the enterprise, and is often called the "golden record" or the "single version of truth." According to Gartner, master data is the consistent and uniform set of identifiers and extended attributes that describe the core entities of the enterprise, and are used across multiple business processes [Gartner, 2016]. In its truest sense, master data is the single and authoritative source of business data. Master data falls generally into three types:

- People, including customers, employees, suppliers, and agencies
- Things, including products, parts, devices, and assets
- Concepts, including contracts, warranties, GL accounts, profit centers, and licenses

TRANSACTIONAL DATA

While master data is about business entities (typically nouns), transactional data is about business events (usually verbs). Transactional data holds relevancy to the external world. Transactional data includes business documents created using the reference and master data to record a specific business event or transaction. This data pertains to discrete business transactions or events involving the trade of goods, services, or both.

Incidentally, the majority of the volume of data that is managed in an enterprise is found in transactional data. For example, purchase orders issued to the seller control the purchasing of products and services from external suppliers. Another example is the bill of lading (BoL) document, which is created only when the customer has received the goods. Other instances of transactional data are business transactions such as purchase orders, deliveries, invoices, and work order notifications, to name a few.

METADATA

Metadata is "data about data." In other words, metadata is used to describe another data element's content. ISO 15489 defines metadata as data describing context, content, and structure of records, and their management through time. Metadata mainly labels, describes, or characterizes the other three types of data (i.e. reference data, master data, and transactional data). Unlike the other three types of data, metadata has no real business utility, and is always married to one or more of the three types of data. Hence it is important to realize that metadata is simply "data about data," and not the data in itself. Metadata is further is classified into three types:

- Technical metadata, used to describe the data structures. Examples are field length, type, size, and so on.
- Business metadata, used to describe non-technical aspects of the data and their usage. Examples are report name, document name, class, XML document type, and others.
- Log metadata, which describes details on how, when, and by whom the data object was created, updated or deleted. Examples are timestamp, created date, and changed date. The log data or log files which are automatically created represent time-stamped documentation of particular events, and are very useful in improving the IT system for preventive maintenance. For example, in an ERP system, the audit log files record chronologically all activities that affect the integrity of a specific data element. The figure below shows the audit log for some Sales order 2596377 line item 10 in the SAP ERP application.

Changes in Request 0002596377

ID	Date	Item	SLNo	Sales Promotion	U
☐	17.11.2014			Total incompletion status of all items: Delivery changed	V
☐	19.11.2014			Released credit value of the document changed	L
☐	19.11.2014			Release date of the document determined by credit management changed	L
☐	19.11.2014			Credit management: Risk category changed	L
☐	19.11.2014			Overall status of credit checks changed	L
△	17.11.2014	10		Price has been created	V
☐	17.11.2014	10		Rounding Difference changed	V
☐	17.11.2014	10		Net price changed	V
☐	17.11.2014	10		Item credit price changed	V
☐	17.11.2014	10		Item credit price changed	V
☐	17.11.2014	10		Condition pricing unit changed	V
☐	17.11.2014	10		Net price changed	V

Audit log sales order line item

The relationships among the four types of data are shown in the figure on the facing page.

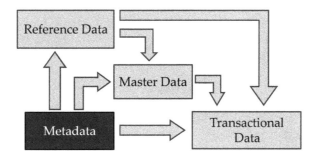

Relationships among the 4 types of data

As metadata is the "supporting" data for the three other types of business data elements, the key characteristics of the three main types of business data are shown in the table below.

Serial Num	Parameter	Reference Data	Master Data	Transactional Data
1	Volume of records	Low	Medium	High
2	Life span	High	Medium	Low
3	Frequency of change	Low	Medium	High
4	Utility span	Enterprise-wide and company	Lob and company-wide	Function-wide
5	Variety of users consuming this data type	High	Medium	Low
6	Data structure	Structured and semi-structured	Structured	Structured and Semi-structured
7	Management location or system	Master data management system	Master data management system	Application systems

There are other types of data that are less often discussed when it comes to the operation of businesses. For example, experimental and scientific data that is generated for scientific investigation or research within an enterprise is typically not relevant to the direct operation of the business. Another example is field data from plant control SCADA (Supervisory Control and Data Acquisition) systems, i.e. the data collected in an uncontrolled in-situ (or "on site") field environment. This field data, which is of the time-series or continuous data type, allows agencies to record series of data points measuring a physical phenomenon. Closely associated with field data is streaming data, i.e. data generated from mobile devices and web applications. Streaming data gives enterprises visibility into many aspects of their online business, such as service usage for metering and billing, server utilization, website clicks, and geolocation of devices.

Against this backdrop, the ANSI (American National Standards Institute) ISA 95 (International Society of Automation) standardization has segregated business activities and systems into four levels. This four-level structure is applicable to most industry sectors, as shown in the figure below. In ISA 95 terms, this book deals with fourth level (i.e. data in business systems).

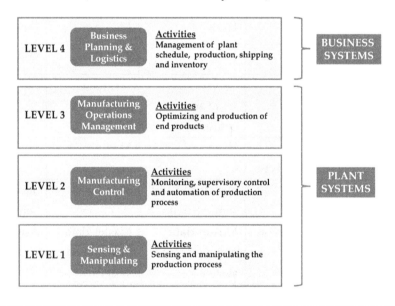

Systems as organized by ANSI/ISA 95

To summarize, I define business data as "data pertaining to the operations of the primary and secondary business functions, within an enterprise whose primary purpose is to generate profit. Running of business operations results in the management of data entities which can be one of the four types (metadata, reference data, master data and transactional data), and these data elements can be directly or indirectly traceable to business operations and the three purposes of data."

KEY CHARACTERISTICS OF BUSINESS DATA

Now that we have clearly defined business data, what are its key characteristics? While many articles have been written on characteristics of quality data (such as accuracy, validity, timeliness, and more), these characteristics are primarily from an IT perspective with emphasis on storage and processing. From the business perspective, though, data is more about consumption than storage and processing. Below are some of the key characteristics of business data.

- **Capture of business data is purpose-driven.** As mentioned before, business data has three main purposes: insights, compliance, and customer service. Even if the origination of data is unwarranted or unplanned, business data capture is always justified by a purpose, whether it is captured by people or by machines. Purpose essentially explains what the data represents and how to interpret it. For example, a purchase order (PO) is not a technical object with just one field in the database. A PO has a specific business purpose; it is a legal document issued by the buyer to the seller with the terms and conditions for buying the product or service. A PO, in turn, has numerous attributes such as vendor code, item code, amount, currency, delivery date, and more. All these attributes or fields and their ensuing data values provide a specific purpose to the business data element (i.e. the purchase order). For example, the data value "USD" in the currency field in the PO means that the item was purchased in US Dollars.

- **Business data is business process-driven.** As mentioned before, a business process is an activity or a set of activities that accomplishes a specific business objective. Hence all business data is directly or indirectly associated with business processes. These business activities are recorded by capturing appropriate data elements. While reference data, master data, and transactional data are directly associated with a business process, metadata is indirectly associated with the business process. For example, recording an equipment failure is driven through the work order (transactional data) that includes capturing equipment details (master data), location of where the equipment is installed (reference data), and the time and the impact of equipment breakdown (transactional data). Essentially, data is integral to the business process, and vice versa.

- **Business data has short time horizon utility.** While data per se has little value to the business, it is quality data that boosts business performance. However, even the insights derived from quality data typically have short lifecycles, and the value and relevancy of data tends to depreciate over time. The rate at which depreciation of data quality happens depends upon the type of data (i.e. reference data, master data, or transactional data), and how relevant the data can remain over time. For example, the relevancy of a purchase order, which is a piece of transactional data, is really only relevant until the invoice is paid to the supplier. But the relevancy of a vendor contract, which is a type of master data, remains relevant until the contract term end date.

- **The relevancy of business data increases when shared.** Data origination and capture in an enterprise is usually an expensive process. In addition, most enterprise business processes revolve around a set of coordinated business activities where the output from one stage is carried forward to the next. Invariably, data — especially master data and reference data — is shared across the enterprise to save cost and time while creating transactional data, as the transactional data element uses many of the fields from the master data and reference data. For example, a customer invoice (which is a transactional data element) uses customer and item details (which are examples of master data) as well as currency and unit of measure details (which are reference data). If data is already in use and managed well, there is generally an increased appetite within the organization to re-use the data for other purposes. For instance, if a product's master data is effectively used by five LoBs within the enterprise, there is a logical case for the sixth LoB to leverage the same product code. However, the ability of the organization to efficiently share data is based on a common set of policies, procedures, and standards governing data management. For example, while an item code can be used in purchasing in the purchase order, the same item code can be shared in the MRP (Materials Requirements Planning) process — but only if these two departments communicate well.

- **Business data follows a lifecycle.** The data lifecycle refers to the process of managing business data securely throughout its "life," from origination through purging, across different application systems, databases, and storage media. The lifecycle of data can ultimately be a lineage which describes where a piece of data came from, the mechanism by which it was validated and processed in the data storage system, how it was integrated with other systems, and finally when and where it was consumed appropriately. The ten steps of the data lifecycle, encompassing both IT and business activities, will be covered in detail in Chapter 3.

- **Business data is non-fungible.** Fungible, in general, means that an asset can be freely exchanged or replaced with another of same nature. While IT systems — especially COTS (commercial off-the-shelf) and cloud SaaS (software as a service) solutions — are normally fungible and can be commoditized, the data that powers the IT systems is not. Specifically, the business data (especially the master data and transactional data) is a non-fungible or irreplaceable asset. While master data and transactional data are specific to the business enterprise and the business process, reference data is relatively fungible (i.e. replaceable) as it is driven by common standards. For example, the attributes of the vendor master data are specific to the business enterprise and the business process, making the vendor master data non-fungible. However, the data pertaining to the UoM reference data can be exchanged between businesses if they follow the ISO standards, thereby making the UoM data element fungible. This essentially means that a business data element of one type is never equivalent to another piece of data, even if it is of the same type. According to Bill Gates, Chairman of Microsoft, "virtually everything in business today is a commodity, except how a company manages its information" [Kalakota and Robinson, 1999].

- **Business data accessibility is controlled by security rules.** Business data needs to be protected from corruption, loss, and unauthorized access. While this holds true for all data — business or personal — business data is especially sensitive since financial data, sales figures, and other key business data can potentially provide competitive advantage to the enterprise. At the same time, personal data like SIN (Social Insurance Number) numbers, bank account details, and other attributes need to be protected for data privacy laws and regulations. From the data management perspective, both personal and business "data at rest" and "data in motion" need to be protected by various mechanisms for authentication, authorization, and confidentiality.

- **Business data has defined ownership.** With business data there is typically a single entity (an individual or an organizational element) that is responsible for data ownership. Data ownership is the act of having legal rights and control over data elements. For reference data and master data, the ownership model is normally centralized, as the data element is shared within the enterprise. On the other hand, ownership for transactional data is typically at the LoB level or at the business function level.

- **Business data quality degrades over time if not governed.** Entropy, one of the most fundamental laws of physics, essentially states that unless energy from the outside is applied, the amount of disorder in an enclosed system will increase over time if not explicitly controlled. In simple words, entropy is a process in which order deteriorates with the passage of time. Restated in data management terms, entropy means that the quality of data held in IT systems will deteriorate unless concrete steps are taken to maintain its quality. In other words, if the business data is not governed properly, there will be deterioration in data quality due to formatting errors, typing mistakes, software bugs, unverified external data sources, among others. Chapter 5 covers enterprise business data quality in detail, including the key data quality dimensions and the reasons for the degradation of data quality.

- **Business data deals with end states and milestones.** Most business data represents the final results of a business processes or key milestones within the business process. Examples include total units produced, total hours consumed, materials received, and final contracted agreement. This transactional end-state data is stored in a database in the IT system; this database has the capability to be "rolled back" if not completed properly. In addition, most business data is typically processed in a structured format, in applications where the processing is divided into individual, indivisible operations called "transactions." Chapter 3 covers the important technical aspects pertaining to the management of business data.

ONE DATA, MANY VIEWS, MANY CLASSES

Converting the data into business value is strongly stakeholder-driven, as these stakeholders typically provide the context or purpose. For example, a product group might be used by the sales department to organize the sales campaign, while the same product group might be used by the finance team for financial posting to general ledger (GL) accounts. So the same data element can be viewed in two different ways by two different stakeholders.

For example, a BALL BEARING is an engineering component for a technician, while the same BALL BEARING is a cost element tied to a GL account for an accountant. Beyond simply classifying business data as reference data, master data, transactional data, or metadata, business data can also be classified in different ways. What follows is a list of different aspects of data, along with ways that different stakeholders might define and describe those aspects, based on their unique vantage point.

PURPOSE

As mentioned earlier, stakeholders see three main purposes in business data: insights, compliance, and customer service. Based on the purpose, a particular data element can be seen from different angles. For example, while the data element "Safety Stock" can be used by the marketing department to avoid stock-outs and keep customer service and satisfaction levels high, the same field can be used to determine insights on unforeseen variation in supply and demand. Another example is the "Vendor SIN" data element. While this data element is needed from the compliance perspective for tax purposes, the same field can be used to find duplicate vendor records, improve data quality, or formulate appropriate vendor segmentation strategies with the clean vendor records.

ORIGINATION

From the data origination view point, business data can be seen from two main views.

- **Structured Data**. Structured data is the data that is organized in a formatted repository (typically in a database) so that the data elements can be uniquely identified for effective processing and analysis. Research shows that just about 20 percent of the data managed in an enterprise is structured data [Hurwitz et al, 2013].

- **Unstructured Data**. Data that is not stored in any predefined data structure is termed unstructured data. Unstructured data includes e-mail messages, word processing documents, videos, photos, audio files, presentations, webpages, RSS feeds, and more. Market intelligence firm IDC estimates that 60 to 80 percent of data created and stored today is unstructured data [Vijayan, 2015].

But does the structure of data, affect the view points of the stakeholder? Does everyone view the data structure in the same way? Let us consider the example of a vendor Purchase Order (PO). When the PO is issued by the buyer to the vendor, the PO is in a document format (i.e. unstructured data). In most enterprises, this PO is created by drawing fields from various database tables. While the buyer and vendor view the PO as unstructured data, the IT developer and the database administrator view the PO as a structured set of fields from various database tables. The table below highlights the key differences between structured and unstructured data.

Features	Structured Data	Unstructured Data
Representation	Structured data is easily and uniquely identifiable	Unstructured data has no identifiable structure
Storage or Persistence	In databases	In file structures or content repository
Metadata	Syntax such as data type and format	Semantics such as description and markup
Example	Data captured in databases and spreadsheets	Images, text, video and voice

PROCESSING

Business data is stored and processed using business rules in IT systems. From the computer programming or processing perspective, the various data types can be real (decimal), integer, Boolean, text or string, image, video, or audio. These data types determine which operations that can be performed on the data. A typical data processing system may involve combinations of:

- Conversion — converting data to another format
- Migration — migration of data from one data source to another source
- Validation — ensuring that data is "clean, correct, and useful"
- Sorting — arranging data items in some sequence
- Aggregation — combining multiple data elements and reducing it to its main points
- Analysis — the collection, organization and presentation of data

Hence when the stakeholder is working on processing data during conversion and migration, he or she views data from the database perspective. But when the stakeholders are working on sorting, the purpose or view is for arranging the data elements in a specific order.

ANALYSIS

Data analysis involves converting raw data into information useful for decision-making. This decision-making can be based on qualitative or quantitative data. Qualitative data analysis is used to draw conclusions from unstructured data like text, images, audio, or video. Qualitative data is data that is descriptive. Quantitative data which are basically numerical used to draw conclusions from structured data which comes from database tables for analysis. Data analysis is different from analytics; Chapter 8 covers business analytics in more detail.

But again, will every stakeholder view the qualitative or quantitative data in the same way? This is not always the case. For instance, qualitative data can be arranged into categories which are not numerical. For example, the priority of the sales orders can be classified as critical, high, medium, and low — sales orders that are high in priority are always more valued than orders which have low priority.

In other words, if the qualitative data can be arranged into categories, then there is a potential to quantify the values.

TIME HORIZON

There is always has a time lag between origination and capture of business data. This lag can range from a few milliseconds to even years in some rare cases. In fact, the term "real time data" is an oxymoron as there is always some amount of time lag or delay between origination and capture, no matter how minute. Based on the time horizon, data can be seen from three main perspectives.

1. Descriptive data summarizes what happened
2. Predictive data use historical data to predict or forecast the future
3. Prescriptive data provides recommendation on the future courses of action

SENSITIVITY

Inappropriate handling of business data could result in penalties, financial loss, and invasion of privacy, among other consequences. Hence business data is assigned a level of sensitivity within the enterprise, depending on the degree of access and the consequences if it were to be compromised.

- **Restricted data.** This includes regulated and personal data which have the highest level of sensitivity, including SINs, credit card numbers, bank accounts, health information, and the like.

- **Confidential data.** This includes data that have medium sensitivity, including data for internal use such as employee details, product designs, non-disclosure agreements (NDAs), financial information, contracts, trade secrets, and more.

- **Public data.** Public data is any data that can be freely used, reused, and re-distributed with no existing local, national, or international legal restrictions on access or usage. Public data has low level of sensitivity and examples include data for public consumption such as a company's balance sheets, details of its products and services, or its senior management profiles, among others.

For example, if a company is trying to launch an innovative product, it might not want to share the details of the product in public domains to avoid competition. Hence the company might keep the product details restricted. But once the product is out in the market, the company might choose to share the product details in the public domain to increase the awareness of the product.

OWNERSHIP

Another way to classify business data is based on who owns it. Data ownership refers to both the possession of and responsibility for data. The control of business data includes not just the ability to access, create, modify, package, derive benefit, sell or purge data, but also the right to assign these access privileges to others. Data ownership within a business can exist at three levels:

- **Enterprise-owned data** is shared across different departments in the company. These data elements (which are usually reference data and master data) have the highest level of process ceremony and control. For example, within the Procurement LoB, the enterprise-owned data can be currencies, plants, and payment terms.

- **Line of businesses (LoB)-owned data** is managed by specific departments in the company. These data elements (which are usually the transactional data) have the some degree of process ceremony and control. For example, within the procurement department, the LoB-owned data can be contracts and purchase orders.

- **Business function-owned business data** is managed and consumed within departments, by a few users. These data elements have the least amount of process ceremony and control. For example, within the procurement department, the business function-owned data could include goods receiving slips.

TREATMENT

According to Gartner's PACE-Layered application strategy, there must exist differentiated management and governance processes for managing applications and data within those applications. Gartner has defined three application categories, in order to help enterprises develop appropriate strategies for the management of applications and data:

- **Systems of Record (SoR).** SoR are established packaged applications or legacy homegrown systems that support core transaction processing and manage the organization's reference and master data. In a typical enterprise, these systems have a long lifecycle of over ten years. In addition, the rate of system change is low because the business processes running in these systems are well-established, common to most organizations, and often are subject to regulatory requirements.

- **Systems of Differentiation (SoD).** SoD applications enable unique company processes or industry-specific capabilities. They have a medium lifecycle of one to three years, but they need to be reconfigured frequently to accommodate changing business practices or customer requirements. These applications are typically focused on LoBs and have application and data integration with the SoR. Today SoD are almost synonymous with systems of engagement (SoE) — enterprise systems which are more decentralized, incorporate technologies which encourage peer interactions, and which often leverage cloud technologies to provide the capabilities to enable those interactions.

- **Systems of Innovation (SoI).** These systems manage new applications that are built on an *ad hoc* basis to address new business requirements or opportunities that are specific to business functions. These are typically short lifecycle systems with life spans of up to 12 months. The applications and the data are used mainly for standalone business processes.

LIFECYCLE

Business data follows a lifecycle with ten key stages or functions. Eight stages are relevant to business: origination, capture, validation, processing, distribution, consolidation, interpretation, and consumption. Two stages are relevant for IT function: storage and security. This means each stage or function has distinct data management processes based on any given stakeholder's needs; these processes address documentation, quality assurance, ownership, and more. The next chapter covers the ten key stages or functions of data.

SECURITY

From the security or data loss prevention (DLP) perspective, business data can be of two classes:

- **Data at rest**. Data at rest is data that is not actively moving from device to device or network to network. Data at rest refers to data which is stored physically in any form including databases, data warehouses, spreadsheets, archives, tapes, off-site backups, and mobile devices.

- **Data in motion**. Data in motion or "transit" refers to data being transmitted across a network. The network can be a public or untrusted network, such as the internet, or a private network, such as an enterprise Local Area Network (LAN).

As discussed above, business data can be classified into many views depending on the stakeholder needs and perspectives. The figure on the facing page shows the ten different stakeholder views or perspectives for the same data element.

Many views of one data element

CONCLUSION

Today's business data holds the key to make decisions, comply with standards, policies, and regulations, and improve customer service. The business data that is integral to the business process can be broadly classified into reference data, master data, and transactional data. The management of data and information starts with good stakeholder management that hinges on striking a balance of business processes, capabilities, resources, and metrics, with the right technologies. Speaking of technologies, it is the SMAC technologies that have played a significant role in the recent years for business to unlock value from data. The next chapter looks at the key aspects that allow the business stakeholder to leverage value from data.

Chapter 3: Discerning Data in Systems

IT and business are inextricably interwoven. We cannot talk meaningfully about one without talking about the other.

Bill Gates
Founder of Microsoft Corporation

In the previous chapters we have seen why business enterprises such as GE, Monsanto, Nestle, and more see value in data and invest in technologies to manage them. But who in the business is actually putting money into information systems and technologies? In this regard, two main trends are shaping the technology investments in enterprises.

On one hand, in recent years, the investment in technology has not necessarily come from the IT department, as businesses are also investing in technologies. Gartner estimates that in 2017, the budget for digital technology investment of the CMO (Chief Marketing Officer) will be more than that of the CIO. According to PwC, 47% of technology spending today is outside the CIO's budget; it comes from the internal business units [Curran and Antao, 2015]. Even though the rest of the 53 percent is under the CIO's discretion, this IT spending is also driven by the need to meet business requirements; business leaders want IT to be focused on business results. Hence it is imperative for the business to understand the basic concepts and techniques in IT systems, as they are putting their stakes into these systems.

However, the gap between IT and business teams has been historically wide due to differences in goals, culture, rewards, and non-appreciation of each other's body of knowledge. This rift has often resulted in expensive and complex IT systems with high total cost of ownership (TCO) and poor return on investment

(ROI) for the enterprise. According to Paul Strassmann, a well-known corporate information systems executive, "aligning information systems to enterprise goals has emerged as the number one concern in surveys of business executives" [Strassmann, 1998].

As such, the purpose of this chapter is to help the business user better understand key IT concepts, so that he or she is better equipped to derive more value from data.

BUSINESS DATA LIFECYCLE

Business data has a limited life span and follows a defined lifecycle. The data lifecycle integrates data and information with people, business processes, and systems. Each stage in the data lifecycle demands different strategies, poses complex challenges, and provides opportunities to the enterprise. The data lifecycle encompasses the end-to-end effective and efficient management of business data with appropriate policies and procedures throughout its lifecycle. Most business data goes through eight key lifecycle stages: origination, capture, validation, processing, distribution, aggregation, interpretation, and consumption.

ORIGINATION

In most cases, business data originates in an unstructured format. The source of origin can be in two main forms: humans or machines. When data comes from humans, it could be from a single person, or from a group as a workflow mechanism. When data originates from machines (including the internet), the rate and the volume at which the data originates is significantly higher than what is capable by human or manual means. Machine-generated data is the lifeblood of the "Internet of Things." This data has no single form; the type, format, metadata, and frequency always relate to some particular business purpose, and the machine that originates the data.

CAPTURE

Whether facilitated by humans or machines, origination is the process of acquiring new data or updating existing data in a machine-readable format. The machine-readable data is initially captured in binary format. It is then translated into a human-readable or ASCII (American Standard Code for Information Interchange) format in IT systems. The data in most cases is formatted and saved in databases of IT systems as structured data. But recently, data has increasingly been captured as unstructured data in IT systems. Regardless of the way the data is captured in IT systems, data capturing typically occurs at the point of data origination, and can be a manual or an automatic process.

- Manual data capture (MDC) is appropriate for low-volume data records that need to be captured on an *ad hoc* basis. Furthermore, MDC is usually performed when human discretion is needed for data capture.

- When data volume is big, defined, and predictable, data is usually captured automatically into computer systems using Automatic Identification and Data Capture (AIDC) technologies. These mechanisms include bar codes, RFID (radio-frequency identification), smart cards, and video and audio recognition software. While some of the data that is automatically captured is intentional, a significant amount of data is "shadowed." A data shadow is a dataset that is a by-product of the automatic data capture process. The data in the shadow normally includes data pertaining to authentication, sensors, communication metadata, and more. Because of this high volume of data, AIDC technologies contribute significantly towards "Big Data."

Again, in both MDC and AIDC methods, there is always a time lag between data origination to capture.

VALIDATION

Once the data persists in IT systems after capture, it must be validated. Data validation is the process of ensuring that the computer programs in the IT system operate on quality data that meets business requirements. Some amount of data validation (especially for structured data) happens during data capture, by ensuring adherence to the data dictionary. But a significant amount of validation is carried out by the transactional application programs before the data is ready for processing. Furthermore, if the data element is subject to internal or industry standards, validation could be performed manually. For example, the CASS (Coding Accuracy and Support System) software utility developed by the USPS (US Postal Service) validates US postal address to USPS specifications.

PROCESSING

Processing involves systematic actions such as classifying, sorting, searching, and calculating, such that the data is transformed into meaningful information. The majority of the processing takes place in transactional application systems. Processing is usually the first step in realizing meaningful patterns from raw data. Processing structured data is fairly straightforward, since the processing logic is managed by the application programs. On the contrary, unstructured data requires some structuring before it can be processed.

DISTRIBUTION

Data distribution (also called data integration) is the transfer of data from one format (or system, or type) to another format (or system, or type). This step is primarily associated with data movement or Enterprise Application Integration (EAI) technologies, which move data from one transactional application to another via the application's programming interfaces (APIs); this is done in order to align with the rules of a particular business process. Current EAI technologies support both synchronous and asynchronous data as well as business rule integration. However in the recent years, Data Virtualization (DV) technologies are increasingly seen as an alternative to EAI technologies. In essence, DV allows an application to retrieve and manipulate data without requiring technical details about the data, such as how it is formatted or where it is physically located.

AGGREGATION

This step combines data from different sources into one canonical or common data model by consolidating (or "aggregating") large quantities of data. Unlike in EAI technologies, here the application's logic is normally skipped, with data movement carried out by extract, transform, and load (ETL) technologies directly from the databases. The purposes of consolidating data are to reduce duplicates, introduce standardization, perform validity checks, and clean erroneous data, ultimately presenting data in a unified (and thereby more valuable) form. The products of consolidation or the ETL process are typically data marts and data warehouses (DWH) that go on to be used by business intelligence (BI) systems.

INTERPRETATION

Based on Benjamin Bloom's taxonomy of learning, data interpretation can be defined as the combination of analysis, synthesis, and evaluation. Analysis ensures that when the information is broken down, it can be traced back to the individual data elements. Synthesis is the process of building information from data — namely, finding patterns. Finally, evaluation includes combining the outcomes from synthesis and analysis to make judgments for a given purpose. Along with appropriate data visualization tools, data can be interpreted in 3 different forms: transactional reports, BI reports, or analytics reports. Chapter 8 discusses these three types of reports in greater detail.

CONSUMPTION

This data lifecycle function is all about realizing results from data. As mentioned before, business data is used for three main purposes: decision making, compliance, and customer service. From the decision-making perspective, data consumption includes deriving insights and suggesting recommendations for business actions. The use of data for compliance ensures that businesses are abiding by industry standards, security policies, and government laws.

Customer service involves taking care of the needs of both internal and external customers of the enterprise by providing stakeholders with data on demand.

IT Functions

Keep in mind that each of the above eight lifecycle activities are performed in IT systems that involve secure data storage, which includes back-up, archival, purging, and disaster recovery (DR). Because of these added elements, we can add two more functions to our data lifecycle: storage and security. Whenever data and information are used in business processes, security and storage must accompany it at every stage of the process.

STORAGE

Data storage is the physical data storage in IT systems. There are two main kinds of data storage: primary and secondary.

- Primary data storage refers to the memory storage that is directly accessible to the processor, including internal memory (registers), fast memory (cache), and main memory (RAM) placed on the motherboard. Data in the primary memory is volatile and is non-removable.

- Secondary storage involves storing data for long-term use. It includes memory devices that are not a part of the motherboard. Secondary memory structures are non-volatile devices that hold data until it is deleted or overwritten. Common examples of secondary storage devices are magnetic disks, optical disks, hard disks, flash drives, and magnetic tapes. With secondary storage, a RAID (redundant array of independent disks) is a technology that connects multiple secondary storage devices to facilitate back-up, archival, and disaster recovery (DR).

Storage also covers the archiving and purging of data. Archiving is transferring data from active use to inactive use; purging is permanently deleting data from storage. Because the cost of storage is dropping dramatically every year, and compliance requirements are regularly becoming more stringent, enterprises are archiving data more often than purging it.

SECURITY

Data security entails protecting data from destructive forces and unauthorized users or systems, in order to maintain its integrity. From the IT perspective, data security encompasses measures on authentication, authorization, and confidentially, with the ultimate goal to prevent unauthorized access and protect data from corruption and loss. Data security is applicable whether the data is in motion or at rest. Key "data in motion" protection techniques are:

- An **SSL** (Secure Sockets Layer) is used to establish an encrypted link between a web server and the browser.
- **FTPS** is FTP (File Transfer Protocol) with added SSL for security. FTPS uses a control channel and opens new connections for data transfer.
- **SFTP** is SSH (Secure Socket Shell) File Transfer Protocol. While SSH is a network protocol that provides a secure way to access a remote computer, SFTP was designed as an extension of SSH to provide file transfer capability. So SFTP uses only the SSH port for both data and control.

The important "data at rest" protection techniques are:

- **Physical control** is the restriction of physical or in-person access to data center.
- Access **control** is achieved by the process of authentication and authorization on applications.

- **Masking** is the process of hiding original data or obfuscating original data with random characters or data.
- In **encryption**, the plain data, referred to as plaintext, is encrypted using an encryption algorithm, generating cipher text that can only be read if decrypted.
- **Tokenization** involves substituting a sensitive data element with a non-sensitive equivalent (called a "token") that has no meaning or use.
- **Scrambling** is the process of mixing up sensitive data. This process is irreversible, so that the original data cannot be discerned from the scrambled data.
- **Anonymization** is the removal of sensitive information before processing.
- **Database controls** are building access controls in databases.

In total, there are ten data lifecycle activities; eight of them are focused on business and two are IT-focused. The ten data lifecycle activities are shown in the figure below.

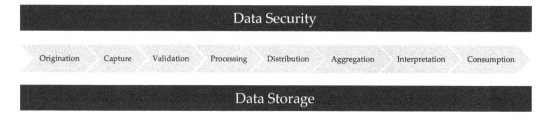

Data lifecycle activities

IT Systems

Up until now we have seen the term "system" often used in this book. What exactly is an IT system? Fundamentally, an IT system is a set of interrelated and interdependent components that forms a functioning whole within a defined boundary. These components continually influence one another to achieve the system's goal.

While the system is subject to constant change, it usually maintains an internal steady state called "homeostasis," despite the changing external environment. But the functioning of the system invariably stops when any one component is removed; the functioning of the system changes when the characteristic of any one or more components is altered significantly. An automatic hand dryer can be considered a system because the hot air (i.e. output) comes out as long as the hands are kept under the machine.

In the context of an IT system, the key components of a system include hardware, software, process, data, users, and a feedback mechanism. The software or application manages the data for the business process, while the hardware or infrastructure facilitates secure data storage.

So what value do IT systems provide? Overall IT systems or digital technologies bring efficiency and effectiveness in business operations. At the core, IT systems bring six main value propositions:

1. **Consistency**. IT systems provide consistency in the execution of business process by adhering to business rules based on leading industry practices and standards. Without IT systems, for example, a purchasing manager would be issuing purchase orders to vendors according to his own standards which would be very different from another purchasing manager issuing a purchase order.

2. **Repeatability**. IT systems can repeat a business process over and over, and get the same results every time. Together with consistency, repeatability brings facilitates automation and reduces the cycle time to complete a business operation.

3. **Integration.** IT systems can integrate business process across different jurisdictions, business processes, business functions and even business partners to act as a coordinated whole. For example in the automotive industry, traditionally the customer plant utilizes the information

contained within the ASN to determine and confirm goods in transit, verification against the shipment as product is received, and generation of an electronic invoice for supplier payment.

4. **Visibility**. IT systems provide visibility as they capture business process details along with data. This provides the foundation for measuring business progress thereby creating accountability.

5. **Scalability**. IT systems can scale business operations and can handle a growing amount of work in a very cost effective manner. In addition, IT systems have to continue to function well when it is changed in scope or size in order to meet the business need. Basically scalability in IT systems can be upward or downward. For example, to approve invoices received, IT systems can process millions of invoices a month easily when the business grows. On the contrary, if the business is experiencing a downturn, IT systems can be quickly rescaled to process lower volumes of data and processes.

6. **Security**. IT systems enable business to control access to business process and the associated data by authenticating users and other IT systems, implementing access control for operations and resources, and providing data integrity and privacy.

Recall in Chapter 2 when we discussed ISA 95, including the IT systems that were part of "level 4" relevance for business operations. Within ISA 95 level 4, there are four main types of IT systems that perform the above ten functions of the data lifecycle. These four types of IT systems are:

1. Online Transactional Processing (OLTP) systems
2. Integration Systems, including EAI (Enterprise Application Integration) and ETL (Extract-Transform-Load) systems
3. Online Analytical Processing (OLAP) Systems
4. Analytics systems

While OLTP systems are basically used for recording business categories, entities, and events (such as vendors, currencies, orders, invoices, and payment) and capturing changes in the data elements as they occur, OLAP systems are mainly used for analysis and decision support. The distribution of data from the OLTP to the OLAP systems is managed by integration systems. As an example, the picture below shows the association of ten data lifecycle activities with the four main types of IT systems (including the key IT tools used) in an electricity distribution company in Toronto, Canada.

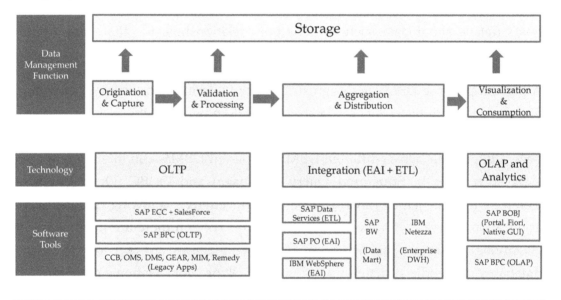

Data lifecycle activities mapped to the IT landscape

IT systems are important as they bring repeatability, consistency, and visibility to the business process. However, it is the data in these systems that really matters to the business. Quality IT systems are of little value if the data quality in these systems is poor. According to Tim Berners-Lee, the inventor of the World Wide Web and one of Time Magazine's '100 Most Important People of the 20th Century', "Data is a precious thing and will last longer than the systems themselves" [Deutsch, Randy, 2015].

DATABASES

Before we look at the above IT systems in detail, it is worth mentioning that one common element in these four systems is the database. Any discussion on data and IT systems without mention of the database is incomplete. Fundamentally, a database is an organized collection of data structures. The metadata of the database is contained in the data dictionary, and the management of data is carried out by the database management system (DBMS). Basically, the DBMS needs the data dictionary to access the data within the database, as the dictionary holds details about data such as definition, relationships to other data, origin, usage, and format.

A general-purpose DBMS is designed to allow the definition, creation, querying, update, and administration of databases. Well-known DBMSs include MySQL, Microsoft SQL Server, Oracle, MongoDB, and IBM DB2. Though a database is not generally portable across different DBMSs, different DBMSs can interoperate with tools such as SQL (Structured Query Language) and ODBC (Open Database Connectivity) or JDBC (Java Database Connectivity), allowing the software application to work with more than one DBMS. Though there are many ways of classifying databases, the two main types of databases are SQL or "relational databases" to handle structured data, and NoSQL or "non-relational databases" to manage unstructured data.

RELATIONAL OR SQL DATABASES

Relational or SQL databases (such as MySQL Oracle, SQL Servers, and SQLite) hold data in defined rows and columns in tables. The data is stored in a structured way with a well-designed schema (i.e. the relationship between tables and field types), including proper relationships that minimize data redundancy and ensure data reliability. Basically, schema ensures that it is not possible to add data until you define tables and field types. For example, a column designed to hold vendor codes might require seven characters; this brings the advantage of rejecting any invalid vendor codes. However, if you need to change the schema (to include vendor codes with more than seven characters), then the table structure must be altered using the Structured Query Language (SQL).

In simple words, a relational database can be visualized as a set of multiple tables; each table contains rows and columns where data is stored. In the tables, rows are data records and columns are attributes or fields. For example, a CRM (Customer Relationship Management) database would include a table for the customers, with columns for name, address, phone number, and so forth. Another table within that same CRM would capture details pertaining to the sales transactions, such as sales order, product identifier, date, sales price, and more. All relational tables in the database must follow two key integrity rules in order to ensure that data is accurate and accessible:

- **Entity integrity**. This rule says that all the rows of a table should be distinct, to avoid ambiguity while accessing the rows of that table. This rule is enforced by setting up a "primary key." The primary key is a field that has data values that uniquely identify each row in the table; the data value in the field cannot be blank.

- **Referential integrity**. This rule says that if a foreign key is defined on a table, then a data value matching that foreign key value must exist as the primary key of a row in some other table. Fundamentally, the foreign key defined in the second table refers to the primary key in the first table. This rule ensures that changes cannot be made to data in the primary key table if those changes break the link to data in the foreign key table.

NON-RELATIONAL OR NOSQL DATABASES

Non-relational or NoSQL databases (such as MongoDB, CouchDB, Redis, and Apache Cassandra) do not have defined data models, as their data are in single document files. If the data requirements are not clear or if there are massive amounts of unstructured data, then non-relational or NoSQL databases are preferred, as they offer much greater flexibility than relational or SQL databases. NoSQL databases have gained prominence due to the explosion in IoT and Web technologies which bring unstructured data from sensors, social sharing, photos, blogs, location/GPS information, online activity, and more. As NoSQL databases consume extra computational effort and more storage than SQL databases, they require different data management technologies and solutions (such as Hadoop). However, NoSQL doesn't mean that the database does not use SQL; it just means that in addition to relational tools, other tools are also available for data analysis. There are four main NoSQL database types:

- **Document databases** pair each key with a complex data structure known as a document. These documents can contain many different key-value pairs, or key-array pairs, or even nested documents.

- **Graph stores** are used to store information about networks of data, such as social connections.

- **Key-value stores** are the simplest NoSQL databases. Every single item in the database is stored as an attribute name (or 'key'), together with its value.

- **Column stores** are optimized for queries over large datasets; they store columns of data together, instead of rows.

SQL OR NOSQL?

Now the key question is: which databases matter for business today? Fundamentally, SQL and NoSQL databases complement each other. For example, to get the most from NoSQL databases, they should be combined with SQL solutions into a single data infrastructure that meets the manageability and security demands of today's business enterprise.

Overall, while SQL and NoSQL databases use a common set of tools, the purposes for which the SQL and NoSQL databases are built are different. When compared to relational databases, NoSQL databases are more scalable and provide superior performance. Today's businesses have to rely on both relational/SQL databases and non-relational/NoSQL databases. For instance, a furniture manufacturer might will issue purchase orders for their vendors on a specific furniture item from their ERP system (which will be a relational/SQL database), and get feedback from Facebook on the same furniture item in a text or unstructured format (which will go into a non-relational/NoSQL database).

Even while NoSQL databases have gained popularity for their performance and scalability, SQL databases are more likely to ensure ACID compliancy (atomicity, consistency, isolation, and durability), which reduces anomalies and protects the integrity of the data. In fact data integrity is one of the key reasons for enterprises to rely on SQL databases. In the healthcare industry, electronic health records (EHRs) rely on structured data elements when documenting critical patient information, by using controlled, structured vocabulary rather than narrative, unstructured text.

In addition, SQL databases are generally preferable if the data is structured and that data structure is unchanging. Essentially, if the business is not experiencing massive data growth (on the order of zettabytes) and is focused on keeping a consistent data structure, then SQL databases are preferred. When it comes to storing large volumes of data that have little structure, NoSQL databases are flexible; they do not set limits on data storage, and they can be supplemented with additional new data structures when required. However, most enterprises do not have this amount and type of data. For example, a leading Canadian energy company had just four TB (terabytes) of data in their structured SAP ERP system after 20 years of deployment. Even in the internet world which is dominated by unstructured data, structured data allows search engines to crawl the websites to understand the website better.

Richard Larson, Professor of Engineering Systems at MIT, says "Today's emphasis on unstructured big data and data analytics may leave some folks thinking that management and policy insights can only arise from the analysis of millions of data entries. Sometimes less is more. In fact, an excess of numbers can engender more headaches than insight."

To summarize, SQL or relational databases are relevant even today for the following reasons:

- SQL databases ensure integrity of the data, which is critical for managing business operations.

- Most enterprises have significant amounts of structured data, and even today are struggling to realize value from it. Many business and IT leaders and information management researchers see deriving value from structured data as a prerequisite to unlock the value from unstructured data.

- As NoSQL databases still need some amount of structure for processing, they still rely on SQL concepts.

NOTE: Going forward, this book will use the term "data element" to refer to a database, table, or field — any data structure that can organize and hold data.

OLTP Systems

We'll start the discussion of the four systems with OLTP (Online Transactional Processing) systems. OLTP systems facilitate fast insertion, updating, and deleting of data pertaining to business transactions. They are used for high throughput inserts or for when hundreds of users concurrently access a system. Invariably, the databases in OLTP systems are relational. The four basic operations that are performed are described by the acronym "CRUD": create, read, update, and delete.

The key value propositions of OLTP applications are availability, speed, concurrency, recoverability, and referential integrity. As OLTP systems perform core business operations, OLTP systems are often decentralized to avoid SPOF (single points of failure). This means OLTP systems are made up of multiple servers (presentation, application and database) to maximize transaction processing and minimize response times.

A CRM system is a good example of an OLTP system. For example, throughout the sales process in a retail store, we capture details such the identity of the customer who bought the item, product details, where to ship, where to bill, among others. Hence the simple OLTP data model for sales must contain tables including currency, stores, customers, products, and sales, ultimately forming a relational database for the "sales" function. The tables CURRENCY and STORES will deal with reference data; tables called CUSTOMERS and ITEMS are related to master data; the table SALES pertains to transactional data. Each of these tables would normally have at least one primary key (PK) field that has values to uniquely identify each row in the table. In addition, nulls are not allowed in the primary key columns; this satisfies the entity integrity rule mentioned in the previous section.

However, the data in the SALES table also includes data coming from other reference, master, and transactional data tables. In this SALES table we will have one or more foreign key (FK) fields that uniquely identify a row of another table. These foreign keys are defined in the second table, but refer to the primary keys in the first table. As mentioned in the previous section, the combination of primary keys and foreign keys enforces integrity in the sales table. The entity and referential integrity rules which are the key features of an OLTP system are illustrated for the "Sales" business function as shown on the following page.

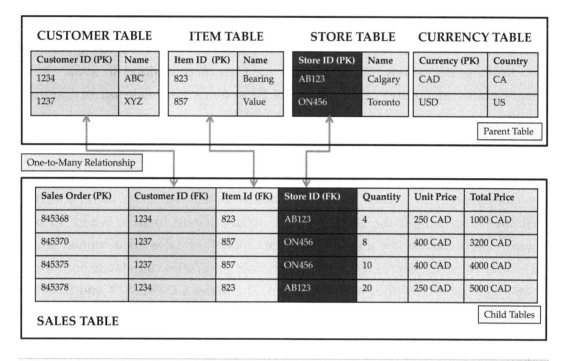

CUSTOMER TABLE		ITEM TABLE		STORE TABLE		CURRENCY TABLE	
Customer ID (PK)	Name	Item ID (PK)	Name	Store ID (PK)	Name	Currency (PK)	Country
1234	ABC	823	Bearing	AB123	Calgary	CAD	CA
1237	XYZ	857	Value	ON456	Toronto	USD	US

Parent Table

One-to-Many Relationship

Sales Order (PK)	Customer ID (FK)	Item Id (FK)	Store ID (FK)	Quantity	Unit Price	Total Price
845368	1234	823	AB123	4	250 CAD	1000 CAD
845370	1237	857	ON456	8	400 CAD	3200 CAD
845375	1237	857	ON456	10	400 CAD	4000 CAD
845378	1234	823	AB123	20	250 CAD	5000 CAD

SALES TABLE

Child Tables

Referential integrity in OLTP systems

Other examples of OLTP systems include the teller application in a bank, a billing application in an electricity distribution company, and a trading system in an oil company, among others.

INTEGRATION SYSTEMS

The second type of IT system is the integration system. Most enterprises have multiple OLTP systems specific to business functions, and these systems vary greatly in terms of business and technical architecture. To have a unified and enterprise-centric view of data and business processes, these OLTP systems have to be integrated. This is achieved by integration systems.

Integration of various IT systems is an expensive and complex endeavor. Gartner predicts that by 2018, more than 50 percent of the cost of implementing 90 percent of new large IT systems will be spent on application and data integration

[Mildeberger, 2013]. While integration systems essentially consolidate and distribute data, they can be broadly classified into two types: EAI (enterprise application integration) and ETL (extraction, transformation, and loading). Both types rely on the concept of mapping data from many disparate OLTP systems to a target system — which could be OLTP or OLAP or analytics systems.

EAI (ENTERPRISE APPLICATION INTEGRATION)

EAI or Middleware address business process integration, allowing OLTP systems to integrate with each other through API (application programming interface) calls. EAI achieves this by encapsulating business rules, data rules, and data into a common data exchange format. EAI involves integration of diverse business applications (usually OLTP systems) within and beyond the enterprise — both synchronously – where data transfer happens without delay and asynchronously – where data transfer happens with some delay. The EAI architecture can be one of three types:

- **PTP (point-to-point) integration**. In PTP integration, business logic and data flow directly from one OLTP application to another. A PTP connection ensures that only one receiver receives a particular message. PTP integration starts simply enough, but becomes complicated as the application landscape gets bigger.
- **Hub and spoke integration**. With hub and spoke technology, data flows through the central point called the "hub." Hubs can simplify integration because they can connect systems with different data formats and data transfer methods. However, hubs also introduce complication, because they become a single point of failure (SPOF) in the integration landscape.
- **ESB (Enterprise Service Bus) integration**. With an ESB, all applications that are part of the integration landscape follow the same standards. They exchange data as messages, using industry standards such as XML (Extensible Markup Language), HTTP (Hypertext Transfer Protocol), SOAP (Simple Object Access Protocol) and more. Any application can plug

into the ESB, as long as it meets the ESB's data exchange standards. ESBs use MQ (message queues) as transports for delivering messages. An ESB is also the backbone for achieving the SOA (service-oriented architecture) which is a set of reusable services to build applications at the enterprise level.

Common examples of EAI or Middleware systems include Microsoft Biztalk, IBM WebSphere, and Mulesoft ESB. Within every EAI, there is another technology called EDI (electronic data interchange), which is used primarily for exchanging business data such as contracts, purchase orders, order status, deliveries, shipments, invoices, and remittances asynchronously as electronic documents in a common standard between business partners. EDI (unlike EAI) does not deal with business process integration or sequencing of business activities.

ETL (EXTRACTION, TRANSFORMATION, AND LOADING)

ETL is the process of extracting the data from homogeneous or heterogeneous OLTP systems, transforming and validating the data, and finally loading the data to the database. This database is commonly called a data warehouse (DWH). The ETL process is often time-consuming; databases may perform slowly due to data concurrency, entity and referential integrity validation, and processing of database indices. Though most DBMS offer ETL capabilities, specialized ETL systems (such as SAP Data Services, Microsoft's SQL Server Integration Services, and IBM's InfoSphere DataStage) are commonly used by enterprises for ETL purposes. The table below shows the differences between the two types of integration systems.

Parameter	EAI	ETL
Target Interfaced System	OLTP systems	OLAP systems
Focus	Business process and system	Data elements
Purpose	Application integration	Data integration
Processing	High numbers of transactions	Large amounts of data
Integration	One-to-one or many-to-many system integration	One-to-one system integration

OLAP Systems (Business Intelligence Systems)

While OLTP systems provide a high degree of data validation and integrity, retrieving data from OLTP systems (especially for reporting) to cater to different views of the stakeholder is time-consuming due to all the references and checks involved. OLAP (online analytical processing) systems enable users to quickly and selectively retrieve and view data from different points of view. At the core, the three main characteristics of OLAP systems are denormalization, aggregation (or abstractness), and multi-dimensionality and the data structure in OLAP systems is known as the data warehouse (DWH).

Fundamentally, for quick and easy data retrieval, we need data structures with little data integrity as data integrity is usually done when the data is captured in the OLTP systems. The data structure that is typically used for data retrieval or reads relies on a technical concept called denormalization, and the denormalized data structure is known as the data warehouse (DWH). A DWH is a federated repository for all the data (typically historical) that an enterprise's various OLTP systems have collected. In fact, a DWH supports an OLTP system by providing a place for the OLTP system to offload data it accumulates; these are services that would complicate and degrade OLTP performance if they were performed in the OLTP system. From the design perspective, the two most prevalent DWH design models are known as the "star schema" and the "snowflake schema."

Both star and snowflake schema segregate business data into dimension tables and fact tables. Dimension tables contain descriptive attributes related to the fact data — specifically to reference data and master data. Dimension attribute examples include product models, product categories, and geographic locations. Fact tables hold the measurable and quantitative data. Specifically, fact tables deal with transactional data that users want to analyze. Examples of fact data include sales price, sales quantity, and time. The fact and dimension tables work together; the fact table holds the data to be analyzed, and the dimension table stores data about the ways in which the fact table can be analyzed.

Let us now come back to the two DWH design models — the star schema and the snowflake schema. The star model gets its name from its depiction as a five-pointed star. This star is formed by a central fact table and multiple dimensional tables that radiate from it, connected by the primary and foreign keys of the database. The star schema is shown in the figure below.

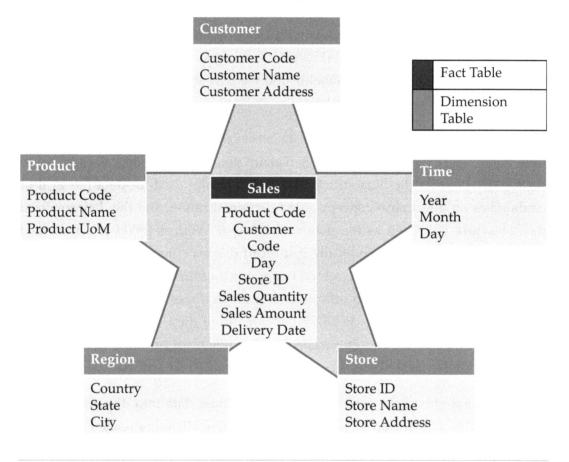

The star schema

The snowflake schema, on the other hand, represents a dimensional model which is composed of a central flat table and a set of constituent dimension tables, which are further normalized into sub-dimensional tables. The snowflake schema is shown in the figure below.

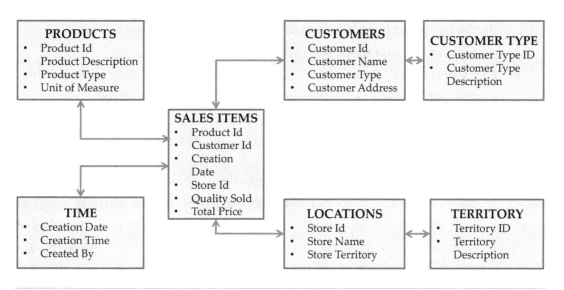

The snowflake schema

So what are the key differences between these two design models? Yahoo's Data Architect, Rohit Chatter, has described four fundamental differences between the star and snowflake schemas [Chatter, 2012]:

1. **Data optimization**. The snowflake model uses normalized data to eliminate redundancy and thus helps to reduce the amount of data. Also, the hierarchy of the business and its dimensions are preserved in the snowflake model, through referential integrity. The star model, on the other hand, uses denormalized data, and the dimensions directly refer to the fact table. So fundamentally the star schema creates more data volumes than snowflake schema.

2. **Business model.** In the snowflake model, the business hierarchy of the data model is represented in a primary key — foreign key relationship between the various dimension tables. In the star model, all dimension tables correspond only to foreign keys in the fact tables. So generally the data integrity with snowflake models is higher than star models.

3. **Performance.** The snowflake model has a higher number of joins between dimension and fact tables; as such, the performance is slower. The star

model has fewer joins between dimension and facts tables, so the performance of star models is faster than snowflake models.

4. **ETL Complexity.** The snowflake model loads the data marts; consequently, the ETL job is made more complex by the dependency between dimensions. The star model, however, loads the dimension table without dependency between dimensions, making the ETL job simpler.

Where do the two models (i.e. star and snowflake) fit into the design of BI or OLAP systems? Choosing a model basically depends on the purpose of your analysis. With the snowflake model, dimension analysis is easier. It makes it relatively easy to answer questions like "how many accounts or campaigns are online for a given customer?" Basically for any analysis based on master data, the snowflake model is preferred. However, the star schema is useful for metrics analysis or transactional data analysis, or asking questions like "what is the revenue for a given customer?"

Note: A cube is a data structure constructed from a DWH to contain the data; a cube is basically an instantiation of the DWH. A cube is organized and pre-summarized into a multidimensional structure defined by a set of dimensions and measures to facilitate queries such as consolidation (roll-up), drill-down, and slicing and dicing of data during reporting.

ANALYTICS SYSTEMS

Closely tied to OLAP or BI tools are the analytics systems. These systems perform descriptive, predictive, and prescriptive reporting. They deal with the discovery, interpretation, and communication of data insights, using techniques from statistics, computer programming, and operations research. Typically, analytics systems can pull data from any sources, including OLTP systems, BI/OLAP systems, spreadsheets, and even unstructured data sources such as documents and text. R, Python, and Microsoft Excel with VBA are key tools within analytics systems, as these programming languages greatly help data analysis and synthesis.

Analytics systems are normally complemented by data visualization (DV) tools as DV tools give visual context to data, by displaying it in infographics, dashboards, geographic maps, heat maps, and detailed charts. The DV tools also provide interactive capabilities, enabling users to "drill into" the data for self-serve ad-hoc querying and analysis. The main purpose of DV is to communicate information clearly and efficiently to appropriate stakeholders. The below figure shows the three stakeholder types, and the four common DV capabilities.

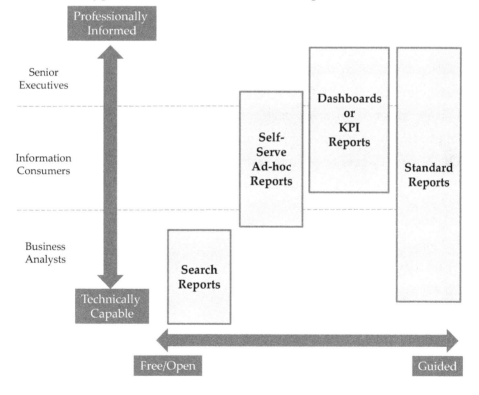

DV capabilities mapped to stakeholder types

Today most OLAP/BI systems come with built-in DV capabilities, like IBM Cognos, Tibco Spotfire, Oracle Hyperion, Microsoft PowerBI, and Tableau.

RELATING OLAP AND OLTP SYSTEMS

Though there are four types of IT systems, from the business user's perspective, the two most important systems are OLTP and OLAP systems. In the enterprise IT landscape, the OLTP system is the business process engine, while the OLAP or BI system is the reporting engine. Key processes of analytic and integration systems are often featured within OLTP and OLAP systems, and are thus rarely the topics of focus in and of themselves. Integration systems are typically under the purview of the IT function and most of the tasks are performed automatically in batches. Also most often the business user might trigger the integration process from the source or target OLTP systems and hence the chance of a business user working directly on an integration system is very slim.

As OLTP and OLAP systems are of primary concern to businesses, in many enterprises, the OLTP and OLAP systems are deliberately hosted in separate servers. This improves system performance, eases the database administration, and makes integration simpler. There are quite a few aspects that are common to both OLTP and OLAP systems. The acronym "ACID" refers to the four fundamental properties of any reliable OLTP or OLAP database:

- **Atomicity:** When a database processes a transaction, it is either fully completed or not executed at all.
- **Consistency:** A transaction either creates a new and valid state of data, or, if any failure occurs, returns all data to its state before the transaction was started.
- **Isolation:** A transaction in process and not yet committed must remain isolated from any other transaction. This ensures that database transactions are securely and independently processed without interference, but it does not ensure the order of transactions.
- **Durability:** Once the transaction is completed, the committed data is saved in the system permanently.

At the same time, there are some key differences between OLTP and OLAP/BI systems, as summarized in this table:

Parameter	OLTP System	OLAP System
Purpose	To control and run core business operations	To help with planning, problem solving, and decision support
Focus	Getting data into the system	Getting data out of the system
Data Source	Operational data generated by one original source	Data that has been consolidated from various OLTP databases
Data Currency	Current	Historical
Data Details	Reveals a snapshot of ongoing business processes	Yields multi-dimensional views of various business activities
Data Model Activity	Create, update, read, and delete or "CRUD" model	Mainly reads data, following the "WORM" model: "written once, read many"
Queries	Relatively standardized and simple queries	Often complex queries involving aggregations
Processing Speed	Very fast	Slower than OLTP systems
Storage Space Requirements	Can be relatively small if historical data is archived	Large due to the existence of aggregation structures and history data
Database Design	Highly normalized with many tables	Typically denormalized with fewer tables

MANAGING THE SYSTEMS

Most business enterprises are constrained by resources such as time, money, and technical capabilities. Hence for efficient utilization of resources, there is a need for differentiated management of these four IT systems. This is where the Gartner PACE model comes into picture. The PACE model is a classification framework that helps with differentiated management of IT systems by categorizing applications into three layers: system of record (SoR), system of differentiation (SoD), and system of innovation (SoI). The PACE layers are shown in the figure below.

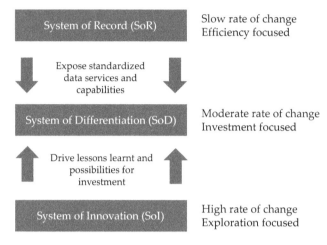

Gartner PACE layers

The word "system" in the context of PACE mainly concerns applications. There are three ways to classify a system: SoR, SoD and SoI:

SOR (SYSTEMS OF RECORD)

Applications or systems can be called SoR if they meet one or more of these criteria:

- These systems empower an enterprise-wide solution, and are used by multiple LoBs in the company.
- These systems are an integrated suite of applications that address core business capabilities.
- These systems can be implemented almost completely out of the box, with little customization or configuration, leveraging best-practice templates for transaction processing.

- Systems under this category would be COTS (commercial off-the-shelf) systems or legacy homegrown systems that have a long lifespan of over 10 years.
- These systems support business processes that are well established and common to most organizations.
- These systems have "single sources of truth" for specific data objects (especially for reference data and master data elements).
- These applications typically push data to SoD and SoI systems.
- The rate of change in these systems is low and system changes are managed every 6 to 12 months as releases. In addition, the stability of these systems is high.
- Any change in these systems has a cascading effect on the dependent IT systems.
- SoR systems typically follow rigorous change control processes.

According to DWH expert Bill Inmon, every SoR shares the following three characteristics [Inmon, 1989]:

1. It provides the most complete, most accurate, and most timely data.
2. It has the best structural conformance to the data model.
3. It is nearest to the point of operational entry and can be used to feed other OLTP systems.

SOD (SYSTEMS OF DIFFERENTIATION)

Applications or systems can be categorized as SoD if they meet one or more of the following criteria:

- SoD applications are specific to one LoB and address one or a group of related business processes.
- Usually SoD applications are custom built as they enable unique company processes or domain-specific capabilities.

- These systems provide competitive advantage and have a medium lifespan of 3 to 5 years. These applications generally receive data from the SoR.
- SoD systems need to be reconfigured frequently to accommodate changing business practices.
- The rate of change or stability in the SoD systems is medium, and system changes are managed every 3 to 6 months.
- SOD systems normally have some degree of change control process.

SOI (SYSTEMS OF INNOVATION)

Applications or systems can be categorized as SoI if they meet one or more of the following criteria:

- SoI systems are built on an ad-hoc basis to address new business requirements or opportunities to enable business transformation.
- These systems generally stand alone.
- These systems typically get data to or from the SoR and SoD systems.
- These systems typically have short implementation timelines with a lifespan of 1 to 3 years.
- These systems support a few users with a function or location in a department or LoB.
- The rate of change in the SoI systems is high, and the stability of these systems is low.

The following table is derived from Gartner's work on PACE layers, and it summarizes the three PACE layers and their key characteristics.

#	Characteristic	SoR	SoD	SoI
1	Strategic Focus	Sustained execution	Competitive differentiation	Business transformation
2	Lifespan	10-20 years	3-5 years	1-3 years
3	Pace of Change	6-12 months	3-6 months	Weekly
4	Business Process	Understood and stable	Understood and dynamic	Ambiguous and dynamic

#	Characteristic	SoR	SoD	SoI
5	Data Integrity	High	High to moderate	Moderate to low
6	Data Integration	Push	Push and/or pull	Pull
7	Sourcing	Integrated application suite	Best-of-breed or suite vendor extension	Specialist niche vendor
8	Investments	Capital	Capital and/or expense	Capital and/or expense

THE BIG PICTURE

The figure below shows how the four systems (i.e. OLTP, integration, OLAP, and analytics) usually work together in an enterprise IT landscape. The enterprise canonical model shown in the figure below is a technology and application agnostic design pattern used to communicate between different data formats.

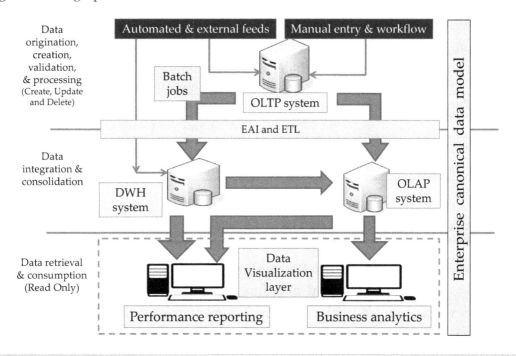

A typical enterprise IT landscape

In this example, the data from the OLTP system can be just integrated into a DWH, which is simply a denormalized table. Standard business performance reports can then be drawn from the DWH. But the data from the OLTP system can also feed into an OLAP/BI system; standard business performance reports and ad-hoc reports can be drawn from the OLAP/BI system using cubes, and viewed using the data visualization (DV) tools. (Note that creating an OLAP cube is not essential to view data in the DV layer. As said before, the DV tools can directly work with a variety of data sources, including OLTP, OLAP, and even Excel spreadsheets.) Finally, the performance reporting or descriptive analytics can come from the OLTP or the OLAP/BI systems, and the business analytics systems normally deal with inferential analytics (i.e. predictive and prescriptive analytics). Chapter 9 covers Enterprise analytics, including descriptive analytics and inferential analytics.

Finally, the associations of the four types of IT systems — OLTP, integration, BI/OLAP, and analytics — are mapped to the three main purposes of data as shown in the table below. For example, the level of association of the OLTP systems is medium compared to the Analytics systems.

Purpose of Data	OLTP	Integration	BI/OLAP	Analytics
Insights	Medium	Very Low	Medium	High
Compliance	High	Low	Medium	Low
Customer Service	High	Very Low	Medium	Low

SYSTEM ARCHITECTURE — THE DATA MODEL

Now that we've discussed the various components in the IT systems such as databases, IT system types, and data lifecycle, we must examine how all these elements work together from a data management perspective. Just as architects consider blueprints before constructing a building, the design of an IT system rests on solid system architecture. One of the key elements of system architecture is the data model, which illustrates the relationship between different data structures within the system. According to ANSI (American National Standards Institute), an organization that fosters development of technology standards, a data model or schema can be one of three kinds:

- **Conceptual data model (CDM)**. A CDM is a high-level description of a business's informational needs. It hides the internal details of logical and physical storage and describes entities, data types, relationships, and constraints.
- **Logical data model (LDM)**. An LDM shows a detailed but technology-agnostic representation of the organization's data. Specifically, an LDM consists of descriptions of entities, attributes, and relationships.
- **Physical data model (PDM)**. A PDM describes the physical means by which data is stored. PDM is concerned with partitions, tablespaces, indexes, clusters, and the like.

At a conceptual or CDM level, data can be modelled as a function of entity, attribute, and value; this model is commonly known as an entity-attribute-value or "EAV" model. The entity is the business object, the attribute includes the parameters or the characteristics of the entity, and value is the quantification of details specific to the attribute of the entity.

To illustrate this EAV model, let us consider a typical sales receipt. When a customer buys five products, the sales receipt lists details of each item purchased, with numerous attributes and values. Here, the data entity is the sales receipt, and the attributes of the sales receipt could include transaction identifier, date, time, store identifier, and others. Each of these attributes will have an appropriate value unique to that individual transaction.

The key point here is that the level of details at which the entity is defined in the EAV model and stakeholder's views and viewpoints that play a key role in the EVM model. In the sales receipt example, if the stakeholder is the customer, the data entity is the receipt. But if the stakeholder is an inventory analyst in the supermarket, the data entity could be any one of the five products on the receipt. If a product is defined as the entity, then the attributes will be product-specific elements such as PLU (price look-up) code or quantity.

Another example of a derived EAV model is when the store-identifier attribute can serve as an entity for a tax analyst. In that case, the attributes for the store location could be city, tax jurisdiction, tax code, and zip code. The potential value for the city attribute could be Calgary or Dallas. Stretching this EAV model further, the value could also be a data entity. For example, if Calgary is an entity for the marketing department, then attributes could be population, state, and per-capita; the value for the population attribute would be about 1.1 million. The EAV data model is shown in the figure below.

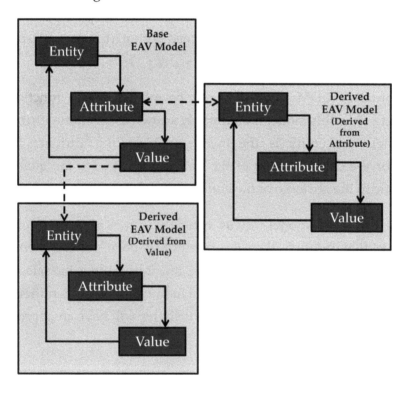

EAV data model

The goal of the EAV data model is to facilitate consistent data definition and classification, in order to optimize data portability and interoperability based on stakeholders' views across the IT landscape. Hence the representation of the EAV model is based on the level of details concerning the stakeholder and has to be conceptual without going into the technical details. This is where the three data models come together. In other words, EAV links the CDM, LDM, and PDM, with solid metadata as the foundation.

CONCLUSION

Today business data is invariably managed in an IT system. Understanding these IT systems will enable the business to get more value from data, and ensure better business-IT alignment. This alignment can provide a positive relationship between the IT function and the business stakeholders, and provide better measures of business performance. These IT systems which address the ten data lifecycle functions could be OLTP systems for recording business events; OLAP, BI or analytics systems for reporting; or integration systems for the transfer and translation of data from the OLTP to the OLAP/BI or analytics systems. However, managing data and information in these systems can take significant cost and effort. Enterprises have to be prudent in making the right investments to realize value from data, carefully considering the benefits, risks, and limitations. Given that data has some limitations as well, the next chapter examines some of the key limitations of data.

Chapter 4: Knowing the Limitations of Data

Not everything that can be counted counts and not everything that counts can be counted.

Albert Einstein
World-famous Physicist

The current wave of excitement about data and related technologies might lead one to think that data could be a panacea for poor business performance. Despite all the attention on data (including millions of dollars spent on data management, business intelligence, and analytics projects), many organizations still struggle to gain value from the investment in digital technologies. In a survey conducted by IBM, 1 in 3 business leaders did not trust the data they used in making decisions. Another survey by the Economist found that 73 percent of respondents trusted their intuition over data when it comes to decision-making [Olavsrud, 2014]. While data definitely has the potential to improve organizational performance, it brings some limitations as well. Hence, it would be prudent to know some of the limitations of data — or rather situations where even quality data might not add much value to the business performance of an enterprise.

KEY LIMITATIONS OF DATA

DATA IS NORMALLY OBSCURED AND BIASED

Today, a significant amount of data that is analyzed by enterprises is structured data that is normally stored in databases within IT systems. The data stored in these databases is usually transformed from an unstructured or "natural" format into a structured format, after the raw data is gathered, curated, and finally stored. This structured format is driven either by the software application (including the database) or by the individual's preferences and experience. For example, in Activity-Based Costing (ABC) analysis, if the application can only capture start and end times (i.e. the duration), but not the actual effort of an activity, then reporting and analytics on that activity would never be possible. Therefore, the data context is either pre-determined or distorted. This means that this "raw data" that is captured, curated, and stored is not only obscure, but also biased.

According to leading statistician Nate Silver, "There is no such thing as unbiased data. We bias the data the minute we start collecting it, as we determine what we will collect, not to mention the types of questions we will ask of it. Bias is the natural state of all data; be it machine or human oriented" [Asay, 2016].

DATA DOESN'T ALWAYS TRANSLATE INTO ACTIONS AND RESULTS

Even if the data quality is good and unbiased, translating data into business insights, strategies, and actions depends on the organization structure, proper training, and empowerment of staff to take actions, among other aspects. A recent Forrester survey found that just 12 percent of the data in an organization is analyzed, 8 percent partially analyzed, while 80 percent of the data is not analyzed at all. Even if the data is analyzed and insights are derived, translating those insights into decisions and actions is based on a number of other business factors and constraints.

I recently drove down one of the main streets in Calgary, Canada, and noticed the gasoline price per liter at Shell (87.9c) is about six cents less than the gasoline price at Esso (93.9c), which is just across the street. While the competitor's data (i.e. Shell's gasoline price) is right in front of the attendant in the Esso gas station, he is not able to change the gasoline prices due to the approval he needs from his reporting manager. Situations like this usually arise because while data relies on logic, decisions are often based on emotions, organizational constraints, organizational structure, and other factors. This means that insights alone very rarely drive actions.

Both for an individual and organization, nothing is more frustrating than having the most timely and accurate data and insights, but still not be able to take any action. **No business value is created by data and insights if they are not acted upon.** If the insights are not put into action, then analytics is not providing any value. According to Thomas Edison, inventor of the motion picture camera and electric bulb, "the value of an idea lies in the using of it" [Gelb, 2008].

RELEVANCY OF DATA IS A FUNCTION OF TIME, SPACE, AND STAKEHOLDER TYPE

Even if quality data is available today, it may not be relevant at a future time, in a different space or jurisdiction, primarily due to changing business needs and government regulations. For example, say within an enterprise, shipments in plant A could be based on delivery priority while shipments in plant B could be based on customer type. So for plant B, delivery priority data is irrelevant or unnecessary. Also stakeholder needs have a bearing on the relevancy of data. For example, cleaned and purged data from stock exchanges may be extremely valuable to financial analysts, but the same curated data would be inappropriate for security analysts fighting fraud. This is why the relevancies of data are often misunderstood, and many enterprises spend a lot of time and effort in managing data that is unnecessary. This problem has been around for a long time. Information systems researchers Martha Feldman and James March reported back in 1981 that managers often ask for data and information that they don't ultimately use [Feldman and March, 1981].

DATA HAS THE POTENTIAL TO CAUSE "ANALYSIS PARALYSIS"

Today we have the technical capabilities to generate, capture, and process huge amounts of data. According to IBM, we create 2.5 quintillion bytes of data every day (1 quintillion is 1 followed by 18 zeros). This ever-increasing volume of data comes in different formats and velocities, and brings higher costs for storage, governance, and retrieval.

According to William McKnight, author of *Strategies for Gaining a Competitive Advantage with Data,* "It is not just spitting out information for the sake of it. It is actually trying to connect the dots between previous transactions, current transactions, and potential future transactions." In a survey by Oracle, over 300 C-level executives said their organization is collecting and managing 85 percent more business data today than it was two years ago. However, 47 percent of them also said that their organization cannot interpret and translate the information into actionable insights. While data is important, it is having the right data that matters.

STAKEHOLDERS' NEEDS PRECEDE METADATA AND DATA DICTIONARY ONTOLOGY

A data element can be consumed in different ways by different stakeholders. For example, while a telephone number field might be used by a sales agent to make customer calls, a tax analyst might use the area code within the telephone number to get tax rates as per jurisdictions. This means the actual use of the telephone number field is more than its intended use, thereby making metadata or data dictionary ontology challenging. In addition, the boundaries between data and information are not always clear. What is data to one person might be information to someone else, and vice versa. For example, to a crude oil commodities trader, slight changes in the sea of data values coming from the exchanges might act as information for taking appropriate action. But to anyone else, they would look like raw meaningless data.

DATA MANAGEMENT IS EXPENSIVE AND TIME-CONSUMING

While businesses strive for quality data to derive insights, getting and managing quality data is time consuming and expensive. In a typical enterprise, every single piece of data must be created, stored, processed, shared, aggregated, cleansed, replicated to Disaster Recovery (DR) sites, and archived — and all these activities take time and money to achieve the desired level of efficiency and effusiveness. According to the research done by Howard Rubin of MIT, 92 percent of the cost of running business in the financial services sector is related to data [Rubin, 2011].

Along with increased cost, it can take years to derive insights from data. Once the data quality is improved, it must continue to be governed throughout its entire lifecycle, to prevent data quality degradation. So if organizations need quality data, then data management should be seen as a continuous improvement initiative at the enterprise level. According to Bill Gates, "The first rule of any technology used in a business is that automation applied to an efficient operation will magnify the efficiency. The second is that automation applied to an inefficient operation will magnify the inefficiency" [Jeston and Nelis, 2008].

DATA MIGHT DISTORT INNOVATION

Data sheds light on past events which no one has any control to change. There is always a time lag between the origination of data to recording of it. Seth Kahan, author of *Getting Change Right*, uses the analogy of driving a car in data-driven decision making. He says, "Making decisions just based on data is like driving your car only by looking in the rear view mirror. During tough times, leaders tend to depend upon the past to make their decisions as they want to be certain about what they are doing. The more certainty an organization wants, the more they go backwards. But the past only shows where you've been, not where you are going or should be going." According to Lara Lee and Daniel Sobol of Harvard Business School, "Data reveals what people do, but not why they do it. Understanding the why is critical to innovation" [Lee and Sobol, 2012].

DATA IS NEVER REAL-TIME; IT IS ALWAYS HISTORICAL

Though many companies talk about performing "real-time" analytics on data, data can never truly be seen in real time. Why? There is always a time lag between data origination and capture. This time lag can be a few microseconds in SCADA (Supervisory Control and Data Acquisition) or PoS (point of sale) systems, or it might be even months in databases of OLTP systems.

On top of this, data is consolidated from diverse systems and aggregated before analytics operations are performed on the BI/OLAP dataset. This means that the time lag is further extended — from microseconds to months or even years. Even though analyzing aggregated data is quite different from analyzing streaming data (i.e. data originating from social media, IoT or sensors), there is still a time lag between data origination and analysis in both cases. Finally, even if a business enterprise manages to get data in technically near-real time, that analysis would be just on a single record. To see trends or conduct prescriptive and predictive analytics, one would need a significant amount of data records; this means that meaningful prescriptive and predictive data analytics can never be in real time.

DATA HAS NO RELEVANCE FOR FIRST-TIME EVENTS

In today's uncertain and volatile business situations, businesses are forced to try new things. Naturally, there is no data available for these first-time events. For example, a company in the US might try to enter a new market in Asia, say India. There is no data available to tell this company if its products or services will work in the Indian market.

Another example of lack of data for first-time events is when an enterprise decides to outsource its IT services. An IT service provider might have a great track record of delivering services to various enterprises. However making a decision whether to outsource based on the data on how the IT service provider is serving other enterprises does not help your enterprise much because the data sets are very contextual. In essence, there would be no reliable data for first-time business ventures. Businesses basically have to rely on intuition, consultation with experts, and computer models and simulations.

DATA CAN MISLEAD DECISION MAKING

Data can be manipulated to mislead decision-making in three main ways:

- **KPIs**. Incomplete KPIs (Key Performance Indicators) are a common source of misinformation. Analytics invariably work most effectively at the enterprise level; as such, analytics need to be implemented with a core set of LoB (Line of Business) dependent KPIs. This is important because LoBs within an enterprise often have conflicting goals, and any KPIs using data at the LoB level might provide a distorted picture of the performance of the enterprise. For example, a marketing LoB might present a KPI that shows increase in customer loyalty. While this KPI might be a positive indicator of performance for the marketing LoB, due to the increased campaign costs, this same KPI has an adverse impact on the financial LoB. In this way, data and KPIs can be used to mislead the organization if the enterprise doesn't have a core set of KPIs that cut across different LoBs.

- **Graphs**. This may happen because the graph designer chooses to give readers the impression of better performance or results than actually exist. In other cases, the reader may be misled by a poor choice of chart selection, or by graphs with inappropriate scales, axes, infographics, and so on.

- **Sample size**. Bias is a systematic error in which a sample is collected in such a way that some members of the intended population are less likely to be included than others. A 2009 investigative survey at the University of Edinburgh found that 33.7 percent of scientists surveyed admitted to questionable research practices, including modifying results to improve outcomes, subjective data interpretation, withholding analytical details, and dropping observations because of gut feelings [Fanelli, 2009].

There have also been numerous cases of data being manipulated for business gains. For example, in 2007, Colgate was ordered by the Advertising Standards Authority (ASA) of the UK to abandon their claim that "more than 80 percent of dentists recommend Colgate." The claim, which was based on surveys of dentists and hygienists carried out by the manufacturer, was found to be misrepresentative as it allowed the participants to select one or more toothpaste brands. The ASA stated that the claim "... would be understood by readers to mean that 80 percent of dentists recommend Colgate over and above other brands, and the remaining 20 percent would recommend different brands." But upon further analysis, ASA understood that another competitor's brand was recommended almost as much as the Colgate brand by the dentists surveyed. The ASA finally concluded that the claim was misleading as it implied that 80 percent of dentists recommend Colgate toothpaste in preference to all other brands [BBC, 2007].

CONCLUSION

In today's interconnected world, with so much data available, decisions don't need to be made on pure intuition. In their 2012 feature on big data, Andrew McAfee and Erik Brynjolfsson of MIT reported that "companies in the top third of their industry in the use of data-driven decision making were, on average, 5 percent more productive and 6 percent more profitable than their competitors" [McAfee and Brynjolfsson, 2012]. However, there are also cases when investing the time and effort to build a data-driven enterprise might be a futile effort — or worse, even harmful. To summarize, data management initiatives could be ineffective in any of the following scenarios:

- There is no senior management commitment to valuing data as an enterprise asset.
- There is no enterprise-wide vision for running and sustaining a data management initiative.
- The insights from data cannot be quickly translated into decisions and actions.
- The relevancy of data changes constantly depending on time, space, and stakeholder preferences.
- There is a need for unbiased details of the business processes and activities.

Chapter 5: Normalizing Enterprise Data Quality

The beginning of wisdom is the definition of terms.

Socrates
Greek Philosopher

In Chapter 3, we discussed how IT systems facilitate data management. Unfortunately, most enterprises have data quality issues of varying sizes and impacts. Stakeholder needs in most data management programs are varied and vague, and most enterprises lack a data-driven culture. For example, when databases are designed, data quality aspects are not explicitly incorporated; database design is focused mainly on application design aspects over data entities, attributes, and relationships.

Generally, data quality is an afterthought in most IT and business transformation initiatives and this results in poor data quality. Organizations that have data quality deficiencies have struggled to achieve growth, agility, and competitiveness. According to Experian Data Quality, a boutique data management company, inaccurate data affects the bottom line of 88 percent of organizations and impacts up to 12 percent of revenues [Levy, 2015]. In 2002, the Data Warehousing Institute (TDWI) stated that poor data quality costs American business $600 billion annually [Eckerson, 2002]. This number went up in 2010 as a report by Ovum, a global analyst firm, estimated that poor data quality costs US businesses a staggering $700 billion per year [Sheina, 2010].

While achieving data quality is complex and time consuming, one of the fundamental challenges arises from the many definitions of "data quality."

Currently there is no universal agreement on what exactly "data quality" means, and which attributes constitute the key data quality dimensions. Hence, this chapter first looks at defining data quality, and then analyzes the key reasons for poor data quality.

DATA QUALITY DIMENSIONS

As mentioned, there is no one universal definition of data quality. One of the leading advocates of quality, Philip Crosby, defined quality as "conformance to requirements" way back in 1979 [Crosby, 1979]. But from the business enterprise perspective, data quality is more about ensuring that the data is useful for performing business transactions. Dr. Thomas Redman believes "data is considered to be of high quality if they are fit for their intended use in operations, decision making and planning" [Redman, 2016].

To define data quality comprehensively, it is important to understand the key dimensions of data quality. Based on the work of the Data Management Association (DAMA), this section examines the different dimensions of data quality for any business enterprise. The word "dimension" is used to identify aspects of data elements that can be defined, quantified, implemented, and tracked. Remember that a "data element" can be reference data, master data, transactional data, or even metadata.

COMPLETENESS

Completeness is the degree of usage of the attributes of a specific data element. Given that data origination and capture is an expensive and time-consuming process, data values for all attributes or fields will not be typically managed for any data element in an enterprise. As such, data completeness involves striking a balance between the effort and time it takes to populate and manage the relevant attributes of the data elements versus the utility that the values in the data element bring to the business.

For example, in many business processes, in the customer master database, the customer's first name and last name are mandatory, while the middle name is optional. In most situations, any effort to update the middle name will cost time and money for very little business value. So the customer data record can be practically considered complete, even if the data value for the middle name is null.

CONSISTENCY

Consistency means that data values across all tables and databases for a specific data element within the enterprise system landscape (or outside the enterprise system landscape) are the same. For example, the GL account for customer deposits in the CRM system should have the same value in the ERP system as well. Consistency in the enterprise IT landscape can be seen from two perspectives:

- **Data value consistency.** Here, the data values are the same across the enterprise IT system landscape. For instance, if the customer identifier is the same in the CRM system and in the shipping system, then the data value is termed consistent.
- **Data traceability consistency.** This case deals with the integrity of the data during data movement and transformation, between systems or in the same system. Data traceability consistency typically is tied to business rules. One example of data traceability consistency is that purchase orders cannot be issued for the vendor if the supplier contract is closed or if the vendor is blocked from doing any business with the enterprise. Another example of data traceability consistency is when an employee status is terminated in the IAM (identity and access management) system, the employee also has no access to the ERP system.

CONFORMITY OR VALIDITY

Conformity (also called validity) refers to data that adheres to specifications, standards, or guidelines, including data type, description, size, format, and other characteristics. For example, in many companies the product code description follows a *noun-modifier-attribute(s)* format — this is a common naming convention for describing items. Though this format is not commonly defined in the data dictionary, any data in violation of this format would be considered low-quality due to inconsistencies in the naming standards.

UNIQUENESS OR CARDINALITY

Uniqueness (also called cardinality) points out that there are no duplicate values for a data element. For example, there might be two vendors that are recorded in the system as Weatherford Inc. and Weatherford Canada, although in fact they are the same business entity. Uniqueness is equivalent to saying that every data record must have a unique primary key, and the value this attribute holds can never be NULL. NULL indicates that a data value does not exist in the database. Uniqueness or cardinality can be described at three levels:

- High cardinality means that a column contains a large percentage of unique values. Examples of fields with high cardinality are identification codes, email addresses, and phone numbers.
- Medium cardinality values are columns or attributes with values that are not commonly repeated. Examples include postal codes and payment plans.
- Low cardinality means that the column contains many duplicates. Low cardinality values include status flags, Boolean values, and gender.

In enterprise databases or tables, all these three types of cardinality coexist. For example, a database table that stores customer bank account information, the "Account Number" column will have very high cardinality, while the customer gender column will have low cardinality (as the column will likely only have "Male" and "Female" as values). Another example of high cardinality is the nine-digit Data Universal Numbering System (DUNS) issued by Dun & Bradstreet that uniquely identifies a business entity in the United States.

How does high cardinality or uniqueness affect data quality? Technically, primary key columns have high cardinality, to prevent duplicate values from being entered. This means it will not be possible to assign two different customers the same customer code. In addition, the primary key field greatly speeds up queries, searches, and sort requests, thanks to database indexing. If the measure of data quality is speed of processing, then it is preferred to query data fields that have high cardinality or uniqueness, and the primary keys usually have high cardinality. In a line, data fields with high cardinality enable faster querying due to database indexing.

ACCURACY

In measurement science, accuracy refers to the closeness of a measured value to a standard or true value. Accuracy is closely related to precision, which is the degree to which repeated measurements under unchanged conditions show the same results. For example, if data originates as 57.75 liters, but it is captured as 57.8 liters, there is a loss of precision.

In the context of data quality, accuracy is the degree to which data truly reflects the business category, entity, or event. However, like the data completeness quality dimension, accurate data involves a trade-off between the time and effort needed to achieve accuracy and the utility of the precision.

In the above example, there was a loss in precision of 0.05 liters, as the measuring instrument could only provide up to first decimal accuracy. Capturing the readings with two decimal place accuracy would require an investment in an advanced and expensive measuring instrument. As such, the analyst must carefully consider whether the small increase in accuracy would really be worth this investment.

CORRECTNESS

Closely related to accuracy is correctness. Correctness is freedom from error or mistakes. It is of Boolean nature; something is either correct or not, and there cannot be a degree of correctness. Correctness is the conformance of a data value to the accepted reference. A customer's bank account number needs to be correct; even a mistake of one character could cause a significant impact to business. Correctness and accuracy go hand-in-hand. For example, the supplier's phone number needs to be correct, while the supplier's name needs to be accurate.

ACCESSIBILITY

Data accessibility refers to how easy (or not) it is to access or retrieve data within a database from the storage repository in the system. Data accessibility is very important from the business perspective, especially if business stakeholders need to accurately and quickly analyze data. The ability to effectively search, retrieve, and use data at all times for business operations can be considered a key characteristic of good data quality. Technically there are two main ways data is accessed in the IT system:

- In random access, retrieval of data happens anywhere on the disk.

- In sequential access, each segment of data has to be read sequentially until the requested data is found. Sequential files are usually faster to retrieve than random access, as they require fewer seek operations.

DATA SECURITY

Closely related to accessibility is data security. Data security entails protecting data from destructive forces, including unauthorized users or systems. Data security also includes the ability to detect cyber threats such as hacking, scams, or malware, by using suitable security tools for data protection. As mentioned in Chapter 3, data security mechanisms are required when data is at rest, in use, and in motion.

Furthermore, data security does not always need to be in the actual production system; a production system is an environment that is used by the end-users for daily business operations. Sometimes non-production systems (where software development and testing of software programs is done by the developers and IT administrators before moving the changes to the production system) also manage a significant amount of the actual production data. In 2011, research by Stuart Feravich, a respected solution expert, reported that 70 percent of surveyed enterprises use live customer data in non-production systems [Feravic, 2011].

CURRENCY AND TIMELINESS

Fundamentally, data quality is time-sensitive; data values continuously change during the data lifecycle. Currency (or "freshness") refers to how "stale" the data is, and how much time has elapsed since it was created or last changed at the data source. According to David Loshin, a recognized thought leader in the area of data quality, currency is the degree to which data is current with the world that it models [Loshin, 2010]. For example, if vendor payment terms have not been updated for years, the data involved would be termed low-quality, as there could be a potential opportunity to renegotiate the contracts with the vendor for better deals.

Related to currency is timeliness. Timeliness refers to whether the most current data value is readily available when it is needed. From the enterprise IT landscape perspective, timeliness is the rate of dissemination of data. Timeliness depends on business criticality and impact. For example, online availability of item stock must be immediately available to inventory management, but a four-hour delay could be acceptable for clearing vendor invoices in the vendor invoice clearing system. Due to increasing demands for quick data-driven decisions, timeliness is increasingly seen as a critical dimension of data quality in today's business environment.

REDUNDANCY

Data redundancy is a condition created within a database or data storage technology in which the data element is replicated and captured by two separate IT systems in two different locations. Redundancy is a deliberate and planned mechanism that enterprises use for backup and recovery purposes. The purpose of this replication is to increase the reliability of the system and thereby improve data quality. Redundancy is closely tied to duplication, as duplication occurs when the same record is repeated in the same table within the database in the same system. While redundancy is a desired characteristic, duplication is not.

COVERAGE

As we've seen, data management is complex, time-consuming, and expensive. As such, the ability of data to cover multiple diverse business needs is always desirable. Reference and master data have high coverage (or "comprehensibility") as they are usually shared in the enterprise, while transactional data has less data coverage as they are specific to one LoB or business function.

Data coverage that promotes data sharing, however, is tied to the business process. For instance, in a telecom company, a 10 percent error rate in customer address might be acceptable for telemarketing. But if billing decides to share the same data values, it might be unacceptable. Data quality can be considered high if the span or coverage of a data element includes multiple business processes.

INTEGRITY

Data integrity includes ensuring that data is recorded exactly as intended, and that when data is retrieved, it is the same as it was when originally recorded. Basically, data integrity ensures that data is not compromised. While data integrity can be enforced as a part of the data governance process, the DBMS can also help by implementing a series of integrity rules to complement data governance processes.

We discussed two types of data integrity from a database perspective in chapter 3 and they are:

- **Entity integrity** defines a row as a unique entity for a particular table. It concerns the concept of primary keys.

- **Referential integrity** preserves the defined relationships between tables when rows are entered or deleted. Referential integrity makes sure that foreign keys and primary keys values are consistent across tables.

However, from the business data perspective, business-defined integrity (the third type of data integrity) ensures that data truly reflects the intended purpose in business operations. For example, one of the most common "anomalies" seen in the Procure-to-Pay (P2P) business processes occurs when purchase requisition (PR) is validated and approved by finance personnel. This situation normally happens when the finance LoB is more influential than the procurement LoB in the enterprise. While a PR is an internal agreement between the requisitioner and the buyer, finance is typically involved in the invoice verification and payment stages which happen later in the P2P cycle. Involving finance in the PR process along with the procurement not only affects the business-defined integrity, but also increases the P2P cycle time. In this example, there is impact on the business-defined integrity if finance would view the procurement spend categories as an internal control mechanism, when procurement would view the same spend categories as part of external mechanisms to respond and align spend categories to market demands.

From the data quality perspective, data integrity ensures that data remains intact and unaltered. It also describes data that can be traced and connected to other data, and ensures that all data is recoverable and searchable.

The figure on the following page gives a holistic view of the 12 data quality dimensions for a business enterprise.

Data quality dimensions

The implementation of the 12 data quality dimensions involves (among other aspects) leveraging the data governance processes and the capabilities of the DBMS. A few points to be noted regarding the implementation of these 12 data quality dimensions:

- It's possible to describe many more than a dozen data quality dimensions. However, these 12 should be applicable to most enterprises for business performance.
- Realizing a high level of data quality for each of these dimensions takes time and effort. It could take months just to determine the current level of data quality. Hence, the 12 data quality dimensions should map to specific business requirements and KPIs, if any steps are taken to improve them.

- The 12 data quality dimensions are described at the most granular level (i.e. at the data record or attribute level).
- All these data quality dimensions are desired attributes for data quality. For example, duplication is not included in the list as it is an undesirable data quality attribute. (Of course, the desirable attributes like uniqueness and cardinality presented here prevent data duplication.)
- Compliance with these 12 data quality dimensions is not mandatory for an enterprise, but it does improve business performance. As mentioned earlier, though, improving all 12 data quality dimensions will include a trade-off between time, cost, and quality. Consider our previous example; updating the customer's middle name for 500,000 customers might improve the completeness dimension for the telemarketing department, but it will also cost a lot of time and effort for relatively few business benefits.

CONSEQUENCES OF POOR DATA QUALITY

So what are the consequences of not complying with these 12 data quality dimensions? What would happen if the data quality in the enterprise is poor given that many enterprises have poor data quality ultimately impacting business performance? In this backdrop, based on the work of David Loshin, there are four categories where poor data quality impacts business performance [Loshin, 2010].

1. **Financial impacts.** Financial impacts due to poor data quality result in increased operating costs, decreased revenues, missed opportunities, reduction or delays in cash flow, and others. For example, if GL accounts are not assigned to the right product categories, then it is difficult to assess which product segments are profitable and which are not.
2. **Marketplace impacts.** These impacts are associated with missing expectations in the marketplace due to compromises in business-defined

integrity. This ultimately results in decreased organizational trust, low confidence in management reporting, and delayed or improper decisions.

3. **Productivity impacts.** Productivity impacts operational efficiency due to increased workloads, decreased throughput, increased cycle time, to name a few. As a simple example, what is the impact if the product description does not adhere to the noun-modifier format or the conformity data quality dimension? Inconsistent product description results in duplicate product master records. This means the same physical product which is codified in different ways results in product assignment to different GL accounts in the contracts, purchase orders, invoices and other transactional documents. This "domino effect" ultimately results in increased workloads to the staff as reconciliations and data clean-up is needed for during management reporting.

4. **Risk and Compliance impacts.** Risk and Compliance impacts due to poor data quality can increase exposure to compliance and financial risks, thereby decreasing the ability to execute in the marketplace. Key impacts include credit assessment, cash flow, capital investment government regulations, industry expectations, internal company policies, and so on. As an example, how does the payment term data element (used in vendor masters) affect compliance and business performance? The vendor payment terms not only determine the due date for clearing vendor invoices, but also improve the cash flow and the working capital requirements of the enterprise.

DATA DEPRECIATION AND ITS FACTORS

Generally, any asset — tangible or intangible — tends to depreciate over time. From the accounting perspective, depreciation refers to the decrease in value of assets so that the company allocates an asset's cost over the duration of its useful life. Technically, for intangible assets such as brands and intellectual property, the process of allocating costs over time is known as "amortization." Given that data is considered an intangible asset, the term amortization is more appropriate when it comes to data quality degradation.

Data decay or degradation refers to a gradual loss in the quality of data. In terms of the data quality dimensions just described, when any of those data quality dimensions are compromised, data is said to be decaying or degrading. Information management researchers Scott Tonidandel, Eden King, and Jose Cortina indicate that in a typical enterprise, data degrades between two to seven percent every month [Tonidandel et al, 2015].

According to Gartner, poor quality data is costing organizations on average $14.2 million annually, and 40 percent of business initiatives fail to achieve targeted benefits because of poor data quality. According to Experian Data Quality, 77 percent of companies believe that their bottom line is affected by inaccurate and incomplete data [Levy, 2015]. As discussed before in chapter 1, businesses are increasingly looking to digital technologies for improved business performance. But if quality data is not available, then these digital technologies or IT systems will have severe limitations in providing business effectiveness and efficiency.

The process of improving the 12 data quality dimensions and preventing data quality degradation is based on three main factors:

1. **Context.** Context depends on the purpose of data — how a specific data element is used in the enterprise. Ultimately, the context or purpose of the data determines the specific data quality dimension that can be used to most effectively raise the quality level of the data. For example, from the analytics or decision-making perspective, the data quality dimensions that are most critical are currency, accessibility, conformity, and consistency. But from the compliance side, say for SSAE-16 (Statement on Standards for Attestation Engagements) certification, the data security dimension is very important. So if the main purpose of some data is to make business decisions, there would be relatively little attention paid to security, resulting in the degradation of the security data quality dimension.

2. **Lifecycle.** As discussed in Chapter 3, the data lifecycle is a series of ten stages involved in successful management of data and information. The data lifecycle (or "data lineage") has a significant impact on data quality; lifecycle touches systems, applications, business processes, and stakeholder roles and responsibilities. Fundamentally, data is hardly stationary. When data flows between systems, it is subject to change in values, format, and usage. This affects data integrity, ultimately causing lower data quality in the enterprise.

3. **Governance.** Successful implementation of any strategic initiative (including data quality initiatives) is a human process. When there are specific goals to achieve, and when the data element is subject to varied forces that could potentially jeopardize data quality, control or governance of data is absolutely essential.

In Chapter 2, while discussing data entropy, it was noted that the quality of data held in IT systems will deteriorate unless steps are explicitly taken to maintain its quality. At the highest level, data governance is a set of processes that ensures that important data assets are formally managed throughout the enterprise. Given that data governance is an evolutionary process for a company, the effectiveness of the data governance processes takes time to mature. This means that in the interim, data quality levels might not be very effective. Chapters 7 and 9 explain the role of governance not only in data quality, but also in effectively enabling data for business performance.

CAUSES OF POOR DATA QUALITY

Having analyzed the 12 different dimensions of data quality and the three key factors that affect data quality, let us consider the key reasons that cause the data quality dimensions to decay or depreciate. In general, there are two main classifications of data decay: physical and logical.

Physical data decay is data loss from the storage medium. Examples include server crashes, hard disk corruptions, data records getting purged without a trace, and more. Physical data decay is instantaneous, and out of one's control. The most common solution to physical data decay is regular backup of the database or recovery of the system in an alternative or secondary data center.

Logical data decay is commonly due to the compromises that different data quality dimensions are subject to. Logical data decay is the main reason why business data cannot be transformed to an enterprise asset effectively. So what are the situations that cause logical data decay? Below are the some of the common causes of poor data quality.

DATA SILOS RESULTING FROM ORGANIZATION SILOS

As mentioned before, business data is one of three main types: reference data, master data, or transactional data. While reference data and master data are typically enterprise-wide and shared, transactional data is specific to LoB and business functions. However, if the reference data and master data are managed by multiple LoBs, the chances of poor data quality increase as each LoB views a data element from their unique business perspective. For example, if the finance LoB owns the product master data because they clear suppliers' invoices and maintain the UoM (unit of measure) as pallets, that particular UoM is not of much use to the warehousing LoB where the products are stocked in boxes.

The root cause of this compromising phenomenon is usually organizational silos, wherein the LoBs do not believe in sharing data or do not see the need to share data with the rest of the organization. This "silo mentality" reduces the efficiency of the overall business operations, and is mainly attributed to a conflicted top leadership team. As written by Patrick Lencioni in his book *Silos, Politics and Turf Wars*, "Silos and the turf wars devastate organizations. They waste resources, kill productivity, and jeopardize the achievement of goals." He goes on to advise leaders to tear down silos by moving past behavioral issues and address the contextual issues that are present at the heart of the enterprise.

INTERPRETATION AND CONSUMPTION OF DATA HAPPEN IN DIFFERENT WAYS

According to Ted Freidman, Gartner's VP of research, "Data quality is a business issue and not an IT matter. Data quality requires businesses to take responsibility and drive improvements" [Saves, 2008]. However, within a business, the intended use of data might be very different from the actual use; data is contextual and is always tied to the business process and role of the data consumer. For instance, the phone number field in the customer master data is usually a shared data element throughout the entire sales process. The shipper can use it to contact the customer while the tax analyst can use it for validating the customer jurisdiction code along with the tax codes — even though the telephone number was not originally meant for tax calculation. For example, a telephone number that starts with 416 is assigned to the Toronto region, but tax analysts might use the number 416 to validate the tax codes as these tax codes are based on jurisdiction. This effectively means that if the telephone number is not maintained, the tax analyst might complain of poor data quality — even though the telephone number field was never intended to validate and calculate taxes.

FREQUENCY OF USE AND THE NUMBER OF USERS

Sharing data increases the number of data consumers, and all of those consumers come with varied and implicit needs. For example, the order status in a sales order might provide the sales director the sales pipeline of the business. If the accounting analyst then decides to use the same data element to improve the prediction of future sales, the delivery dates and payment terms must also be maintained in the sales order. The more people use data, the more data elements must be managed and governed. Satisfying the diverse requirements of multiple data consumers invariably results in increased data management, with different data quality dimensions to satisfy. This increases scope and management, ultimately resulting in data becoming more vulnerable to quality problems.

POOR BUSINESS CASE FOR DATA ORIGINATION AND CAPTURE

Going back to our previous example, one might ask — why can't the delivery dates and payment terms be maintained when creating the sales order, or for that matter, why can't all the data fields just be populated? Populating database tables and fields for adherence to the data quality dimension of completeness does not necessarily guarantee high data quality. Populating the database fields takes time and money. More importantly, usage of the data fields within the database must be tied to business processes and user needs. For instance, if the procurement department decides to update the terms of payment in the vendor master database to 45 days, it is important to ensure that the account payable and treasury teams are aligned to clearing the supplier invoices within 45 days.

DATA SEARCHING AND RETRIEVAL CHALLENGES

Sometimes the unavailability of data is perceived as poor data quality. The issue could be due to the data element value itself being missing, or it could be due to the way the search is performed by the users. For example, say that a business user is trying to look for a product code "SKF ROLLER BEARINGS" by entering the search parameter "BEARING." If the product is maintained as "BRG RLR SKF 6312" in the IT system, the user will not get any product codes for SKF ROLLER BEARINGS in the search results. Most of the issues in searching can be attributed to factors such as lack of formatting, inconsistent taxonomy, lack of standards, missing characteristics, poor data governance, database constraints, or poor training.

SYSTEM PROLIFERATION AND INTEGRATION ISSUES

For most businesses, a system of record (SoR) is the authoritative source for data entities. Data in the SoR is interfaced to target applications called systems of differentiation (SoD), where specific business processes are carried out. As an enterprise usually carries a mix of these SoR and SoD systems, it is imperative to have an enterprise-wide data model. The root cause of system proliferation in an enterprise is organization silos.

If there is no enterprise-wide model, the multiplicity of systems can jeopardize data integrity due to differences in semantics, syntax, business processes, timing of the data extracts, system bugs, and more. For example, units of measure (or "UoM") often vary depending on which business entity is involved. A flange might be quantified in an enterprise's SoR as "each," with a UoM of "EA." The CRM system (an example of a SoD), on the other hand, might deal with boxes of flanges rather than individual units, so they might quantify flanges in units of "BX." Furthermore, the warehouse might stock flanges in pallets, so their SoD might quantify them in a UoM called "PT" for pallet.

Even if some data fields are maintained in the source SoR system, the values might change when these data objects are interfaced to target OLTP applications which handle specific business processes. For example, the master data team in an oil and gas company might describe the flange as "FIXED 23/4" CF FLANGE" with a UoM of "EA" (each). But the sales LoB might change that UoM in the CRM system to "PK" as the flanges are sold in packets. The warehouse technician might then change the UoM in the warehouse application to "BX" as the flanges are stocked in boxes. This ultimately results in data integrity issues as the same product has different UoMs in different systems.

Each of these UoM values is correct from the individual stakeholder and system perceptive. The differences due to business processes and system proliferation enable the respective departments to contextualize the data to meet their specific needs affecting data integrity. Fundamentally the ACID (atomicity, consistency, isolation, and durability) model and metadata definitions are more vulnerable to compromises during EAI and ETL integration.

DIFFERENT VALUE PROPOSITIONS BETWEEN CONSUMERS AND ORIGINATORS OF DATA

Typically, consumers of data have more issues with data quality then producers of data. This reflects basic human nature; when you create something, you develop a sense of ownership over it. In the previous example, the problem with the value UoM of "EA" for the flange is seen by the sales and the warehouse LoBs as problematic, as they want to use a different UoM (PK or BX). In addition, data quality problems become visible and even get amplified when data gets propagated to different business functions, stakeholders, and systems.

DATA RULES AFFECT BUSINESS OPERATIONS

While business rules define things like categories, entities, events, and constraints, data rules define database attributes such as field length, type, format, and others. For example, if there is a data rule defined in the IT system that field length for product description is restricted to 25 characters, if some actual product description is 43 characters long, then complete details of the product cannot be maintained. This affects the data completeness, accuracy, and correctness dimensions, ultimately affecting data quality. This example shows that data rules impact business performance making the relationship amongst the data entities and events more complex.

Another scenario where data rules affect business operations arises when an enterprise purchases data from external agencies. Many enterprises assume that data quality will be high when purchased from agencies such as AC Nielsen, IHS, Bloomberg, and others. But unfortunately, that is not necessarily the case. According to Frank Dravis, former VP of Firstlogic and SAP, data vendors suffer from the same aging, context mismatch, field overuse, and other data quality issues as enterprises. If the data purchased from external agencies is not validated upon receipt, the enterprise is essentially abdicating its internal data quality standards to those of the vendor [Dravis, 2004]. Even though business rules govern data rules, sometimes the data rules or system limitations impact business performance.

DATA QUALITY IS TIME-SENSITIVE

Although most business processes are asynchronous and nonlinear, the timing of data availability (i.e. timeliness and concurrency data quality dimensions) might cause data quality issues. For example, let us imagine a purchase order (PO) is created with INCO (International Commercial) term CIF (Cost, Insurance & Freight). **International Commercial Terms** are pre-defined commercial terms that make international trade easier by helping traders in different countries understand one another. Between the time that the PO is issued to the supplier and the time that the goods are delivered by the supplier, supplier negotiations could result in the INCO term being changed to CFR (Cost & Freight). Consequently, the goods receiving and accounting teams will potentially have a challenge reconciling the INCO term codes between real document values.

Inherently, data values change over time. For example, it is estimated that 60 percent of the phone records in US change each year; if the data records related to the telephone fields are not kept current, this affects data quality. Furthermore, companies change; they start, grow, acquire, rename, go bankrupt, and spin-off. If regular data validation is not performed, the quality of data degrades.

RESULTS OF DATA QUALITY IMPROVEMENTS ARE NORMALLY TRANSIENT

Even if data is of very high quality during capture, things change. Factors such as business needs, entity relationships, metadata definitions, data structures, and system configurations continuously change over time. Basically, data quality degrades if not controlled or governed regularly. The data quality degradation is typically gradual, if checks to measure and control data quality are not maintained throughout the entire data lifecycle. During the interview for this book, Gartner's Vice President Mario Faria said, "Data governance plays a key role in data quality and data quality initiatives cannot be successful without effective data governance. There has to be a strong synergy between the two initiatives and functions. However for both data governance and data quality initiatives to be successful, the performance of these initiatives should be tied to the financial goals and metrics of the enterprise".

DATA CONVERSION AND MIGRATION ISSUES

In his book, *Data Quality Assessment*, author Arkady Maydanchik says "Databases in business enterprises rarely begin their lives empty." Often, data origination and capture starts from data conversion or migration from some legacy database. Data conversion and migration is a risky, time-consuming, and complex undertaking. This is fundamentally due to the tight interdependency between the three layers in the system: user interface, business rules, and database.

During data conversion and migration, the data structure in the database layer is the main focus, with little attention paid towards the business rules (i.e. application) and user-interface layers. The main purpose of data conversion and migration is to get data into enterprise systems. For example, in one supplier contracts conversion and migration project from SAP Enterprise Resource Planning (ERP) to the Contracts Lifecycle Management (CLM) application, the contracts were successfully migrated, but the business rules or criteria for selecting the system of record for contracts between the ERP and CLM systems was not considered. The impact was that business users were able to edit contract data in both the CLM and ERP systems, resulting in data inconsistency and multiple versions of the same contract in two different systems.

INTERFACE FEEDS

Interface feeds — especially EAI data feeds — are big and regular data exchanges between OLTP systems. Two main interface feed issues that impact data quality are:

- When the source OLTP system is subject to system changes, updates, and upgrades, the data structures and data models usually change. This in turn impacts the data feeds from the source IT system to multiple target systems.
- Interface feeds quickly spread poor-quality data, as they are normally automated and work on large data sets. Any bad data quality that gets into the source system will invariably trickle down to the target system(s). These "bad" records will be used in business activities in the target system, resulting in more data getting corrupted. This impact is more severe when the quality of reference data and master data is impacted, due to its association with other data elements.

SYSTEM UPGRADES

Often data elements are used for wrong purposes, not filled, converted into a form acceptable to the system, and so on. Basically during manual data entry users try to force feed data by tweaking data rules. Business processes and IT programs may be built upon these anomalies, causing potential data quality issues. For example, as discussed earlier a piece of programming code might exist to take the first three characters of the customer's telephone number to assign the tax code. However during system upgrades, especially on the COTS (commercial-off-the-shelf) systems, programs are designed and tested against what data is really expected to be and not what data really is.

MANUAL ERRORS

One of the biggest sources of poor data quality is the data that is entered, edited, and manipulated by people. In this regard, the most common cause of poor data quality is manual data entry. This normally comes from cumbersome and inconsistent data entry forms, paper-based documents, and other manual processes. Manual errors can also be caused by lack of training or simple carelessness. In some cases, data curation will take a tremendous amount of time, in an effort to improve the accessibility and timeliness of data quality dimensions. A common example of a place with much room for errors is when multiyear, multimillion-dollar supplier contracts are entered with significant amount of clauses, terms, and conditions. In a survey by TDWI (The Data Warehousing Institute), 76% of the survey respondents said "Manual data entry is the number source of poor data quality" [Eckerson, 2002].

POOR DATABASE DESIGN

Data integrity cannot be ensured if the database design itself is poor. No amount of data governance will help if the database design pertaining to data integrity is poor. The following aspects if not appropriately addressed will result in adversely affecting data integrity. These aspects are:

- **Data normalization.** Data normalization refines the data definitions, eliminates repeating groups, and unnecessary dependencies. Normalization is the process of refining tables, keys, columns, and relationships to create an efficient database specifically for querying and searching.
- **Referential integrity.** Referential integrity protects data from corruption. Referential integrity means that the foreign key in any referencing table must always refer to a valid row in the referenced table. Referential integrity ensures that the relationship between two tables remains synchronized during updates and deletes. If appropriate rules are not followed, the result is poor database design.
- **Business rules.** Business rules or software programs control data capture, validation, and processing. The software programs can sometimes force capture of data values which might be contrary to the data dictionary definition or DBMS configuration.
- **Data rules.** This includes range checking, field validation, and other forms of data validation. Any violation of data rules results in poor database design and ultimately poor data quality.

DATA PURGING AND CLEANSING

Data purging is the erasing and removing of data from the storage space. As said before, data is interpreted and consumed in many ways. In most cases the use and users of the data element might not be clearly defined, so the data purging and cleaning initiative might begin after consulting only a selective group of stakeholders.

For instance, in one actual data purge project, a team decided to purge the serial number values after consulting only the engineering and purchasing teams. This data element did not matter to these two teams, as they did not use the serial number data element in their business activities. But, the serial number data element was used extensively by the asset management and quality engineering teams, so this purging exercise seriously affected their business operations.

CONCLUSION

It is estimated that enterprise data doubles every four years. According to Eric Schmidt, Chairman of Google, every two days we create as much data as we did from the dawn of civilization up until 2003 [Johnston, 2015]. This situation will result in more challenges with getting quality data and ultimately deriving business value and performance.

Given that every data and information management initiative rests on the assumption of sound data quality, ensuring quality data in the enterprise is of paramount importance. According to Dr. Redman, data quality initiatives in the enterprise should be pursued holistically, considering the purpose, business processes, systems, stakeholders' roles and responsibilities, and the organizational response mechanism to utilize data effectively. The next chapter looks at identifying the key data elements using the GQM framework for a successful data management initiative.

Chapter 6: Leveraging GQM for Information Management

What gets measured gets managed.

Peter Drucker
American Management Consultant

As discussed in previous chapters, many enterprises spend a significant amount of time and effort in data management initiatives. But most often enterprises do not accomplish the desired outcomes. Most of the data that is originated and captured is unwanted and never used in decision making, compliance, or serving the business customers. As most businesses do not have a clear plan on what to do with data, ultimately a great deal of data is captured with practically little utility for the business.

A recent a survey at the Compliance, Governance and Oversight Council (CGOC) summit found that one percent of corporate information is on litigation hold, five percent is sitting in a records retention category, and a mere 25 percent has any business value. This means that approximately 69 percent of all the data collected and maintained by most enterprises has no business or regulatory value at all [Savitz, 2012]. So why capture and manage data when it is not required? What can an organization do to manage data that is relevant for business performance? This chapter looks a popular performance measurement framework called Goal-Question-Metric (GQM), which is used to proactively identify and manage the key data elements that can make data management initiatives effective. To illustrate the application of the GQM framework in data management, two real world case studies are used to illustrate how the GQM framework was actually applied in business initiatives.

DEEP DIVE OF THE GQM FRAMEWORK

The Goal-Question-Metric (GQM) framework was devised by Victor Basili, Caldiera Gianluigi, and Deiter Rombach in the 1990s for software measurement. But today, GQM is applied in areas outside software metrics, as it provides a simple and straightforward method for defining goals, refining them into questions, and formulating metrics for data collection, analysis, and decision making. The core concept of the GQM is that it's integral to involve the right stakeholders in the data process, to ensure that the right goals, questions, and metrics are formulated [Basili et al, 1994]. Fundamentally, the GQM framework is based on eight principles:

- **Goal-driven.** Define measurement goals in line with the project goals
- **Context-sensitive.** Consider context when defining measurement goals
- **Top-down.** Refine goals in a "top-down" manner into measures via questions
- **Documented.** Explicitly document measurement goals and their refinement
- **Bottom-up.** Analyze and interpret the collected data in a "bottom-up" manner, in the context of the goal
- **People-oriented.** Actively involve all stakeholders in the measurement program
- **Sustained.** Measure for systematic and continuous improvement
- **Reuse-oriented.** Describe the context to facilitate packaging and reuse of knowledge gained

Implementation of the GQM framework results in a contextual measurement model that is specific to the stakeholder's value proposition, with three levels as explained below. At all three levels the stakeholder plays a key role.

CONCEPTUAL LEVEL — THE GOAL

A goal is a desired result that a person or an organization envisions, plans, and commits to achieve within a finite amount of time in a particular environment. The goal defines the context of the problem or the opportunity statement. Research by Professor Edwin Locke, an American psychologist, suggests that goal setting with specific quantification among group members can serve as an effective tool to achieve a shared objective. According to psychology researchers Gary Latham and Marie Budworth [Latham and Budworth, 2007], setting goals affects organization outcomes in four main ways:

- **Choice**. Choice helps to direct efforts to goal-relevant activities
- **Effort**. Goals can lead to greater effort and better results
- **Persistence**. Individuals and team are more likely to work through setbacks if pursuing a goal
- **Cognition**. Goals can lead individuals to develop and change behavior

Clearly, goal setting in an enterprise can address problems and improve business performance. According to Douglas Hubbard, author of *How to Measure Anything*, "A problem well stated is a problem half solved."

OPERATIONAL LEVEL — THE QUESTION

Once the goal statement is formulated, a set of questions is used to characterize the achievement of that specific goal. Questioning is the core component in learning. In business, good questions can make the difference between a successful and a failed endeavor. Asking good questions is considered one of the most important skills in business. According to business management guru Peter Drucker, "the important and difficult job is never to find the right answer; it is find the right question" [Dyer et al, 2011].

From the GQM perspective, the questions generated should define the goals in a quantifiable way, help to clarify and refine the goals, and capture the variation in the understanding of the goals that exists among the different stakeholders. Think of formulating questions as using the Google search engine; just like the right keywords get the desired results, asking good questions and answering them can be far-reaching and potentially game-changing for a business enterprise.

QUANTITATIVE LEVEL — THE METRIC

GQM proposes a set of metrics that is associated with every question. Basically, metrics indicate quantitative assessment of performance to track conformance to the goals. The metrics hold the key to data management, as the metrics link the goal statements to the data elements. For example, if the business goal is to reduce the customer churn by five percent, the goal can be validated if there are data elements available to capture customer master records including their termination status value.

Most business enterprises regularly use KPIs (Key Performance Indicators) that are most important to track business performance. One of Canada's largest integrated energy companies uses the following seven KPIs to get a snapshot of the business performance:

Metric	Unit	Current Quarter	Year-To-Date Actual	Full Year Target
Total Recordable Injury Rate	#	0.48	0.55	0.90
Production	mboe/day	315.8	328.6	324.5
Refinery/Upgrader Throughput [1]	mboe/day	239.5	270.3	303.4
Operating Costs/Barrel				
- Upstream	C$/boe	13.90	13.59	16.62
- Upgrading/Refining [1]		9.19	8.13	7.31
Capital Expenditures	mm C$	617.6	1,074.4	1,928.6
Return on Capital Employed (ROCE) [2]	%	-2.5%	-2.5%	4.9%
Return on Capital in Use (ROCIU) [2]	%	-3.0%	-3.0%	6.0%

A snapshot of current measurements of a company's KPIs

Note: "mboe" stands for one thousand barrels of oil equivalents.

However, the mapping among goals, questions, and metrics is not one-to-one. When implementing the GQM framework, for each goal, there can be several questions; for each question, there can be multiple metrics. Broadly, a typical GQM implementation has four main phases: planning, definition, collection and interpretation. This is shown in the figure below.

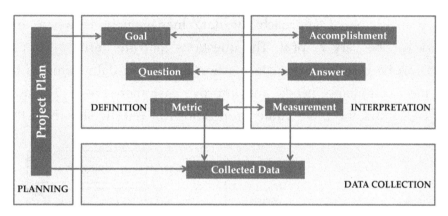

A typical GQM model

NOTE: While the terms measures and metrics are used synonymously in business, technically they are different. According to Merriam-Webster dictionary, a measure is an amount or degree of something and a metric is a standard of measurement which is derived or calculated from the measure. Basically the term metric brings a performance flavor to it and help measuring progress against defined goals. For example the total number of hours worked is a measure, while productivity is a metric. However throughout this book, we will use the terms metric and measure interchangeably.

LEVERAGING GQM FOR DATA MANAGEMENT

Every data management endeavor should formulate a solid goal statement, ask relevant questions, and evaluate outcomes using appropriate metrics. Father of modern science Galileo said "Measure what is measurable and make measurable what is not so." Within the area of data management, Gartner believes, "a metrics based approach to assessing data quality helps to remove assumptions, politics and emotions often associated with data management issues. This gives organizations a factual basis to justify, focus and monitor their information management efforts" [Friedman and Smith, 2011].

Refining a metric-based approach for data management is where the GQM framework can be very helpful. The questions that are derived from the goal statement can be used to formulate metrics and collect data elements to derive insights, meet compliance needs, and improve customer service. The association between GQM and the three value propositions of data is shown in the figure below.

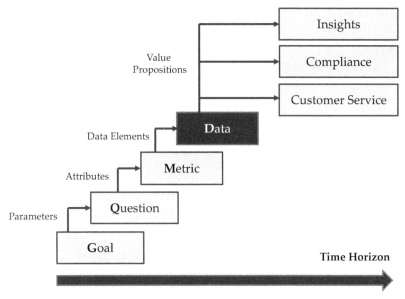

Aligning GQM to business purposes

Though the GQM framework gives an excellent structure for effective data management, implementation of any framework (including GQM) requires instantiation of the framework; this instantiation is commonly known as the model. The following 10 steps explain the derivation of a stakeholder-driven, GQM-based data management model that utilizes the GQM framework. As mentioned earlier, the purpose of deriving the GQM model is to identify the data elements that matter for business performance.

STEP 1: CONDUCT STAKEHOLDER ANALYSIS

Identifying the stakeholders' value propositions and categorizing the stakeholders is often considered the first step in strategic planning. Stakeholder categorization helps in understanding the attributes, relationships, and interactions not only between stakeholders, but also between different organizational elements in the system. Stakeholder analysis can be performed in a four-step process:

1. **Identify**. Within an enterprise, there are different stakeholders with various levels of interests to pursue data management programs. Some will be positive and optimistic, while others will be negative or pessimistic. A few will be even neutral. So, the first step is to **identify** business stakeholders who seriously believe that data can improve business performance.

2. **Categorize**. The second step is **categorizing** the stakeholders into groups by understanding their needs, attributes, interactions, and interdependencies. This could be as simple as classifying the stakeholders based on business functions, geographic locations, or on the consumption of data.

3. **Access**. The third step is **assessment.** Proper assessment of the stakeholders will help you to understand their influence, importance, knowledge, and specific needs. Assessment should map each stakeholder to the ten data lifecycle functions mentioned in Chapter 3. The stakeholders should include not only those who generate and capture data, but also those who govern and eventually consume data.

4. **Engage**. The final step is **engaging** the stakeholders. Even if the participating stakeholders believe that data is important for the enterprise, do they have the resources and time to deliver the project? Analyzing tens

or hundreds of terabytes of structured and unstructured data is tough and time-consuming. Stakeholders must not only see the potential merits, but must also be willing to invest time and energy. If stakeholders are not properly engaged, ready, and willing, chances of success in the data management initiative are very low.

To summarize, the main purpose of conducting stakeholder analysis is to understand the right players, their value propositions, their importance, and the communication strategies in the data management initiative. Many real world data management projects take months of effort but end up with little practical use in the company — mainly because stakeholders and the appropriate mechanisms with which to use the data were not identified.

STEP 2: FORMULATE THE STAKEHOLDERS' GOAL(S)

Once the stakeholder analysis is done, the next step is formulating the goal statement that reflects the needs of the stakeholder. Defining the goal is a fundamental step in problem solving. While the stakeholders' needs are normally stated as business goals, the goals from the GQM perspective are stated as measurable goals. Having the measurement perspective helps data management initiatives greatly, as measurement involves data planning, capture, and interpretation. In this step, the goal statement (from the stakeholder and measurement perspective) is constructed by utilizing the GQM goal template. This template includes five dimensions: object, purpose, focus, viewpoint, and environment:

- **Object**. The object is the business category, entity, or event that will be measured and analyzed. As mentioned Chapter 2, the business category is the reference data, the business entity is the master data, and the business event is the transactional data. Objects of measurement or analysis can include:

- o **Products**. Artifacts, deliverables and documents that are produced in the data lifecycle
- o **Processes**. Activities normally associated with times, such as planning, implementing, or validating
- o **Resources**. Items used by processes in order to produce their outputs, including systems, money, and personnel

- **Purpose**. The **purpose** expresses what will be measured. It is the reason to achieve the goal and should reflect the three purposes of data.

- **Focus**. The **focus** is the issue or the particular attribute of the object that will be analyzed.

- **Viewpoint**. The **viewpoint** provides information about the people or business stakeholders who will interpret and use the metrics. According to TOGAF, while a *view* is what you see, the *viewpoint* is where you are looking from - the vantage point or perspective that determines what you see [Desfray and Raymond, 2014].

- **Environment**. Finally, the **environment** describes the context in which the measurement and data management endeavor will be performed. The context could be the business segment (enterprise, LoB, or business function), time frame, or geographic location, to name a few.

For the most part, business enterprises operate within constraints. These constraints can be fiscal limitations, location limitations, time limitations, resource limitations, or any other constraints that affect the achievement of the business goal. However, the GQM-based goal statement does not always capture the business constraints very well. Hence, the goal statement that is formulated using the five GQM dimensional elements can be further refined and validated with SMART criteria. The SMART criteria were first used by George Doran in 1981 at the Washington Water Power Company in the US [Doran, 1981]. SMART emphasizes that every business objective or goal should be:

- **Specific**. Define the specific area for improvement.
- **Measurable**. Quantify the indicator of progress based on data and metrics.
- **Assignable**. Specify who will execute the goal statement. This ensures that goal statements are action-oriented.
- **Realistic**. State what results can be achieved with the assigned resources. This dimension will also ensure that there are data elements available to capture the metrics and realize the goal.
- **Time-related**. Specify when the result can be achieved, and reflect the accessibility and the timeliness data quality dimension.

The implementation of the GQM model might be complicated if the goals are abstract or the business stakeholder's value proposition is varied. If the goal is very broad, it is better to break the goal statement down into multiple smaller goals, and apply the ten-step methodology individually to each of them. The drawback of this breakdown is that it leads to the creation of multiple data models, which require efficient rationalization and abstraction.

Realizing a goal statement that includes value propositions of marketing and finance LoBs will be challenging, as these LoBs typically have conflicting business goals. While marketing wants to increase revenues by maintaining high inventories so that the products are readily available when the customer orders, finance prefers to keep inventory low so that inventory costs are minimized. So in this case, it is highly unlikely to have a good goal statement that brings the marketing and finance stakeholders together — especially if the purpose (one of the five dimensions in the goal statements) is to keep the inventory levels optimized. As such, it is always better to keep the stakeholder community focused, specific, and relatively homogeneous.

STEP 3: IDENTIFY THE PARAMETERS IN THE GOAL STATEMENT

This step identifies the key characteristics or parameters in the goal statement. A parameter is a definable element in the goal statement that is considered essential to understanding and accomplishing the goal. There are different sources that must be consulted to identify the parameters in the goal statements:

- The first source includes the five dimensions in the goal statement (i.e. object, purpose, focus, viewpoint and environment) as well as the five elements of the SMART criteria.

- The second area which can provide clues to identify parameters are the business categories, entities, and events that impact the goal statement. These business categories, entities, and events can be identified by value stream mapping (VSM). The VSM (also known as material and information flow mapping) is based on the flow of information throughout the delivery of the product or service to the customer. Below is a simple VSM for a downstream oil company operating in US and Canada.

	Hydrocarbon Supply, Trading and Transportation	Hydrocarbon Processing in Refineries	Distribution & Commercial Sales	Retail Operations & Customer Service
	Parameters	**Parameters**	**Parameters**	**Parameters**
Categories	Distribution Channel Division Purchasing Organization	Unit of Measure (UoM) Production Facility	Rack Meter Vehicle Meter Sales Organization	Warehouse Facility
Entities	Products Suppliers Trading Partners Trading Contracts	Products Bill of Materials (BoM) Equipment	Products Railcar	Customer
Events	Purchase Orders	Operating Plan Notifications Work Orders	Pipeline Nomination Deliveries Shipments	Invoices

Example of value stream mapping (VSM)

- The third source of parameters is the specific verbs and phrases in the goal statement. Fundamentally, action words and phrases create a definite call to action. Examples of action words in the business and data management context include "compare", "estimate", "utilize", and so on. For example, in a simple goal statement such as "reduce manufacturing defects by 18 percent," the key parameter is "reduce."

STEP 4: TRANSLATE THE GOALS AND PARAMETERS TO QUANTIFIABLE QUESTIONS

Moving from goals and parameters to quantifiable questions is a crucial phase in the GQM model, as the answers to these questions help to determine whether the goal can be achieved. Within data management, questioning helps to improve business performance because it prompts us to explore, discover, and innovate. In an article in Harvard Business Review (HBR), psychologists Tom Pohlmann and Neethi Thomas state that "the unfortunate side effect of not asking enough questions is poor decision-making" [Pohlmann and Thomas, 2015]. According to Thomas Davenport, one of the best-known thinkers on data management, "the key to frame the decision, is asking questions about the data and the methodology, working to understand the results, and using them to improve outcomes for your organization" [Davenport, 2013].

Since questions are so critical to drive business performance, how do we get started with formulating good questions? Based on the work of Eric Vogt, an innovation expert, the basic architecture of powerful questions has three main dimensions — scope, assumptions and constraints, and construction — and all three dimensions center on the purpose or the goal [Vogt, 2016].

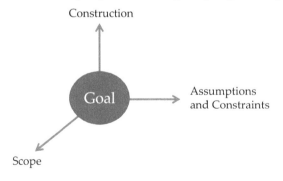

Question architecture

- **Scope**. Scope helps to define boundaries, establish responsibilities, and set up procedures for how the questions formulated will be verified and approved. One key way to define the scope is to list out the deliverables and the benefits that the data management initiative is expected to provide. While identifying what is in the scope is important, it is also important to clearly list out items that are *not* in the scope of the data management initiative. Scope management facilitates clear expectation alignment and communication when constructing questions.

- **Assumptions and constraints.** Almost all questions will have some degree of assumptions and constraints. Assumptions are normally events that need to occur for a goal to be delivered, while constraints are events that might restrict, limit, or regulate the outcome of the goal. Areas where assumptions and constraints normally arise include schedule, budget, skills, market conditions, and so on. However, some powerful questions can challenge even existing assumptions and constraints. For example, in the question, "How should we create new markets for our products and services?" one assumption is that stakeholders have agreed that they have capabilities and resources to respond to the market demand. A question on "How do we inform the supplier on the proposed change in the payment schedule that will be implemented in three months?" provides a time constraint on delivering the objective.

- **Construction.** Once the scope, assumptions, and constraints are addressed, the final step is taking those inputs and constructing the actual questions. Before you can formulate the questions, you must identify the phenomenon to be studied. This means the question should be specific and associated with the goal statement. The construction of a question can make a critical difference either in opening the minds or narrowing the possibilities. Most groups working on constructing the questions follow the below hierarchy.

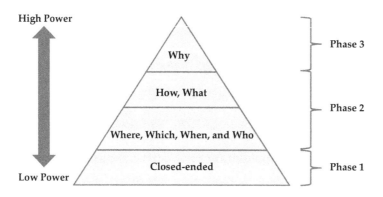

Hierarchy of question types

The basic premise is that any question can be converted into a more powerful question by moving up the pyramid as shown in the figure above. Moving from simple dichotomous questions to reflective and open-ended questions result in powerful insights. The first phase of questioning starts with simple "yes or no" questions. Questions that include words like "would," "should," or "are" all lead to "yes or no" answers. While dichotomous questions often result in incomplete answers, they help in filtering or narrowing the scope of questions.

This brings us to the second phase with open-ended or exploratory questions; questions that pertain to where, which, when, who, how and what, provide detailed and meaningful answers. The most important benefit of open-ended questions is that they usually allow more than one anticipated answer to be found. When you ask people to explain things with exploratory questions, they often reveal problem-solving strategies, hopes, fears, concerns, and much more.

The next phase of questioning relies on "why" questions to understand reasons, behaviors, and responses. The quality of "why" questions can be further improved using the 5WHY technique, which considers the cause-and-effect relationships underlying the goal statement. In the 5WHY technique, you uncover the nature of the problem and its root cause by asking "why" in an iterative fashion no fewer than five times. How does the 5WHY technique actually work? Talichi Ohno, the creator of the 5Why technique, is quoted using the following example to demonstrate using 5WHY for root cause analysis [Ries, 2011]:

1. Why did the robot stop?
2. The circuit has overloaded, causing a fuse to blow.
3. Why is the circuit overloaded?
4. There was insufficient lubrication on the bearings, so they locked up.
5. Why was there insufficient lubrication on the bearings?
6. The oil pump on the robot is not circulating sufficient oil.
7. Why is the pump not circulating sufficient oil?
8. The pump intake is clogged with metal shavings.
9. Why is the intake clogged with metal shavings?

Because there is no filter on the pump.

Hence as seen above, the root cause of the problem is "NO FILTER ON THE PUMP."

Once the questions are formulated based on this three-dimensional architecture, it helps to look at the questions from a different perspective. Psychologists Tom Pohlmann and Neethi Thomas propose that questions can be of four different types: clarifying, adjoining, funneling, and elevating. These four types of questions can be explained by the four-block grid below.

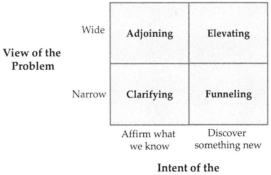

The four fundamental question types

- **Clarifying questions.** These questions help to better understand what has been actually said and uncover the real intent. Clarifying questions help us understand the goal better and lead us toward follow-up questions.
- **Adjoining questions.** Adjoining questions are used to explore related aspects of the goal or problem. Sometimes too much focus on the goal statement inhibits our asking more exploratory questions, but taking time to ask exploratory questions can help us gain a broader understanding.
- **Funneling questions.** While adjoining questions address the breadth, funneling questions go deeper. These types of questions understand how the question was formulated in the first place, challenge assumptions, and constraints, and understand the root causes of problems.
- **Elevating questions.** These types of questions highlight the bigger picture. These questions are used to derive connections and patterns between individual questions.

Typically, a big list of questions will be produced by the end of this step, after considering the 3-dimensional question architecture and the four question types. This big list of questions should be ideally reduced to fewer than 15 questions for better management [Southekal, 2014]. To achieve the reduced list of questions:

- Make sure every question can be associated to the parameters of the goal statement.
- Select those questions that have high influence and impact to business performance.
- Use the paired comparison analysis (PCA) technique: ask a sample set of stakeholders the importance of every question relative to the others. PCA helps in setting priorities where there are multiple options and limited resources. It involves pairing each question with each of the other questions in the set and then making a choice between the two questions. The result of these paired questions is a set of items, rank-ordered in terms of which items you have chosen more often. If there are 15 questions, you have a rank-ordered of 225 (i.e. 15X15) items. This technique is very useful

in the absence of objective and historical data on which to base priorities [Southekal, 2014].

STEP 5: ANSWER THE QUESTIONS AND DERIVE THE HYPOTHESIS

In this step, it's time to objectively, accurately, and correctly answer the closed-ended and open-ended questions selected. Closed-ended or dichotomous questions are those which can be answered by a simple "yes" or "no," while open-ended or exploratory questions are those which require the subject's own knowledge and expertise to produce more than a simple one-word answer. For answers to these open-ended questions, it is better to get more responses from multiple stakeholders to reduce bias. Also, getting answers from multiple stakeholders might lead to more powerful questions you never asked.

From the answers to the questions, it's possible to formulate multiple hypotheses. Of course, in some cases, a few questions might not have clear answers. In these cases, hypotheses can be used to explain the phenomena. A hypothesis is a possible answer to a question; the key variables identified in the hypothesis can serve as starting points for further analysis. The hypothesis is a statement that expresses probable relationship between variables, determining the outcome. From the data management perspective, forming a hypothesis means identifying the relationship between the data elements and the goal statement — a relationship that can be validated or tested. For example, the goal of reducing customer churn can be better accomplished by capturing customer status from the customer master data, rather than relying on order status, which is transactional data.

Validating the hypothesis involves careful consideration of two key statements called the null hypothesis and the alternate hypothesis. The null hypothesis serves as a benchmark to illustrate that there is no relationship between the variables, while the alternate hypothesis runs contrary to the null hypothesis, and is used to illustrate a clear relationship between the variables. Regardless of whether the questions give clear and definite answers, it is always better to use questions to formulate a hypothesis, as hypotheses help in the derivation of the attributes pertaining to the goal statement.

STEP 6: DERIVE ATTRIBUTES FROM THE QUESTIONS, ANSWERS, AND HYPOTHESIS

The attributes or variables that are found within the hypothesis should be technical, business-related, and associated with data elements (which could be business categories, entities, or events). The selected questions with their respective answers and hypotheses should be mapped to specific attributes. This will help define any metric "M" as a three-tuple M = (a, b, c) where "a" is the attribute to be measured, "b" is the measurement scale, and "c" is the unit of measure (UoM). Remember that any metric is a function of an attribute.

While goal parameters described in Step 2 deal with verbs or action words, attributes normally deal with nouns such as time, weight, distance, region, and the like. Identifying these attributes helps in deriving the metrics, as metrics are basically the result of activities that occur for a particular attribute. The attribute selected from the hypothesis should:

- Be a noun
- Have a specific measurement scale
- Be a function of jurisdiction or location and time

For example, one business question could be "How do I protect my Canadian business customers against data privacy?" The answer could be compliance to PIPEDA laws. So what is the attribute here and how does it map to the three salient features discussed above? The attribute here is **compliance**. The term "compliance" is a noun which is the first feature. Though it does not have a UoM, it has a nominal type of measurement scale (namely "yes" or "no") and this addresses the second feature. Lastly, coming to this feature of the attribute, the compliance certification is specifically valid for the Canadian jurisdiction until the customers transact with the business enterprise.

Another business question could be "What are the strategies to increase revenue by 10 percent in the mid-west region of the US in Q2 of 2018?" The response could be to invest (say 100 million USD) to set up a distribution center in the state of Illinois. The attributes here are **100 million** and **distribution center**. The first term or attribute "**100 million**" is a noun, has a UoM of USD, has a ratio type of measurement scale, and is valid for the Illinois jurisdiction before Q2 of 2018. The second term or attribute "**distribution center**" is also noun, has no UoM but has a nominal type of measurement scale with **distribution center** as the value, and is valid for the Illinois jurisdiction before Q2 of 2018.

STEP 7: DERIVE METRICS FROM THE ATTRIBUTES

Metrics are the things being measured to ensure progress towards the goal. Metrics determine the behavior and performance of the business. At the core, any unit of measurement is called a metric. According to John Hauser and Gerard Katz, Professors of Marketing at Sloan School of Management in MIT, "Every metric, whether it is used explicitly to influence behavior, to evaluate future strategies, or simply to take stock, will affect actions and decisions" [Hausera and Katz, 1998].

But there might be some critics who say that everything cannot be measured. According to Douglas Hubbard, "Anything can be measured. If a thing can be observed in any way at all, it lends itself to some type of measurement method. No matter how "fuzzy" the measurement is, it is still a measurement if it tells you more than you knew before. And those very things most likely to be seen as immeasurable are, virtually always, solved by relatively simple measurement methods" [Hubbard, 2014]. Hubbard believes "immeasurability" is just an illusion caused by three basic types of misunderstanding about measurement problems:

- The object of measurement (i.e. the thing being measured) is not understood. Understanding the object of measurement simply requires being specific. Hubbard suggests using the clarification chain to analyze and define intangibles so that they can be replaced with more clearly understood tangibles. Basically, the clarification chain is a series of connections that should bring us from thinking of something as an intangible to thinking of it as a tangible. The clarification chain when applied on the object of measurement has three main dimensions:

  1. If the object of measurement matters at all, it is detectable
  2. If the object of measurement is detectable, then it must be detectable as an amount
  3. Finally, if the object of measurement can be detected as an amount, it can be measured.

- The concept or the meaning of measurement is not understood. The key element here is using the measurement to reduce uncertainty and not necessarily the elimination of uncertainty. Hubbard emphasizes that measurements are pragmatic observations and never eliminate uncertainty and hence all realistic measurements in science, engineering, actuarial science, and economics are expressed as "probability distributions." Simply put, a probability distribution is a range of possible outcomes and their possibilities.

- The methods of measurement techniques used by science generally are not well understood. Hubbard believes after intangibles have been clarified by developing unambiguous definitions and the measurement process is better understood, many more things appear to be measurable. .

Coming back to the GQM, the term "metric" in the GQM can mean a base measure, a derived measure, or a composite of measures. A base measure captures data pertaining to a single attribute and is functionally independent of all other measures. For example, the total number of widgets produced in a production shift is a base measure. A derived measure captures data about more than one attribute. An example of a derived measure can be machine utilization which is the difference of machine availability (attribute 1) and machine downtime (attribute 2). Lastly, a composite measure is a combination of base and/or derived measures to provide a more holistic view of business performance. Let us say a manufacturing business unit or LoB produced 90,000 widgets utilizing 1,500 machine hours (1,550 hours of machine time available – 50 hours of machine downtime). To calculate the productivity, you would divide 90,000 by 1,500, which equals 60. In this example, productivity is the composite measure, total number of widgets produced is the base measure, and the machine utilization hour is the derived measure.

Given that there are hundreds of metrics available for a given attribute, the metrics selected should be:

- **Practical.** Every business stakeholder must be able to understand the metric and how it measures business performance. In addition, the data elements with values for calculating the metric should be available in the enterprise IT system landscape.
- **Simple.** The selected metric must be simple to use, and it should be easily decomposable with targets, control limits, ranges, and thresholds. The data should be comparative across time periods, stakeholder groups, or categories, in order to understand how the business is performing. For example, "Increased order-to-cash conversion by 10 percent from last week" is more meaningful than "We are at 2 percent conversion."
- **Precise.** Compared to the other three types of measurement scales i.e. nominal, ordinal, and interval, a metric with ratio scale type gives a more precise status of the business, and is easier to act on. Step 9 explains the measurement scales in detail.
- **Cost effective.** The metric and the mechanism to capture the data for the metric should be easily and readily available. For example, APICS has developed the Supply Chain Operations Reference model (SCOR) for 250

metrics. These metrics are categorized into five performance attributes: reliability, responsiveness, agility, costs, and asset management efficiency [Ayers, 2003]. So in this case, it is better to re-use these SCOR metrics, instead of developing new ones.

- **Few in number**. Good business performance rests on a few vital KPIs. However, some companies directly define KPIs without going over the first six steps. These companies struggle to identify the goals that these KPIs address and face challenges when implementing those goals, as the KPIs do not rest on solid foundation. Research by Bernard Marr and his team at AP-Institute finds that "less than 10 percent of all the metrics that are collected, analyzed and reported in businesses are ever used to inform decision-making. 90 percent of the metrics are wasted, or worse, used to drown people in data while they are thirsting for insights." Marr believes that the most effective KPIs are closely tied to strategic objectives and help to answer the most critical business questions [Marr, 2015].

STEP 8: APPLY THE REVERSE GQM OR MQG FRAMEWORK (METRIC-QUESTION-GOAL)

Once the metrics are selected, a "reverse GQM" or MQG (Metric-Question-Goal) framework should be applied to ensure that the metrics really answer the questions and align to the stakeholder's goals. This step is needed because sometimes the "top-down" GQM approach ignores what is feasible, especially on the mechanisms to collect the data elements. Hence a "bottom-up" MQG approach to validate the GQM model is also essential. In addition, most enterprise IT systems these days are packaged commercial off-the-shelf (COTS) applications with predefined data structures. Knowing the key data elements in these applications helps to determine what data can be readily captured to realize the metrics. For example, the product master in the SAP ERP application has over 300 fields from 10 different database tables. Knowing that these fields are always available helps to capture data and derive metrics, and realize the stakeholder's goals.

STEP 9: DERIVE THE DATA ELEMENTS FROM METRICS OR ANSWERS

Data elements can come from the metrics or from the answers determined in Step 5. But data elements derived from metrics help businesses focus on optimizing resources that are important. This is mainly because metrics unite answers and the variables in the hypothesis, to come up with a rationalized and optimized set of data elements at a conceptual level. In other words, as data elements derived from metrics are rationalized and optimized, the chances of having duplicate data elements are significantly reduced.

In Step 6, we identified the Unit of Measure (UoM) and the measurement scale associated with the attribute related to the metric. The scale type and the UoM of the metric can be the starting points to determine the appropriate data elements. These data elements might already exist in the system or they might have to be created. If the data elements already exist in the IT systems, they could be reference data, master data, or transactional data (from the OLTP system perspective) or they could be fact or dimensional tables (from the OLAP and BI systems side).

Coming to the measurement scale type, there are four measurement scale types popularly known as "NOIR" [Stevens, 1946] Basically, measurement scales are used to categorize different types of data variables. The four scale types are:

- **Nominal or categorical** scale types are used for labeling and have no quantifiable significance. Examples include vendor name and customer type.

- **Ordinal** scale type refers to data elements that have a natural ordering. Examples are purchase order priority and customer satisfaction score.

- **Interval** scale type is like the ordinal scale type, except that the intervals between each value are equally split. For example, the difference between 500 and 600 kilograms is the same as the difference between 850 and 950 kilograms.

- **Ratio or numerical** scale types tell us about the order, the exact value between units, and they also have an absolute zero — which provides a wide range of both descriptive and inferential statistics to be applied. Examples of ratio scale types are a safety stock with 7000 kilograms, a lead time of 14 days, and so on.

Scale type inherently holds a significant amount of details which help derive value from data. So how do these four scale types help to derive value from business data? Let us consider an example of a data element called "delivery priority," which is a part of the sales order. If we decide to manage this data element as a **nominal or categorical** scale type, then the potential values could be regular, new, or strategic. These values are just labels with no relevancy or significance for analysis. The most these values can help with is categorization.

But we can move up the data value chain by implementing a natural ordering with **ordinal** scale type, including potential values for delivery priority such as low, medium, high, and critical. This means the delivery priority for "critical" priority orders are more important than the delivery priority of "low" priority orders.

The next level in the data value chain can be reached by including more details or granularity with an **interval** scale type, with values say from 1 to 10; 10 being the highest delivery priority and 1 being the least. This implies that the orders with delivery priority of 6 are three times more important than orders which have the delivery priority of 2.

Finally, **ratio or numerical** scale type is the most valuable because we can specifically have timeframes such as 1 day (for urgent orders), 3 days (for standard orders), and 7 days (for normal orders). This means that one could know precisely how much time it takes to deliver the customer's order. Unlike nominal or ordinal scale types, data entities with interval and ratio scale types usually come with a Unit of Measure (UoM).

As we move up the data value chain from nominal to ratio, we enable the data model to include more and more specific and tangible details. When we have a data value for the data entity as "regular" (nominal scale), it is very subjective and holds fewer details. But we can definitely derive more insights (and decisions and actions) if the data value is "3 days" (ordinal scale) rather than "regular." This is specific and brings a promise of deriving more insights; if the goal is to derive insights from data, framing the right measurement scale type for the data entity is very important.

All this means that if the purpose of data is to derive insights, then the data element that should be captured should have the ratio scale type. If the delivery time frame has to be reduced by five percent then the goal can only be realized and validated if the data value captured is of ratio scale. The relationship of the four data types with details, value, cost, and proximity in deriving business insights is shown in the figure below.

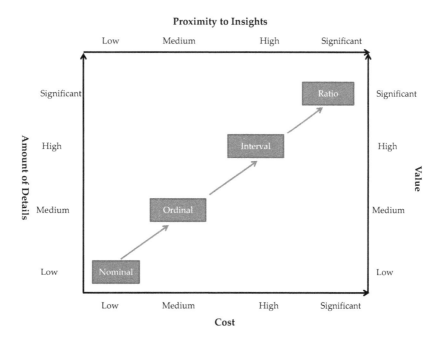

STEP 10: PROFILE THE DATA ELEMENTS AND BUILD THE DATA MODEL

Once the data elements are identified, these data elements must be profiled. According to Ralph Kimball, an expert in Data Warehousing (DWH), "Data Profiling is a systematic analysis of the content of a data source" [Kimball et al, 2011]. Data profiling clarifies the data type, structure, relationship, content, and derivation rules of data. Specifically, data profiling involves assessing the data elements against the data quality dimensions to get a better perspective on how and by whom the data elements are used. Data profiling also ensures that the stakeholders identified in the first step of the GQM model derivation are the actual stakeholders of these data elements, and play an important role in the data lifecycle.

The next phase after data profiling is building the data model. A data model should clearly illustrate the structure of data at the physical level. Specifically, the physical database model shows all system details, the business data type, and the table structures, including column name, column data type, column constraints, primary key, foreign key, and relationships between tables. For COTS or Cloud SaaS applications, it is imperative to properly configure the application to meet the enterprise data model standards. This is essentially the "consistency" data quality dimension, involving data value and data traceability, which was discussed in Chapter 5. A good data model helps to better communicate the alignment between the data fields and the stakeholder goals. If the data elements are in the scope of the OLTP systems, then the EVM model is the preferred data model. If the data elements are relevant for the OLAP/BI or analytics systems, then the star or snowflake model is appropriate.

To summarize, GQM helps to proactively identify, manage, and govern data elements based on the goals of the business stakeholders. One does not capture data elements and govern them just because there are technical capabilities available to store and process data. Just capturing and managing data without a strong goal would be expensive in the long run. Every reference data, master data, and transactional data element should have a customer and a clear goal. If the data elements are captured and managed with no utility for the business, it is a complete waste of enterprise's resources and time. The application of the 10 Steps in the derivation of the data management model based on the GQM Framework is shown in the diagram on the facing page.

A Simple GQM Example

Below is a simple example of how the GQM framework can be put to good use. Let us say that a utilities company has a goal to reduce indirect procurement spending by 10 percent in the current financial year. Here the procurement LoB stakeholders wish to improve business operations with reduced procurement spend.

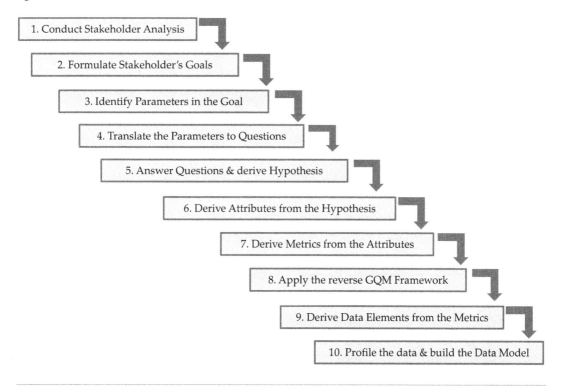

1. Conduct Stakeholder Analysis
2. Formulate Stakeholder's Goals
3. Identify Parameters in the Goal
4. Translate the Parameters to Questions
5. Answer Questions & derive Hypothesis
6. Derive Attributes from the Hypothesis
7. Derive Metrics from the Attributes
8. Apply the reverse GQM Framework
9. Derive Data Elements from the Metrics
10. Profile the data & build the Data Model

From this goal statement, the key parameters (i.e. the verbs) are identification and controlling of spending. From these parameters, different questions can be derived to realize the goal. Some questions could include: What are the top spend categories? Who are the top spend vendors? What is the average time to issue a purchase order? What is the total goods delivery time? Why do we spend 70 percent of the budget on just four spend categories?

The answers to these questions can be used to formulate the hypothesis, and relevant attributes can be determined. The attributes for these questions include budget, time, and vendors. These attributes can now be tied to different metrics. One key metric that emerges from these questions is the procure-to-pay (P2P) cycle time. Upon further analysis of this metric, there are five data elements that need to be managed: payment terms for the suppliers, lead time for goods delivery, MRP type (i.e. the procedure used for planning the material), the location where the material needs to be delivered, and finally the location from where the supplier ships the material (due to INCO terms implications).

As evident in the following figure, the implementation of the GQM framework is contextual and is based on specific stakeholder goals, questions, and metrics. So, if the business metric is procure-to-pay (P2P) cycle time, only five data elements matter. Therefore if the procurement LoB is spending a considerable amount of effort on capturing, formatting, and curating other data elements (say, capturing the engineering drawing number, cleansing supplier address, or re-classifying the general ledger accounts), then the effort is completely futile if the metric that matters for business performance is P2P cycle time.

Essentially, in order to derive value from data, one must first identify the data elements that matter in realizing the goals of the business stakeholder. The coming sections look at two real-world case studies where the GQM models were used for realizing business performance. The identities of the organizations are not shared for confidentiality reasons.

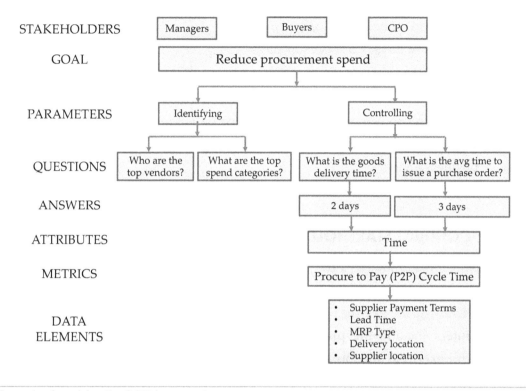

Example of applying the GQM framework

CASE STUDY 1: APPLICATION OF THE GQM FOR INSIGHTS

To further illustrate the implementation of the GQM for effective data management, an SAP Portal implementation project for a bank is considered as a case study. The bank's strategy was to have an SAP Portal for high frequency, customer-facing transactions for the tellers, branch managers, and back office personnel. The bank has close to 5,000 employees, assets of over $25 billion and about 700,000 customers. This case study demonstrates how by using GQM, the data elements helped the SAP Portal project to be delivered successfully. The key project details were:

- **Budget**: $2.1 million CAD
- **Duration**: 6 months

- **Industry**: Financial services
- **Contracted days**: 1,520 person-days

Key project stakeholders:

- **Initiators**: sponsor and business transformation lead
- **Implementers**: program manager, project manager, developer, testers, and business analysts
- **Beneficiaries**: users i.e. tellers.

STEP 1: CONDUCT STAKEHOLDER ANALYSIS

The table below summarizes the three different types of project stakeholders and their value propositions for the success of the SAP Portal project. **Initiators** are stakeholders such as the project sponsor and the management team. **Implementers** include the project manager, business analysts, developers, and testers who executed the project. **Beneficiaries** are the actual users of the SAP Portal application, who desire a functional, reliable, user-friendly, and secure application. From the data management perspective, beneficiaries represented the ten data lifecycle functions, including stakeholders who consumed data. The table below presents the stakeholder analysis, including primary and secondary value propositions.

Stakeholder Group	Project Members	Primary Concerns	Secondary Concerns
Initiators	Project sponsor Senior management	Schedule and cost	Scope
Implementers	Project manager Business analysts Developers Testers	Scope	Schedule and cost
Beneficiaries	Product champion Super users Tellers	Quality	Features

STEP 2: FORMULATE THE STAKEHOLDERS GOAL(S)

A goal statement was formed, encompassing the five dimensions of the GQM framework and the SMART concept. This goal statement was: "track the **SAP Portal project** objectively to **deliver the scope** successfully with respect to **size, schedule, cost,** and **quality** from the viewpoint of the **stakeholders** and provide **management visibility during the project duration**."

STEP 3: IDENTIFY THE PARAMETERS IN THE GOAL STATEMENT

Along with the five dimensions in the goal statement, the other key parameters in the goal statement are to **track** and **deliver**. Upon further examination of the goal statement, the SAP Portal project was decomposed into three business sub-entities: product management, process management, and resources management. Each of these elements affected the outcome of the project. In all, there were ten parameters that came from the goal statements.

STEP 4: TRANSLATE THE GOALS AND PARAMETERS TO QUANTIFIABLE QUESTIONS

Using the 3-dimensional question architecture and the 4-block classification, 204 questions were derived. The list was further pruned using strategies described earlier and 12 questions were finally selected. These questions were:

1. How do we estimate the functional size of the project?
2. How do we know the size of the project after development?
3. How much will this project cost?
4. How complex are the deliverables?
5. What is the estimated duration of this project?
6. What is the current stage of the project?
7. What are the schedule and effort variances?
8. What is the delivery effectiveness in the project?
9. What is the current level of quality?

10. What is the impact or the amount of re-work pertaining to cost of quality?
11. What is the mean time to failure (MTTF) or process stability?
12. What are the risk levels with respect to schedule, cost, and quality?

STEP 5: ANSWER THE QUESTIONS OBJECTIVELY

As most of these questions are exploratory in nature, the answers to the questions were collected from multiple stakeholders within the project. This helped to reduce the bias to a large extent, and bring in consistent and aggregated responses.

STEP 6: DERIVE HYPOTHESES AND ATTRIBUTES

As mentioned before, a hypothesis has classically been referred to as an educated guess and most hypotheses are written in "if...then" format reflecting the goals and parameters; in other words both independent variables (the factor control in the experiment) and dependent variables (the factors you observe or measure in an experiment). In this case study, the hypothesis was: "If the IT project is measured holistically and objectively, then the IT project can be effectively tracked and successfully delivered." From questions, answers, and hypotheses, attributes relevant to achieving the goal were identified. The five attributes identified from the 12 questions are **size, complexity, cost, schedule,** and **quality**.

STEP 7: DERIVE METRICS FROM THE ATTRIBUTES

Given that hundreds of metrics are available within the realm of software engineering and IT project management, five important factors were considered in the selection of appropriate metrics:

1. **Application at all project phases**. Metrics selected could be applied in all the IT project phases, i.e. requirement elicitation, design, development, testing, and deployment.
2. **Objectivity**. Objective metrics are preferred over subjective measures to bring consistency in the measurement process.

3. **Level of measurement scale types**. The ratio and interval scale types (which have the most granular level of information) were preferred over others.

4. **Availability in existing tools**. A metric that is already proven (i.e. well researched, validated, and implemented in IT tools) is selected over others for easier and quicker implementation.

5. **Flexibility in implementation**. The measures identified were flexible because it was assumed that refinement and adaptation would be needed during implementation.

Considering the above five criteria, the answers to the 12 questions and five attributes resulted in eight KPIs:

#	KPI	Definition	UoM	Scale Type
1	Lines of Code (LOC)	The physical count of any programming statement	Dimensionless	Ratio
2	Function Point (Fp)	The amount of business functionality provided to the business user	Dimensionless	Ratio
3	McCabe's Cyclomatic Complexity	Measures the system complexity by counting the available decision paths in the program	Dimensionless	Ratio
4	Schedule Performance Index (SPI)	An index showing the efficiency of the time utilized in the project	Dimensionless	Ratio
5	Cost Performance Index (CPI)	The efficiency of the utilization of the budget in the project	Dimensionless	Ratio
6	Sigma Level (Cpk)	Indicates the effectiveness or stability of the entire project delivery process; a higher Cpk indicates a process that is less prone to defects	Dimensionless	Ratio

#	KPI	Definition	UoM	Scale Type
7	Defect Density (DD)	The ratio of the number of open defects to the size of the software component	Dimensionless	Ratio
8	Defect Removal Efficiency (DRE)	Indicates the rate at which defects are resolved	Dimensionless	Ratio

STEP 8: APPLY MQG FRAMEWORK

Once the eight KPIs were selected, a reverse GQM or MQG (Metric-Question-Goal) framework was carried out to ensure that the metrics answered the questions and aligned to the stakeholder needs.

STEP 9: DEFINE DATA ELEMENTS FROM THE METRICS

Data values pertaining to the eight metrics were collected, mostly from data elements available from the IT systems within the project.

STEP 10: PROFILE THE DATA ELEMENTS AND BUILD THE DATA MODEL

The table on the facing page also includes the data model for the GQM model.

The eight KPIs were regularly used to track the project, derive insights, and take corrective actions such as fast tracking, crashing, resource leveling, budgeting, and buffer management. Some of the corrective actions taken in the project were:

- Increased testing and assigning skilled developers for more complex work

- Deliverables with poor DRE and low SPI functions were put on the "Max-Attention" list for close monitoring of the project's progress

- Deliverables with low complexity and low SPI were given more priority

- Deliverables with low Cpk were given low priority, as they needed significant change in the project management process

Sl # FDD Name	Lines of Code (LOC)	Function Points (FP)	Total McCabe Complexity	Complexity Type	CPI	SPI	Total Test Cases (Opportunities)	Defects Open and unresolved (Test Cases)	DPMO	Sigma Level	DD	Total Defects	Defects Removed	DRE
1 PT_EH_01-Deposit & FDD Maintenance	2390	11	309	High	1.15	1.00	34	2	58824	3.07	0.18	34	32	0.94
2 PT_EH_01-LO-Deposit & FDD Maintenance - Change A/c Holder	1195	6	155	High	0.79	1.00	27	2	74074	2.95	0.36	27	25	0.93
3 PT_EH_04-Registered Plans & TFSA - Contract Details	2988	14	341	High	0.68	1.00	10	1	100000	2.78	0.07	27	7	0.26
4 PT_EH_08-Registered Plans & TFSA - Contract Maintenance	1793	8	394	High	1.11	1.00	24	2	83333	2.88	0.24	24	19	0.79
5 PT_EH_09-Loan - Account Details	971	5	126	High	1.30	1.00	20	1	50000	3.15	0.22	20	18	0.90
6 PT_EH_10_16_18-Loan - Make Payment - Lumpsum - Payout	2600	12	370	High	0.86	1.00	15	2	133333	2.61	0.16	23	14	0.62
7 PT_EH_14-Loan - Disbursement - Loan Maintenance	2183	10	353	High	1.00	1.00	20	8	400000	1.75	0.78	20	12	0.60
8 PT_EH_17-Loan - Payout Scenario - Loan Maintenance	1643	7	291	High	0.96	1.00	10	3	300000	2.02	0.42	12	7	0.59
9 PT_EH_20-View Estatements	1307	6	243	High	1.63	1.00	35	3	85714	2.87	0.49	35	32	0.91
10 PT_EH_24-Transfers	18841	88	1494	High	1.10	1.00	117	2	17094	3.62	0.02	270	115	0.43
11 PT_EH_26-Fees	2335	11	241	High	0.95	1.00	45	12	266667	2.12	1.10	45	33	0.73
12 PT_EH_27-Supervisor Overrides	1167	5	104	High	1.35	1.00	32	12	375000	1.82	2.20	32	20	0.63
13 PT_EH_32_33-Overdraft Protection Details & Maintenance	4982	23	687	High	1.30	1.00	45	9	200000	2.34	0.39	51	33	0.65
14 PT_EH_60-Deposit & FDD Account Details	1419	7	193	High	1.65	1.00	7	1	142857	2.57	0.15	11	6	0.56
15 PT_EH_61-Registered Plan Payments incl Close Accounts	10724	50	1426	High	1.30	1.00	120	25	208333	2.31	0.50	133	95	0.71
16 PT_EH_62-Deposits - Close Accounts	1643	8	212	High	1.87	1.00	26	2	76923	2.93	0.26	26	24	0.92
17 PT_EH_64-FDD Funding for Non-Registred Products	2241	10	289	High	1.00	1.00	17	1	58824	3.07	0.10	19	15	0.80
Overall	60322	282	7218	High	1.04	1.00	624	88	141026	2.58	0.31	808	490	0.61

Project Status as on July 31st, 2010 (Project Ending: All three iterations completed)

CASE STUDY 2: APPLICATION OF THE GQM FOR COMPLIANCE TO INDUSTRY STANDARDS

While the first case study illustrated the use of the GQM to derive project insights for decision-making, this case study features an item master data project for industry compliance in an oil and gas company. The compliance standards were provided by PIDX (Petroleum Industry Data Exchange) and UNSPSC (United Nations Standard Products and Services Code). The company has close to 4,000 employees, revenues of over $25 billion, and an indirect procurement spend of about $9 billion. The other key project details were:

- **Budget**: $3 million CAD
- **Duration**: 6 months
- **Industry**: Oil and gas
- **Scope**: 125,000 item masters managed in SAP ERP

Key project stakeholders:

- **Initiators**: Chief Procurement Officer (CPO) and Master Data lead
- **Implementers**: Data Architect and Business Analysts
- **Beneficiaries**: Data Governance Analysts and Purchase Requisition Analysts.

The GQM-based, information-managed model was derived using the GQM framework as explained below.

STEP 1: CONDUCT STAKEHOLDER ANALYSIS

Initiators include the CPO and the Master data lead who sponsored the project. **Implementers** are the Data Architect and the Business Analysts, who executed the project. **Beneficiaries** are the actual users who desire an industry-compliant master data for items procured externally. From the data management perspective, beneficiaries represented the ten data lifecycle functions, and included stakeholders who consumed data. In this project, the beneficiaries included the purchase requisition analysts who analyze and consume data, and the data governance analysts who are responsible for the remaining ten functions in the data lifecycle.

STEP 2: FORMULATE THE STAKEHOLDER GOAL(S)

The measurement goal statement based on the five dimensions of the GQM framework, and the SMART concept was to "**Improve item master data quality** with respect to **PIDX and UNSPSC standards** to address **item master description inconsistencies** from the view point of the **procurement stakeholders** and **provide data quality and compliance** during indirect procurement."

STEP 3: DERIVE THE PARAMETERS FOR THE GOALS

Apart from the five dimensions in the goal statement (which are highlighted above), the other two parameters are to **improve** the item master data quality and **comply** with PIDX and UNSPSC standards.

STEP 4: TRANSLATE THE GOALS TO QUANTIFIABLE QUESTIONS

From the seven parameters in the goal statement, nine questions were finally derived using the 3-dimensional architecture and the 4-block classification. These nine questions were:

1. What is the count of the active item master data?
2. What is the rate of change in the creation of the item master data?
3. What is the description format for compliance?
4. What is the current percent compliance?
5. How does compliance to standards help in procurement?
6. How can we agree on a name across different business units and systems?
7. What is the impact of non-compliance?
8. Who will manage the item master data description for compliance?

9. Where will these standard item masters be used?

STEP 5: ANSWER THE QUESTIONS

In this step, the questions listed in step 4 were answered objectively. As most of the questions are exploratory in nature, multiple stakeholders were interviewed and answers collected.

STEP 6: DERIVE HYPOTHESIS AND ATTRIBUTES

This step entailed the identification of the attributes from the questions, and answers, and ultimately led to a hypothesis. In this case study, the hypothesis was: "If the item master data description inconsistencies have to addressed, then the item master data quality can be effectively improved and complied." In this case, the attributes relevant to the goal were:

- Completeness
- Consistency
- Conformity
- Accuracy
- Duplication
- Integrity (entity and domain)

STEP 7: DERIVE METRICS FROM THE ATTRIBUTES

The relevant metrics or KPIs for these six attributes were:

#	KPI	UoM	Scale Type
1	Item Master Data Count	Dimensionless	Ratio
2	Non Compliance to PIDX and UNSPSC	Dimensionless	Ratio
3	PIDX Compliance	Dimensionless	Ratio
4	UNSPSC Compliance	Dimensionless	Ratio
5	GTIN: UNSPSC Compliance	Dimensionless	Ratio

STEP 8: APPLY THE MQG FRAMEWORK

Once these metrics were selected, a reverse GQM or MQG (Metric-Question-Goal) was carried out to ensure that the metrics answer the questions and align to stakeholder needs.

STEP 9: DERIVE DATA ELEMENTS FOR THESE METRICS

The relevant data elements for these KPIs were:

- Item code: the attribute that uniquely identifies the item master
- PIDX Category: the specific PIDX category with which the item master will be associated
- Item Description: the details of the item master
- PIDX Attributes Fields: the item attributes as per PIDX standards
- UNSPSC Attribute Field: a four-level hierarchy coded as an eight-digit number for commodities
- EAN/UPC Codes: the GS1 bar codes that are printed on almost all products in the world

STEP 10: PROFILE THE DATA ELEMENTS AND BUILD THE DATA MODEL

The data model for the six data elements pertaining to the five KPIs were:

#	Data Element	Data Type	Fieldname	Type	Length	Key
1	Item code	Master Data	MATNR	Character	18	Yes
2	PIDX Category	Reference Data	MATKL	Character	4	No
3	Item Description	Master Data	MATKX	Character	40	No
4	PIDX Attributes Fields	Master Data	Multiple Fields	Character	3 to 40	No
5	UNSPSC Attribute Field	Master Data	Custom field	Character	8	No
6	EAN/UPC Code	Master Data	EAN11	Character	8	No

CONCLUSION

Ubiquitous access to data, low cost of data storage, and improved processing capabilities are enabling enterprises to collect, manage, and govern data that is not clearly aligned to business performance. To succeed in this environment, the enterprises need to build lean and efficient data infrastructure based on solid business goals. Achieving these goals requires asking powerful questions and tracking the right metrics. The GQM model is a natural choice as it unites the goals of the enterprise, with the right questions and appropriate metrics. The ten-step data management model based on the GQM framework can help us in identifying the key data elements or fields that can be used for effective and efficient data management.

Identifying the data elements, however, is just one part of the story. To optimize data for business performance, enterprises should holistically look at processes, technology, and the roles of people in managing and governing the appropriate data elements. The next chapter looks at the core building blocks that hold the keys in realizing the digital enterprise.

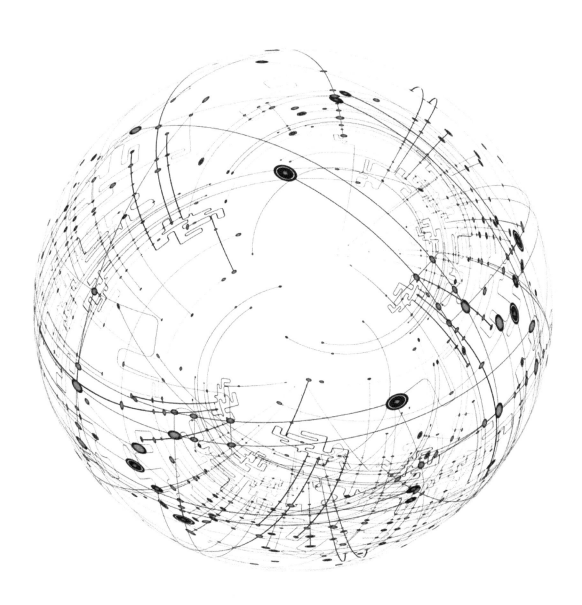

Chapter 7: Building Blocks of a Digital Enterprise

Simplicity is the ultimate form of sophistication.

Leonardo Da Vinci
Italian Polymath

In Chapter 6, we used the GQM model to develop a process to identify the key data elements that are aligned to the goals of the business stakeholders. But there are also situations where data elements are already captured — mostly in an unplanned manner — and businesses are exploring options to leverage value from this data. It is imperative to manage and govern these available data elements effectively to realize the digital enterprise.

Essentially, a digital enterprise refers to an organization where the business activities are mainly driven by data rather than intuition, personal experience, or one-off events. Today, "digital enterprise" is often used to describe organizations that rely on SMAC (social media, mobile, analytics, and cloud) technologies for its internal and external business operations. Given the number of new digital technologies that are available to businesses today, most enterprises want to become digital enterprises to improve business performance. Unfortunately, many enterprises are struggling as they lack sound principles and practices to reach this goal. This chapter considers the core building blocks of an effective digital enterprise.

REFERENCE ARCHITECTURE

According to management consulting firm McKinsey, there are three keys in building a data-driven or digital enterprise. First, companies must be able to identify, combine, and manage multiple sources of data. Second, they need the capability to build advanced technology models for reporting, predicting, and optimizing outcomes. Finally (and most critically), management must possess the muscle to transform the organization so that the data actually yields better results. These objectives can be realized using an approach that successfully puts strategy into action. One of the most popular approaches is to bring together business stakeholders, processes, data, and systems with a solid architecture — specifically, the Reference Architecture.

But what is a Reference Architecture (RA)? In general, an RA is a technology-agnostic package of architectural best practices, that governs and guides implementation of some solution, considering business processes, data, and systems. According to the US Department of Defense [DoDCIO, 2010], Reference Architecture is an organizational asset in:

1. Providing a common language for various stakeholders
2. Providing consistency and repeatability of implementations to solve organizational problems
3. Supporting the validation of solutions against proven reference architectures
4. Encouraging adherence to common standards, specifications, and patterns

So what specifically goes into an RA? A good RA has three main components:

- **Principles**. Principles are guidelines or doctrines that serve the design, build, and deployment phases.
- **Patterns.** A pattern is a generic, proven, and reusable solution to a common problem, based on best practices. Essentially patterns:

- Provide a simple and consistent way to translate requirements into technical solutions
- Assist and speed up the solution development and delivery
- Capture the knowledge and best practices from past initiatives for use in new initiatives
- **Standards**. Standards (or "positions") provide uniformity in methods, processes, and practices.

Principles drive behavior, patterns propel actions, and standards bring consistency and repeatability in behaviors and actions. Implementing the RA provides important benefits including:

- **Risk mitigation**. With Reference Architecture, risks are mitigated by proven architectural foundations that can be reused and adopted to new needs.
- **Cost reduction**. Since the development of solution architecture does not need to start from "square one," solution development costs are reduced.
- **Quality deployment.** Reference Architecture provides core building blocks that are extensively verified and validated over numerous implementations. This improves the overall quality for the deployment of a solution.

So, how exactly does Reference Architecture help in data management? Understanding the RA provides a good background for implementing various data management initiatives. The following sections look at each of the three areas within Reference Architecture, in the context of data management.

PRINCIPLES

Principles are structured sets of rules that collectively guide the organization in the use and deployment of resources. They reflect a level of consensus among the various stakeholders in the enterprise, and form the basis for making future decisions. Derived from TOGAF (The Open Group Architecture Framework), the below section lists the six data-related principles at the enterprise level [Greefhorst and Proper, 2011]. These principles are inter-related and usually most effective in the enterprise when applied as a set. According to TOGAF, a good principle has four main components:

1. The **name** represents the essence of the rule.
2. The **statement** succinctly and unambiguously communicates the rule.
3. The **rationale** highlights the business benefits of adhering to the principle, using business terminology.
4. The **implications** highlight the requirements and impact for carrying out the principle, in terms of resources, costs, and activities.

PRINCIPLE 1: DATA IS MANAGED FOR A PURPOSE

Statement	Data is valuable when managed for a business purpose; business data should align to three purposes - decision making, compliance, and customer service.
Rationale	Enterprises have capabilities to capture a tremendous amount of data. But in the interest of time, quality, and cost, only those elements should be captured, managed, and governed that are traceable to the three main purposes of data (i.e. decision-making; compliance to regulations, security policies, and industry standards, and service to both internal and external customers).
Implications	Just collecting, storing, and analyzing data does not generate any value for the business. The organization structure and the business processes should also be aligned to the purpose for which data is managed, so that the data can enable business performance.

PRINCIPLE 2: QUALITY BUSINESS DATA IS AN ENTERPRISE ASSET

Statement	Quality business data is an enterprise asset to improve business performance.
Rationale	Business data is an asset that has value to the enterprise. It should be carefully managed to ensure quality and accessibility whenever and wherever necessary. The value can be real and measurable if the data element adheres to the 12 data quality dimensions.

Implications	Quality data brings benefits in all areas of business operations of an enterprise. In accounting, quality data can bring savings through a unified approach to credit control and invoicing. A structured approach to managing data in the sales LoB can allow for more effective cross-selling and up-selling, as well as improved customer relationship management. In procurement, quality data can provide better spend visibility and reduce costs. In HR, workforce analytics allows enterprise leaders to optimize human resource management.

PRINCIPLE 3: REALIZING QUALITY DATA TAKES INVESTMENT

Statement	Realizing quality data takes significant time, effort, and organization alignment.
Rationale	Realizing and maintaining quality data is an ongoing endeavor that takes considerable time and effort. Selecting the relevant data quality dimensions, defining the targets, ranges, and thresholds, and implementing and sustaining the initiative are all complex, challenging, and time consuming.
Implications	Realizing a high level of data quality in each of the 12 quality dimensions takes time and effort. Each of the 12 data quality dimensions should map to a specific business need. In addition, stakeholders need to be educated and trained to understand the value and utility of quality data. Hence businesses must be ready to commit sufficient resources to ensure data quality based on a solid cost, risk, and business benefit assessment. The commitment from the senior management to the initiative should be as a long-term continuous improvement initiative.

PRINCIPLE 4: ENTERPRISE DATA HAS CLEAR OWNERSHIP

Statement	Enterprise data has clear ownership and is governed appropriately.
Rationale	Even though enterprise data belongs to the enterprise and not to specific LoBs or individuals, enterprise data should have clear ownership with defined roles and responsibilities for its management. Data ownership is needed to ensure adequate safeguards are in place to manage data quality.
Implications	Data management is not only about capturing and processing data, but about aggregating data from different sources for appropriate consumption by the business. The question of who owns data can get complicated when the data element is shared in the enterprise. In addition, when aggregating data from

	different OLTP systems, the enterprise canonical data model might not completely satisfy the needs of various individual stakeholders. To address this, data governance processes must be a critical component in data management.

PRINCIPLE 5: DATA SHALL ALWAYS BE ACCESSIBLE AND SHARED

Statement	Data is always accessible and shared in an enterprise.
Rationale	Data should be accessible to a variety of users and shared throughout an enterprise, in order to meet a wide range of data and information needs. Sharing quality data helps business performance because the data is already curated and made reliable for each individual user.
Implications	The way data is accessed, shared, and reused must be sufficiently adaptable to meet the needs of a wide range of enterprise users. While data sharing demands a significant amount of governance and collaboration, it has some implications too. These include: • Data sharing should be based in solid data profiling practices. • To enable data sharing, enterprises must develop and abide by a common set of policies, procedures, and standards governing data. • Data sharing will require a significant cultural change as it promotes data democratization. • The principles of data sharing will regularly conflict with the principles of data security. But under no circumstances will the data sharing principle can cause sensitive data, especially restricted and confidential data, to be compromised.

PRINCIPLE 6: ENTERPRISE DATA IS SECURE

Statement	Enterprise data is secure from unauthorized users and systems.
Rationale	Enterprises are accountable for satisfying the needs of a diverse set of stakeholders — both internal and external. This diverse set means the enterprise systems that host the data need to be secure from destructive forces including unauthorized users and systems.
Implications	The implications of data loss can range from loss of business to damage to an enterprise's reputation. Data including customer and supplier details,

	payment information, personal files, and bank account details can be hard to replace, and very dangerous if leaked into the wrong hands. This means delivering, monitoring, and managing security across all data elements and repositories within the enterprise, when the data is at rest, in use, and in motion. Also current technologies such as mobile, cloud, and big data are driving business into uncharted waters, making data increasingly out of the enterprise's control.

The following figure lists these six key principles for a digital enterprise. But these six principles are by no means a complete list. They are meant to serve as a starting point for an enterprise in its digital transformation journey. Depending on the specific circumstances, an enterprise can choose to have appropriate principles added or removed.

Principles for a digital enterprise

PATTERNS

The above six principles or rules can be realized with appropriate practices or patterns. Technically, a pattern can be defined as a consistent and recurring characteristic or trait that helps in the identification of a phenomenon or problem, and serves as an indicator for predicting its future behavior. TOGAF defined pattern as "an idea that has been useful in one practical context and will probably be useful in others." In a line, patterns are reusable solutions based on best practices. The following describes key patterns pertaining to any successful digital enterprise.

BASELINE THE CURRENT LEVEL OF DATA MANAGEMENT MATURITY

Before embarking on any data management initiatives, the first step is to "baseline," or understand where the enterprise currently stands in leveraging data for business performance. Technically, a baseline is a starting point from which implementation begins, improvement is assessed, and comparisons are made. The Data Management Maturity Model (DMMM) developed by Carnegie Melon University helps to evaluate the data management maturity of an enterprise based on 25 process areas [CMMI, 2014].

The DMMM is a comprehensive reference model for fundamental data management disciplines. It provides organizations with a standard set of best practices to assess capabilities, strengthen the data management program, and align improvements with business goals. By providing a structured and standard framework of practices, the DMMM can be leveraged by organizations to build their own roadmap to data management maturity. The term "maturity" relates to the degree of formality and optimization of processes, from ad hoc data management practices, to formally defined steps, to managed result metrics, to active optimization of the data management processes. Basically DMMM facilitates an organization's appreciation for the management of data as critical infrastructure, by increasing capabilities and disciplined practices. A maturity model can be viewed as a set of structured levels that describes how well the behaviors, practices, and processes of an organization can reliably and sustainably produce required outcomes. It can also be used as a benchmark for comparison and as an aid for understanding. The five-level DMMM is shown in the figure below.

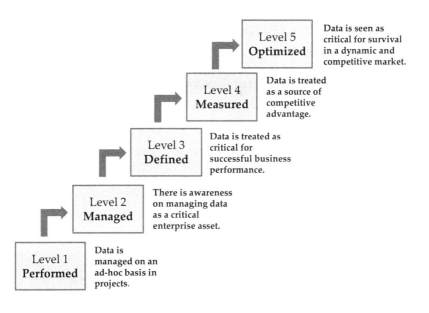

CMMI's Data Management Maturity Model (DMMM)

The below figure is a DMM assessment summary on the 25 process areas (which fall into six domains) for a sample organization.

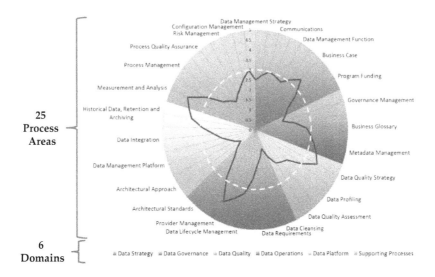

DATA-DRIVEN INITIATIVES SHOULD BE TIED TO A STRONG BUSINESS CASE AND BUSINESS KPIS

For a data-driven initiative to be valuable for business performance, it should be traceable to the three main business purposes discussed before. Any data-driven initiative should ideally be executed as a business transformation initiative. Any initiative in the name of digital transformation outside these three purposes of data should be seriously assessed.

One effective way this pattern can be implemented is by mapping the performance of the data-driven initiatives to business goals and KPIs, using the GQM model. Mario Faria of Gartner, in the interview for this book said, "Every data initiative and activity should be associated with business goals and metrics. For example, if the business goal of a media company is to increase the subscription by 50 percent, then the office of the CDO should be leveraging the data assets to contribute to this goal. If a transportation company wants to reduce the fuel costs by 5 percent, then the data governance and any other data initiatives undertaken should be towards achieving that business goal."

ENTERPRISE GOALS SHOULD PRECEDE LOB GOALS

In many enterprises, data elements are captured in multiple systems of record (SoR) which is akin to creating multiple versions of truth. This situation mainly occurs when the LoBs (such as finance, HR, or supply chain) operate in silos, with their own goals and systems isolated from those of other LoBs. In doing this, LoBs give their own goals more priority than that of the value propositions of the entire enterprise.

This situation results in duplicate data elements, proliferation of systems, poor efficiency, and increased costs for the enterprise. So if the cross-functional enterprise data elements (especially the reference data and master data) are managed by a LoB and not by the enterprise, it results in poor data quality throughout the enterprise. This pattern aims to correct that, and can be implemented by:

- Aligning the goals of the data initiative directly to the goals of the enterprise
- Rationalizing the systems so that core business processes are owned at the enterprise level, and managed by the SoR

At the core, managing data at the enterprise level brings efficiency and reduces costs. Data quality expert Dr. Thomas Redman notes that one important way for businesses to profit is to share data [Redman, 2016]. He says business units that own the data sometimes tend to be excessively possessive, and should be encouraged to share. The goal is to become a content provider (one who sells data to businesses) and or a facilitator (one who aggregates and presents data in a way that enhances the user's experience). Dr. Redman emphasizes repeatedly that there is gold in enterprise data when shared effectively. So if the data needs to be shared effectively, it should be managed at an enterprise level.

MANAGE CORE BUSINESS PROCESSES IN THE SOR

Companies that have challenges deriving value from data usually have multiple SoRs. This results in multiple and inconsistent data definitions due to multiple systems using different data dictionaries and metadata models. If the data dictionary is sourced from a single enterprise-wide SoR, the enterprise data definitions pertaining to origin, usage, format, type, and relationships to other data aspects will be consistent, accurate, and authoritative.

While achieving this state of having a single SoR like an ERP application might seem unrealistic for some enterprises, most successful digital enterprises have managed to achieve it by running core business processes centrally in the SoR. In addition, while the SoR may not completely provide solution for each and every LoB in the enterprise, it is more efficient and profitable than having multiple systems used by each LoB in the long term.

To further support the SoR, the reference data and master data are managed centrally at the enterprise level; the reference data and master data can be managed in the SoR or in a separate MDM (Master Data Management) system. For example, Shell Energy runs all its core enterprise business activities such as HR, finance, and supply chain from the SAP ERP application. This not only provides consistent data definitions, but also provides a single source of truth for the reference data and master data elements in the enterprise.

REFERENCE AND MASTER DATA SHOULD BE BASED ON DATA STANDARDS AND MDM

The reference and master data elements (which, again, should be shared throughout the enterprise) should be based on standards to facilitate portability and consistency in business transactions. These data standards can be defined internally or can be based on industry standards. Technically, data standards are documented agreements on representation, format, definition, structuring, tagging, transmission, manipulation, use and management of data. For example, reference data elements (such as UoM, currency codes, and others) shall be based on ISO codes; product master data elements can be based on GTIN standards and UNSPSC codes.

Closely related to the data standard is the management of standards. In most enterprises, data is scattered everywhere — on applications, shared drives, individual PCs, or even in papers and folders. The challenge lies in knowing what is available, where the data is, how it is used, how the data is consolidated, and more. This can be achieved by managing the reference data and the master data elements in the SoR or the master data management (MDM) system.

While we discussed SoR earlier, what exactly is MDM? According to Gartner, MDM is a technology-enabled discipline in which business and IT work together to ensure the uniformity, accuracy, stewardship, consistency, and accountability of the enterprise's master data assets [Gartner, 2016]. In other words, MDM is the foundation for realizing the 12 data quality dimensions.

The key to implementing these 12 data quality dimensions on the reference data and master data relies on a solid MDM architectural style. There are different styles that can be adopted by an organization when implementing the MDM solution. The top three MDM implementation styles are cross-referenced or registry, coexistence or harmonized, and transaction hub-and-spoke. The table below highlights the key features of these MDM styles.

	Cross-referenced or registry	Coexistence or harmonized	Transaction hub-and-spoke
Definition	In this style, the various source systems publish data to the central hub. The central hub stores only the source system IDs, the foreign keys, and other key metadata values needed for matching. This style uses data federation to build the "virtual" master data from the connected systems.	The coexistence style MDM hub involves master data that is created and stored in numerous spoke systems, but includes a physically instantiated "golden record" in the central hub. The authoring of data is distributed. The data in the spoke systems is harmonized with the central hub after each transaction via APIs or web services.	In this architecture, the hub stores, enhances, and maintains all the relevant master data attributes as the authoritative source of truth. The hub publishes this information to the respective spoke systems via APIs or web services.

	Cross-referenced or registry	Coexistence or harmonized	Transaction hub-and-spoke
Physical location of the master data record	The data in the central hub is the metadata pertaining to the master data that exists in the spoke systems. There is no master data in the central hub system.	Master data is partly in the hub and partly in the spoke systems.	The master data is completely maintained in the centralized hub system, and the spoke system takes a copy of the master data from the central hub.
Example	A bearing in a Salesforce (a popular CRM application) spoke system might be called 1234 with a UoM of Each (EA), while the same bearing in the oracle spoke might be called SKF3690 with a UoM of Packet (PK). In the central hub, you would manually map 1234 = SKF3690 and allow the UoM to be managed in the spoke systems.	A bearing in Salesforce might be called 1234 with a UoM of EA, while the same bearing in Oracle might be called SKF3690 with a UoM of PK. In the central hub, you would define the primary key, and change the values of 1234 in Salesforce and SKF3890 in Oracle to new values, say 567SKF. This unique product code of 567SKF will be distributed to the spoke systems while the UoM of EA and PK will continue to remain in the Salesforce and Oracle spoke systems.	Here all the data is rationalized and managed in the central hub — say Cisco Composite (a popular data virtualization application). The product ID of 567SKF and the UoM of BX (Box) will become the master data elements, with their values interfaced via APIs or web services to the spoke systems. The ID and UoM in the Salesforce and Oracle spoke systems will be always in sync with the centralized Cisco Composite system.

	Cross-referenced or registry	Coexistence or harmonized	Transaction hub-and-spoke
Benefits	The spoke systems can continue to use the same data records and values.	The spoke systems can continue to use the majority of the data records and values that are specific to them.	This architecture provides an enterprise-wide, complete, and accurate view of various master data elements.
Limitations	There is no one view of master data, as every system will have its own way of defining master data; hence reporting will be cumbersome.	There is a partial view of the master data. This requires good governance processes to make the data clean and relevant.	This style takes time to implement, and also requires alignment of different stakeholders. It works well in green-field implementations.

Most master data implementations rely on the transaction hub-and-spoke architecture, as it provides a single, consolidated, enterprise-wide, complete, and accurate view of various master data elements. Below is a real world example, in which an oil refinery is looking to improve their reporting capabilities after implementing the cross-referenced registry style. However, the report developer is finding it challenging to get a consolidated report, because the same product is described and managed in four different ways in four different systems as shown in the image below.

Planner
Aspen PIMS
7.8# CBOB

Plant Manager
Aspen AORA
83.5 SUBGRADE7.8

Accountant
SAP ERP
SUB GRADE

Trader
RightAngle
SUB GRADE RVP 7.8

Master data discrepancies example

On the contrary, P&G, one of the most successful consumer packaged goods company in the world, has implemented a centralized transaction hub-and-spoke global master data system within its SAP ERP system, as most of its core business processes are on SAP. P&G's master data (i.e. product data, customer data, ledger accounts, suppliers, and sales prices) is centralized with a transaction hub-and-spoke architecture and the overall governance and data quality has improved significantly. To complement its master data efforts, P&G has implemented Lean Six Sigma improvement initiatives. According to Adnan Behmen, who is in charge of the P&G's master data team, currently P&G operates at quality levels of 99.9 percent — meaning just one or two defects per thousand. P&G has achieved what many other enterprises have failed to do: a standardized global ERP deployment with a centralized infrastructure that is flexible enough to support its global business plans [Behmen, 2016].

DATA INTEGRATION (EAI AND ETL) SHOULD BE SPECIFIC TO THE DATA TYPES AND THE BUSINESS RULES

A good data integration solution (EAI or ETL) addresses both business and data rules. Data integration architecture in general should be based on business processes, the enterprise OLTP landscape, transaction integrity of data during data flow, and ETL and EAI mechanisms. While reference data and master data can be managed from the SoR system, the volume of these data sets is relatively small. There is a much greater volume of transactional data; the sheer volume of data that flows through enterprise systems can make it challenging to maintain good quality transactional data at all times.

However, the data integration problem takes on a different dimension when enterprises try to integrate on-premises applications with SaaS cloud applications, which have different data models. As an example, the field "payment term" is considered transactional data in Ariba's Procurement SaaS cloud application, while the same field is defined as master data in the SAP COTS ERP application. Thus, integrating the cloud Ariba solution with the on-premises SAP ERP application will create significant data model inconsistencies in the enterprise. Also, maintaining the system connections and the data exchange with the desired level of enterprise security is very challenging when integrating on-premises with SaaS cloud applications.

Application integration has been lost in the "cloud rush," said Benoit Lheureux, vice president of research firm Gartner. To address these system integration issues, Lheureux suggests creating a coherent, disciplined application integration strategy that works across all sources of data — in-house or cloud, behind or outside the enterprise firewall.

This "creating a coherent, disciplined application integration strategy" can be implemented effectively using the Enterprise Service Bus (ESB), which enforces standards-based integration. As discussed in Chapter 3, with an ESB, all applications in the integration landscape follow the same standards and share data as messages using industry standards such as XML (Extensible Markup Language), HTTP (Hypertext Transfer Protocol), SOAP (Simple Object Access Protocol) and more. Any application can plug into the ESB, as long as it meets the standards described in the Web Services Description Language (WSDL).

DISTRIBUTE REPORTING IN OLTP, BI, AND ANALYTICS SYSTEMS

Enterprises need information, knowledge, and wisdom to be successful in the marketplace. An enterprise success is measured by the quality of the results it produces. These results are in turn dependent on the quality of the decisions made, and these decisions rely on the quality of the data which is presented in reports.

Technically, a report is the output of a query against a data set, usually in a predetermined format, which is used to gain insights. From the IT systems side, three kinds of reports matter in an enterprise: OLTP or Transactional (TR) Reports, OLAP or Business Intelligence (BI) Reports, and Business Analytics (BA) reports. In most cases, these three types of reports mean different things to different people. But generally TR, BI, and BA will help in making informed decisions by providing different types of insights:

Perspective	Transactional Reporting (TR)	Business Intelligence (BI)	Business Analytics (BA)
Business Value	TR is focused on creating operational efficiency through problem identification and solving. It does this by giving a snapshot of data from a single OLTP system.	BI is focused on operational efficiency through problem identification and solving. It does this by consolidating and analyzing data from multiple OLTP systems.	BA focuses on identifying future trends in business operations and comparing one metric or KPI to others.
Organizational Focus	TR is tailored towards business functions	BI is tailored to LoB and enterprises	BA is for all; business function, LoB, and enterprise
Time Horizon	TR entails analysis of historical data from specific OLTP systems to make informed decisions on the current business situation. TR will tell what happened based on past results.	BI involves analysis of historical data from multiple OLTP systems to make informed decisions on the current situation. BI will also tell what happened based on past results.	BA typically uses analysis of historical data from multiple sources to make informed decisions about the future state. BA is telling what is going to happen, to anticipate what is coming.
Data Source	Individual OLTP systems	Data warehouses (DWH), where multiple OLTP systems are combined to form a canonical data model	The analysis can be on a single OLTP system, multiple OLTPs, or on the DWH
Data Type	Structured data	Mainly structured, but can include some unstructured data	Structured and unstructured data

Perspective	Transactional Reporting (TR)	Business Intelligence (BI)	Business Analytics (BA)
Data Volume	Small data, up to gigabytes	Medium data, multiple gigabytes to many terabytes	Big data, multiple terabytes to many petabytes
Database Design	OLTP systems are highly normalized (usually 3NF)	BI is based on OLAP. BI is typically denormalized, with fewer tables based on star or snowflake schemas	BA can include a combination of normalized and denormalized tables
Insight Consumption Style	TR is reactive. In TR, reports are created specific to the user and his or her roles or work	BI is reactive. In BI, highly-formatted reports are created and distributed to the department or organization to address KPIs	BA is typically proactive. BA is about letting people "get into the flow" of analysis, explore their data, and ask their own questions
DIKW Model Alignment	Data and Information	Information and Knowledge	Knowledge and Wisdom
Example	What is the rejection rate for supplier X in 2015?	What is the rejection rate for YYY procurement category between 2005 and 2015 for ZZZ category of suppliers?	What will be the average rejection rate if we reduce the lead time by 10% for one-time supplier category?

DATA SECURITY PRACTICES SHOULD BE INTEGRAL TO BUSINESS OPERATIONS

Enterprise data must always be protected from unauthorized access, corruption, and loss. Managing this risk is imperative and takes a deal of effort if the business wishes to be legally complaint. These protection efforts include backups of operational data, disaster recovery (DR), and mechanisms to guard against malware, virus attacks, and system failure.

While the above strategies protect the infrastructure, the application and data can be secured using role-based access control (RBAC) and attribute-based access control (ABAC) solutions. While RBAC employs pre-defined roles that carry specific sets of privileges to which users are assigned, ABAC provides dynamic, context-aware, and risk-intelligent access control to users. The access control policies in ABAC are based on user, resource, object, and environment attributes, and logical statements such as "IF, THEN, ELSE" statements. For example: IF the requestor is a manager, THEN allow read/write access to sensitive data and IF the requestor is a NOT a manager, THEN restrict access.

However, digital enterprises need to strike a balance between employing security procedures and empowering business users with access to data they need for improved productivity. In a recent survey by McKinsey & Company, 70 percent of American users were willing to share personal data for connected navigation, while 90 percent of Chinese respondents would share personal data to enable predictive maintenance.

ENTERPRISE DATA GOVERNANCE (EDG) SHOULD BE AN ACTIVE AND FUNCTIONAL BUSINESS ENTITY

EDG is a real and active working body of business and IT stakeholders. EDG should set up data policies, procedures, and standards, for addressing data-related issues, implement data quality improvement programs, take proactive measures to prevent data-related problems, and facilitate change in how data is consumed in the enterprise. Specifically, EDG should be responsible for ownership of reference data and master data as these are enterprise-wide data elements.

As such, the EDG must be supported by data stewards from the business and data custodians from IT, who together take responsibility for high-quality data. Data steward is a business-driven role responsible for content, context, and associated business rules to help business users with quality data. The data steward acts as a liaison between the IT department and the business consumers by defining data formats, resolving data quality issues, and ensuring that data consumers adhere to defined standards. On the other hand, data custodians are responsible for the safe and secure custody, transport, and storage of data and business rules. Primarily, data custodians are responsible for the technical environment and the database structure.

Hence in order for EDG to be effective, data stewards and data custodians must feel empowered not only to exploit data to the fullest for business benefits, but also to archive and purge data when continued management becomes unnecessary. While EDG focuses on policies, procedures and standards, data stewards and custodians need to focus on tactical coordination and implementation.

The area where the data stewards and data custodians really come together is the monitoring of data quality. As mentioned earlier, data quality degrades over time. As such, data should be monitored for quality throughout its lifecycle with appropriate KPIs. Specifically, data quality monitoring includes setting baselines, thresholds, and targets, ensuring conformance to those values, and effectively communicating the metrics to stakeholders for taking corrective measures.

DATA-DRIVEN CULTURE SHOULD BE ENTERPRISE-WIDE

How does a digital enterprise function? Management guru Peter Drucker once said, "Culture eats strategy for breakfast" [Schein, 2004]. This basically means that an organization's culture can be a powerful force to counteract and resist change, no matter how good the strategy is. The culture of a digital enterprise — at a minimum — lies in using data for business performance, framing questions for discovery, valuing hypotheses over assumptions, and using KPIs to baseline the current status and to track future progress and outcomes. Furthermore, implementing data initiatives is not a one-time project. Becoming a digital enterprise is a continuous improvement initiative program that can only be successful if every business stakeholder in the enterprise has a stake in data. Chapter 9 covers these aspects in more detail as part of change management.

The figure below summarizes the ten key patterns for a building a successful digital enterprise. Of course, this list of ten patterns is by no means complete. They are meant to serve as a starting point for enterprises in their digital transformation journeys. Depending on the unique circumstances, an enterprise can revise the list by adding or removing patterns appropriately. But the key point to remember is that the purpose of any pattern is to facilitate reusability and consistency in deployment across the enterprise, and to prevent one-off implementations that might hamper the overall efficiency of the enterprise.

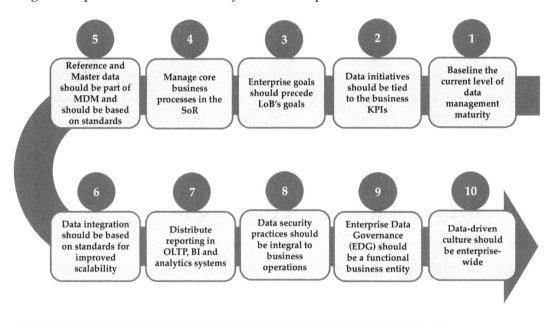

Patterns for building a digital enterprise

STANDARDS FOR DATA MANAGEMENT

As said before, data can be managed at the enterprise, LoB, business function level or even at individual user level. However, without strong governance, data always defaults to the lowest common denominator — the individual user level — and the outcome is generally poor data quality. So if the data must be managed at the highest level (i.e. at the enterprise level), it should be based on mechanisms acceptable to all stakeholders in the enterprise. The vehicle for realizing this is the standards within reference architecture.

As mentioned before, one of the key aspects of reference architecture is a standards-based framework that rests on sound data management and data governance standards and practices. According to ISO, standards are agreements containing specifications and other criteria to serve as rules, guidelines, definitions or characteristics to ensure that the outcomes fit their purpose.

Within data management, common standards address data governance, including associated processes, quality standards, and taxonomies. According to DAMA's (Data Management Association) Data Management Body of Knowledge (DMBOK), data management is the development and execution of architectures, policies, practices and procedures in order to manage the information lifecycle needs of an enterprise in an effective manner. Data management in DMBOK comprises 10 disciplines, as shown in the figure on the facing page.

As shown in this figure, data governance is merely one of the ten data management disciplines. Data governance is a set of processes that ensures that an enterprise's key data assets are formally managed. In simple words, data governance is the act of rule-setting and monitoring to ensure that data is of high quality, and that individuals can be made accountable for any consequences of low data quality.

To enable this, the data governance framework from DGI (Data Governance Institute) provides a logical structure for classifying, organizing, and communicating complex activities involved in making decisions about and taking action on enterprise data.

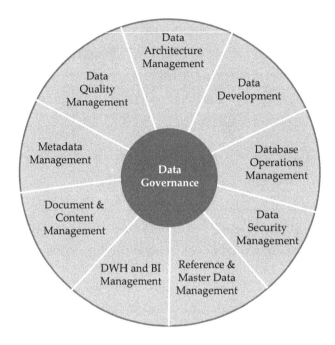

The data governance framework adapted from DGI is shown in the figure below.

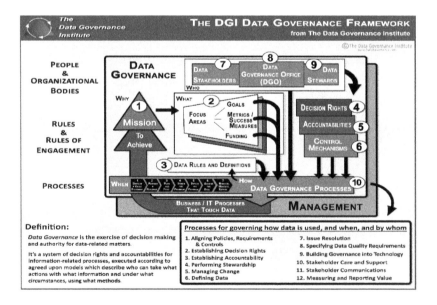

CHIEF DATA OFFICER (CDO)

While data governance focuses on high-level policies and procedures, implementation of data governance is normally shared between the IT and the business. In recent years, in order to ensure that digital initiatives effectively cascade across the enterprise, many organizations have created the Chief Data Officer (CDO) and included EDG function as part of the CDO's office. A recent Gartner report estimates that 90 percent of large organizations will have a CDO by 2019 [Gartner, 2016].

Broadly, the CDO bears responsibility for the firm's enterprise-wide data and information strategy, governance, control, and policy development. The CDO's ultimate goal is the effective exploitation of data assets to create business value. So specifically, what exactly is the role of the CDO? Research by IBM finds that CDOs drive data innovation and optimization efforts in five general ways [Henschen, 2014]:

1. **Leverage**. Finding ways to use existing data.
2. **Enrichment**. Augmenting data by combining internal and external sources.
3. **Monetization**. Finding new sources of revenue tied to data.
4. **Protection**. Ensuring data privacy and security.
5. **Upkeep**. Managing the health of data under governance.

However, setting up the office of the CDO and running it efficiently is not easy. According to Mario Faria, Managing Vice President at Gartner Research, "Currently only 50 percent of the CDOs are successful. People, culture and internal resistance can create formidable roadblocks for the CDO [Henderson, 2016]." While these are valid reasons, the key factors in a successful CDO office lie in two key elements:

- **Alignment.** A CDO's role is strategic and spans the enterprise; the role is not specific to a certain LoB or business function. Though the tasks of a CDO were previously managed by a CIO, the new role of the CDO is more closely aligned with the business. According to Prof. Richard Wang of MIT, "CDO is not an IT role" [Wang, 1992]. If the organization is serious about leveraging data as an enterprise asset, the tasks of the CDO should be aligned with the strategic goals of the organization. In a recent Garner survey, while 38 percent of CDOs report to CEOs, 51 percent still report to LoB heads and 11 percent report to CIOs. A Forbes survey puts digital ownership with the CMO at 34 percent, CEO at 27 percent, and CIO/CTO (who have traditionally led technology roadmaps) in a distant third place at 19 percent [Solis, 2016].

- **Focus.** As mentioned before, an enterprise typically works on different types of data: reference data (for business categorization), master data (for business entities), and transactional data (for business events). While the majority of data issues are visible in transactional data, in most cases, the root cause lies in poor quality of reference data and master data. Hence the CDO and his or her team of data architects, stewards, and custodians should focus on reference data and master data, as these data elements span the enterprise. Their focus should also include finding the right implementation styles, utilizing patterns, introducing data governance mechanisms, and optimizing relevant data quality dimensions, to name a few.

CONCLUSION

Today, almost every strategic initiative in an enterprise is supported by data. If the business wants to run smoothly, data needs to be managed carefully and governed thoughtfully on a long-term basis. Executing a digital transformation initiative is like running a marathon — not just a few sprints. Businesses that have poor data quality and practice ad-hoc data governance practices will find their data locked in silos, produce unreliable reports, and see their core business processes poorly executed.

At the same time, enterprise data management is about individuals and organizations as much as it about databases, applications, and infrastructure. Communicating data principles to diverse stakeholders and building patterns for the digital enterprise takes time, is complex, and is extremely difficult. In order for data to be leveraged appropriately, there should be a good data governance framework where businesses (and CDOs, specifically) own the data and manage the data governance process, and IT supports the business.

Chapter 8: Realizing the Data-Driven Enterprise

If you torture the data long enough, it will confess.

Ronald Coase
Noted Economist

This chapter takes a close look at what it takes to realize the three purposes of data: deriving business insights, complying with industry standards, security policies, government regulations, and finally providing the desired level of services for internal and external customers. While Chapter 7 was mainly concerned with design aspects, this chapter is about implementation. The third purpose of data, improving service levels for internal and external customers, is very specific to the enterprise. Chapter 5 covered different data quality dimensions, so this leaves room for discussing the other two purposes of data — the implementation details for deriving business insights and ensuring compliance.

COMPLYING WITH REGULATIONS USING THE COBIT MODEL

Broadly, compliance is an organization's adherence to laws, regulations, guidelines, and specifications relevant to its business, in order to minimize the risk and improve effectiveness in business operations. As mentioned in the previous chapters, compliance focuses on three main areas: government regulations and laws, industry standards, and internal security policies. This section deals with compliance to government regulations and laws. Examples of government regulatory compliance laws and regulations include the PCI DSS (Payment Card Industry Data Security Standard), HIPAA (Health Insurance Portability and Accountability Act), and the SOX (Sarbanes-Oxley Act), to name a few.

Regulations vary based on jurisdiction and industry type. SOX is US legislation for all public companies in US. While HIPAA is also a US legislation, it is related specifically to the health care industry sector. While PIPEDA (Personal Information Protection and Electronic Documents Act) is the data privacy law in Canada, personal data in Singapore is protected under the PDPA (Personal Data Protection Act), and the EU version is General Data Protection Regulation (GDPR). While it is impossible to list all the government compliance laws and regulations in the world, we need to look at a generic compliance framework that is applicable for most government regulatory compliance laws.

There exist various compliance frameworks, including COBIT (Control Objectives for Information and Related Technologies), ITIL (IT Infrastructure Library), ISO 38500, and Six Sigma. The most popular of these is COBIT, which is published by the Information Systems Audit and Control Association (ISACA). COBIT provides an implementable set of IT controls around a framework of IT-related processes, designed to ensure regulatory compliance.

COBIT links business or compliance goals to IT goals, providing metrics and maturity models to measure their success, and identifying the associated responsibilities of business and IT process owners. Apart from ensuring regulatory compliance, COBIT helps to manage information, increase business agility, lower IT operating costs, and improve compliance with data retention and management regulations.

So how does the management of an IT system using COBIT ensure regulatory compliance? A solid IT system simplifies regulatory compliance across the enterprise, as digital transactions provide legal representatives timely access to data for validating adherence to compliance. Specifically IT systems facilitated by the COBIT processes can promote regulatory compliance in a number of ways:

- **Data security.** IT systems maintain access control of data records. For example, ERP systems can restrict data access to authorized personnel and maintain a record of all personnel who have access to specific data records. Another example is the three-way match in accounting — a procedure used when processing an invoice received from a supplier against the purchase order and the receivable slip to avoid fraudulent invoices. Compliance to three-way matching is ensuring that there are three different persons managing the documents related to purchase orders, invoices, and receivables.

- **Integrity.** The IT systems make it possible to obscure personal data in business documents to protect data privacy. In transactional documents IT systems ensure that the actual data involved contains sufficient detail, is posted in a timely manner, is stored securely, is readily retrievable, and is safeguarded against improper alteration, disclosure, or use. Another example where IT systems ensure compliance is transfer pricing in intercompany business transactions to align with the arms-length pricing when the enterprise conducts intra-company transactions.

- **Automated control.** Most COTS IT systems provide standard business rules against compliance to ISO, Sarbanes Oxley (SOX), and other regulations. This means the IT systems facilitate review and approval of business documents in an automated, controlled, and standardized manner to maintain compliance to regulations. Also IT systems provide automated retention schedules and guidelines so when new business documents are added to the system, records are retained and not prematurely purged or erased. The IT systems also maintain an audit trail of records accessed if there are any questions.

- **Legal hold.** An IT system also simplifies implementing a legal hold in the event of litigation. Secure files can be securely stored to prevent them from being altered during litigation while digital copies of those documents are still available for business operations.

Coming back to COBIT, there are approximately 300 generic COBIT objectives grouped in COBIT-5, which is the latest version. The COBIT-5 process reference model divides the governance and management processes of enterprise IT into two main process domains:

- **Governance.** Governance ensures that the needs of the stakeholder are evaluated to determine specific objectives. This domain contains five governance processes; each of these includes defined "evaluate, direct and monitor" practices. This means that governance should:
  - Evaluate to determine balanced, agreed-on enterprise objectives to be achieved
  - Direct through prioritization and decision making
  - Monitor performance, compliance and progress against agreed direction and objectives

- **Management.** The management domain provides end-to-end coverage of IT. In other words, management plans, builds, delivers, and monitors activities to align with and support the governance objectives. Specifically the four areas in this domain are:
  - Align, Plan, and Organize (APO)
  - Build, Acquire, and Implement (BAI)
  - Deliver, Service, and Support (DSS)
  - Monitor, Evaluate, and Assess (MEA)

The complete COBIT-5 model which includes a total of 37 governance and management processes is shown in the image on the facing page. More details on the COBIT-5 are available at the ISACA website.

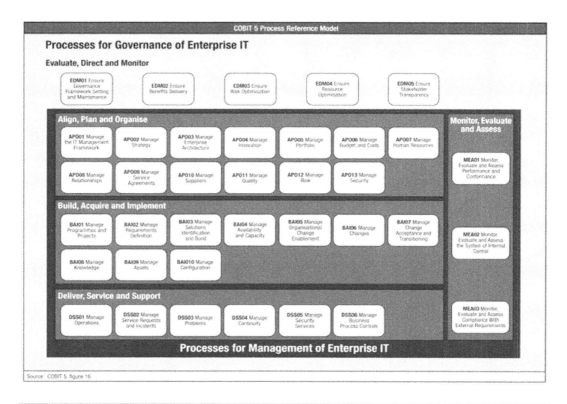

The COBIT Model

COMPLIANCE WITH INDUSTRY STANDARDS

While the previous section discussed regulatory compliance, the second area of compliance involves meeting industry standards. Each industry sector has established numerous standards. These standards provide technology-agnostic, scalable, flexible, interoperable, feature-rich solutions that deliver a return on investment (ROI), whilst also ensuring that future requirements can be supported. Standards also support health and safety aspects — electrical and fire hazard standards are a prime example. At the core, standards provide a technology agnostic, scalable, flexible, portable, and feature rich solutions to drive innovation, increase productivity, and reduce costs. A study by ISO showed that companies involved in standardization of processes, products, and services saw an extra 20 percent growth in annual revenue.

How are industry standards relevant to data management? In a nutshell, standards fuel the development and implementation of technologies that influence and transform the way businesses operate and perform. For example, industry standards based on EDI and XML formats provide a common language, enabling all business partners within a particular industry sector to promote business-to-business (B2B) integration. Another example of an industry standard is the United Nations' Standard Products and Services Code (UNSPSC) taxonomy for over 50,000 commodities, and Global Trade Item Number (GTIN) coding standards for product identification.

Many businesses follow UNSPSC and GTIN standards to manage their commodities and products. A common standard in the supply chain area is the DUNS (Data Universal Numbering System); many organizations require their trading partners to be complaint with DUNS. The Petroleum Industry Data Exchange (PIDX) is a common data standard for e-business across the petroleum industry. While none of these standards have legal or regulatory bearing, almost every industry sector has some standards to enforce efficiency in the business operations.

The facing page contains an example of a globally integrated oil company that combined UNSPSC and PIDX standards to define internal compliance standards for managing master data in their ERP system. While UNSPSC provided industry-compliant taxonomy, PIDX provided the data formatting templates for commodities. The goals of adhering to UNSPSC and PIDX standards were to enable better product classification, improve searching of products by business users, and reduce duplicate data.

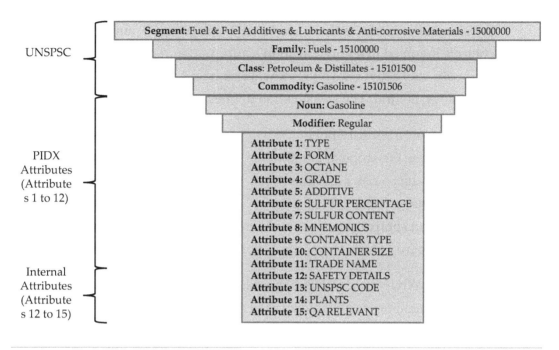

UNSPSC

PIDX
Attributes
(Attribute
s 1 to 12)

Internal
Attributes
(Attribute
s 12 to 15)

Segment: Fuel & Fuel Additives & Lubricants & Anti-corrosive Materials - 15000000
Family: Fuels - 15100000
Class: Petroleum & Distillates - 15101500
Commodity: Gasoline - 15101506
Noun: Gasoline
Modifier: Regular

Attribute 1: TYPE
Attribute 2: FORM
Attribute 3: OCTANE
Attribute 4: GRADE
Attribute 5: ADDITIVE
Attribute 6: SULFUR PERCENTAGE
Attribute 7: SULFUR CONTENT
Attribute 8: MNEMONICS
Attribute 9: CONTAINER TYPE
Attribute 10: CONTAINER SIZE
Attribute 11: TRADE NAME
Attribute 12: SAFETY DETAILS
Attribute 13: UNSPSC CODE
Attribute 14: PLANTS
Attribute 15: QA RELEVANT

The UNSPSC and PIDX for item masters

COMPLIANCE TO INTERNAL POLICIES

The third area of compliance pertains to internal policies of the enterprise. Internal policies are sets of documented guidelines that establish standards in areas pertaining to IT security, safety requirements, and employee conduct, among others. From the data management perspective, the important internal policy is the security of information systems. Ensuring the security of an organization's data and information means adhering to security policies and standards. The important security standards relevant for enterprises include ISO 27001, ISO 27002, SSAE16/SOC 1, SOC 2, and ISO 9001. Compliance to these standards are usually determined and certified by an external auditor in many enterprises.

- **ISO 27001.** This standard formally specifies an Information Security Management System (ISMS), a suite of activities concerning the management of information security risks. An ISMS is a framework of policies and procedures that includes all legal, physical, and technical controls involved in an organization's information risk management processes. ISO 27001 uses a top-down, risk-based approach and is technology-neutral. The specification defines a six-part planning process:

1. Define a security policy.
2. Define the scope of the ISMS.
3. Conduct a risk assessment.
4. Manage identified risks.
5. Select control objectives and controls to be implemented.
6. Prepare a statement of applicability.

- **ISO 27002.** While the ISO 27001 standard provides a checklist of controls, it does not mandate specific information security controls; ISO 27001 is still at a policy level. We need mechanisms that provide guidance for implementation. Therefore, ISO 27002 provides a comprehensive set of information security controls. ISO 27002 contains 12 main sections:

1. Risk assessment
2. Security policy
3. Organization of information security
4. Asset management
5. Human resources security
6. Physical and environmental security
7. Communications and operations management
8. Access control
9. Information systems acquisition, development and maintenance
10. Information security incident management
11. Business continuity management
12. Compliance

- **SSAE 16 or SOC 1.** The Statement on Standards for Attestation Engagements (SSAE) 16 is a regulation created by the American Institute of

Certified Public Accountants (AICPA). It addresses how service companies report on compliance controls. SSAE 16 also covers the requirements of Service Organization Control 1 (SOC1) reports. If an enterprise is compliant for SOC 1 reports, then SSAE 16 compliance is basically redundant. So what do SOC 1 or SSAE 16 reports achieve? A SOC 1 or SSAE 16 report is an audit of the financial statements of the enterprise. SOC 1 reports are divided into Type 1 and Type 2 reports. Type 1 reports on an organization's suitability of design of controls on a specific date, while a Type 2 report evaluates the effectiveness of the control design over a period of time.

- **SOC 2.** Service Organization Control 2 (SOC2) reports on various organizational controls related to five aspects:

  1. Security
  2. Availability
  3. Processing integrity
  4. Confidentiality
  5. Privacy

- **ISO 9001.** This is a global standard for managing the quality of products and services according to eight main principles. These eight principles are:

  1. Customer focus
  2. Leadership
  3. Involvement of people
  4. Process approach
  5. System approach to management
  6. Continual improvement
  7. Factual approach to decision making
  8. Mutually beneficial supplier relations

The important question at this juncture is whether all IT solution vendors follow all of these compliance certifications in their IT products. While some do not, the majority of them follow these compliance certifications. As an example, the table below summarizes the status of these compliance certifications from leading cloud SaaS solution vendors based on 2015 data.

#	Certifications	Azure	Amazon	RackSpace	SAP	Workday
1	ISO 27001	Yes	Yes	Yes	Yes	Yes
2	ISO 27002	Yes	No	Yes	No	No
3	SSAE16 (or SOC1)	Yes	No	Yes	Yes	Yes
4	SOC 2	Yes	Yes	Yes	Yes	Yes
5	ISO 9001	No	Yes	No	Yes	No

Though the above five security certification standards are important and commonly used, any IT security policy is a living document that needs to be continually updated to adapt to evolving business and IT requirements. Institutions such as the International Organization of Standardization (ISO) and the U.S. National Institute of Standards and Technology (NIST) regularly publish and update standards and best practices for security policy formation.

BUSINESS INSIGHTS AND THE DIKW MODEL

Let us now look at the second main topic of this chapter — deriving insights. As mentioned earlier, deriving business insights for decision-making is one of the key purposes of data. First, what is the definition of an insight? Researcher Marco Vriens defines business insight as "A thought, fact, combination of facts, data, and analysis of data that induces meaning and furthers understanding of a situation or issue for benefiting the business" [Vriens, 2012]. Hence from the insights perspective, data should do two key things:

- Confirm or disprove the goal, questions, hypothesis, and KPIs that support a specific decision.

- Probe more relevant goal, questions, hypothesis, and KPIs pertaining to the decision.

Deriving insights from data is often quite challenging, compared to the other two purposes of data. Adherence to standards and improving service levels are pretty straightforward and their outcomes are easily validated. Though there are many frameworks and models that can be used to derive insights from data, the DIKW (**D**ata, **I**nformation, **K**nowledge, **W**isdom) model is one of the most commonly embraced.

According to Russell Ackoff, a systems theorist who developed the DIKW model, the relationship between data, information, knowledge and wisdom can be represented as a "DIKW hierarchy" [Ackoff, 1989]. The first three categories (**d**ata, **i**nformation, and **k**nowledge) relate to past events and are typically system-driven. The fourth category (**w**isdom), which is derived from results of the first three categories, deals with the future and is human-centric. While data is simply raw facts, it is information, knowledge, and wisdom that build insights.

From the perspective of the DIKW model, asking different types of questions can lead to different outcomes. Using **data**, **information** provides answers to "who," "what," "where," and "when" type of questions. **Knowledge** answers the "how" type of questions, while **wisdom** provides a deep understanding with an appreciation of the "why" questions.

When data is framed by context provided by the user, information is discovered. Patterns of information over time constitute knowledge, and knowledge embodied with principles results in wisdom. The figure below, derived from the work of Jonathan Hey, represents the transitions from data to information, knowledge, and finally wisdom.

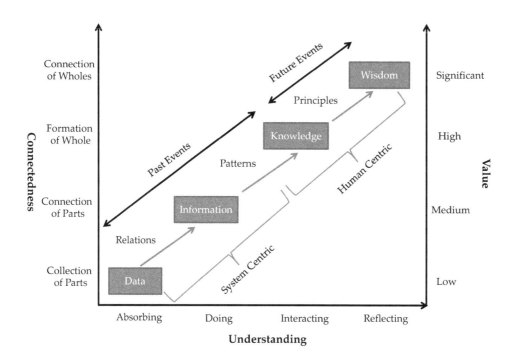

INTUITION AND DECISION-MAKING

Just like the extraction of one gram of gold from tons of mined earth, deriving insights requires processing huge amounts of data from the right business areas. According to Irfan Kamal, author of *Metrics Are Easy; Insight Is Hard*, "Insights are relatively rare. Insights that are actionable and data-driven and create business value are relatively rare. Delivering them requires different people, technology, and skills — specifically including deep domain knowledge."

In the popular book *Blink*, author Malcolm Gladwell argued that snap judgments are often superior to studied, rational responses; there is a wealth of serious research that supports that view. So when deriving insights takes significant time and effort, data-driven thinking is often challenged by intuition-based approaches. In the context of making business decisions, intuition can be defined as the processing of data by the human mind simultaneously rather than sequentially. It is the process of perceiving or knowing things without conscious or rational thought.

So why not just use intuition to make decisions? Why spend millions of dollars in capturing, processing, and deriving insights from data? There is significant evidence that shows that intuition can lead us astray. Firstly, intuition is subjective and personal. Intuition depends on the person's background, experience, culture, feelings, and upbringing; data-driven decisions are based on logic, reason, predictability, and consistency.

Also, in today's business environment of increasing complexity, it is difficult for the human mind to get a comprehensive "big picture" of a business situation. Cognitive science researchers believe that human beings can normally cope with just five to nine pieces of information at a time. This study, commonly known as the "Magic Number," was conducted in 1957 by George Miller, a cognitive psychologist. Furthermore, intuitive thinkers easily get so focused on an instinct that they fail to consider alternative solutions. Business enterprises need to look at all possible solutions to select the best option.

While research supports data drive decision making, what about practical experience? What are the experts saying? Daniel Kahneman, professor of psychology at Princeton, describes decision-making in his best-selling book *Thinking, Fast and Slow*. "We can try to train our gut to produce more reliable responses. While intuition may work at times, it is better simply to recognize the limits of intuition. We can train our intuition to be more reliable. But smarter decisions simply tend to take more effort" [Kahneman, 2013]. So while intuition might produce results faster and ignores certain select gaps and conflicts in data, intuition can be easily misled if too many of the data points are wrong or missing. In other words, intuition is still dependent on data.

According to John Naisbitt, American author in the area of futures studies, "Intuition becomes increasingly valuable in the new information society precisely because there is so much data" [Decelles, 2013]. So even though data has some limitations and deriving insights from data takes time and effort, using quality data to make decisions is still better than relying purely on intuition. According to renowned statistician Nate Silver, "a lot of times when data isn't very reliable, intuition isn't reliable either" [Frick, 2013].

While data may have limitations (as discussed in Chapter 4), intuition also brings significant drawbacks. At the same time, both data and intuition bring lot of benefits to the table. Though the "data vs. intuition" debate has been a recurring theme for years, many current experts believe that the most effective analytics solutions need to make use of both mind and machine. For instance, in the previous chapters we discussed the hypothesis as an educated guess, which is essentially intuition. Tom Davenport says "hypothesis is an intuition about what is going on in the data you have about the world" [Davenport, 2013]. Hence it is best to combine data with intuition and reduce uncertainty in decision making. Jeanne Harris, co-author with Thomas Davenport, on "Competing on Analytics," believes "intuition and data analysis are like two wings on a bird — you need both to soar. It is not data versus intuition. It is both. You will always get a better answer if you use both" [Davenport and Harris, 2007].

ENTERPRISE ANALYTICS

So how does one derive insights? How are insights and analytics related? Analytics (which is synonymous with "reporting") is the use of software-based algorithms and statistics to derive insights from data. Peter Sonderguard, VP of research at Gartner, says "Information is the oil of the 21st century and Analytics is the combustion engine" [Gartner, 2011]. As explained earlier, the three types of reports (OLTP or Transactional Reports (TR), Business Intelligence (BI) reports, and Business Analytics (BA) reports) mainly describe analytics from the IT systems perspective. From the business perspective, on the other hand, enterprise reports can be placed in one of two categories:

- **Descriptive or diagnostic reports.** Descriptive reports look at past performance to determine what happened and why it happened. Transactional reports and Business Intelligence reports are descriptive, as they describe historical business data in a meaningful way.

- **Inferential reports.** Inferential reports help make inferences using data. The inferences can be based on extrapolating the historical data to a future time period, examining trends in different geographical regions, and so on. Business Analytics reports are typically inferential reports, as they deal with the discovery of complex behaviors, patterns, trends, and inferences gleaned from historical data. BA employs techniques and theories from diverse fields such as business, mathematics, statistics, and operations research to extract insights from structured or unstructured data. Inferential reports again can be of two types: predictive reports which give insights of the likely scenarios of what will happen or how can we make it happen and prescriptive reports which reveal what actions should be taken.

Fundamentally, deriving insights requires a combination of visualizing, analyzing, and synthesizing data — this field is known as data science. In short, data science is about extracting insights from structured or unstructured data. The figure on the following page is derived from Gartner's Ascendency Model; it compares the difficulty and the value of different types of analytics [Jugulum, 2014].

Both descriptive and inferential reports will be invariably based on a hypothesis or a question. The output of the report, which provides relationships between different variables, depends on a key concept known as statistical significance. In normal English, "significant" means important, while in statistics "significant" means probably true, or not due to chance. According to Dr. Redman, "Statistical significance helps quantify whether a result is likely due to chance or to some factor of interest" [Redman, 2016]. Basically, a statistically significant result is a result that is not attributed to chance.

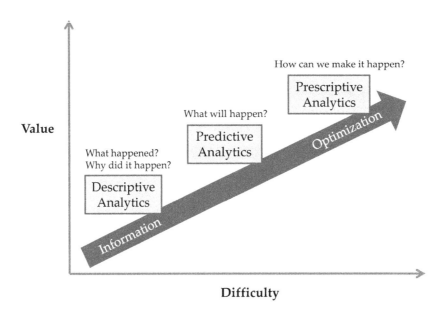

Gartner's ascendency model

Statistical significance is determined using a term called probability value or p-value, which is an estimate of the probability that the result has occurred by accident. A large p-value represents a small level of statistical significance, and vice versa. For example, a p-value of 0.01 means there is just a one percent chance that the result was accidental; at this level, usually the null hypothesis can be rejected.

How does statistical significance come into play with descriptive and inferential business reports? Statistical significance depends on the sample size. Let us say the CPO (Chief Procurement Officer) of a large multi-national corporation operating in the US and Canada (CA) is interested in knowing whether the average purchase order (PO) amount for US businesses is more than the average PO amount for CA businesses, for 2015. This type of hypothesis or question in the data science world is commonly known as "A/B testing" or "split testing."

Let us assume the CPO takes a sample of three POs from each country, and quickly notices a difference in PO averages — around $150,000 for US and $180,000 for CA. But that doesn't mean that the observed difference is statistically significant. With so few POs sampled, the difference could easily be due to random chance. With such a small sample, there is really no way to know if the three POs are really good representatives of the whole bunch.

If instead the CPO takes 30,000 US and Canadian POs, and still sees some difference in the PO amounts, that difference is much less likely due to chance. The more POs are sampled, the more likely that the sample will be representative of the whole lot.

However, collecting data on 30,000 POs takes a substantial amount of time and resources. So the CPO will typically collect samples of 30 POs from each country and calculate the average PO value as well as the p-value. If the p-value is low, say 0.02, which means there is just two percent chance that the result was accidental, the CPO's hypothesis that the average PO amount for US is more than the average PO for Canada would be valid.

However, given the amount of computational processing power available in IT systems these days, descriptive analytics based on sample size is not a strong strategy, as enterprises are able to use the entire population of datasets to derive insights. So statistical significance and p-values are practically irrelevant in descriptive analytics.

But, inferential analytics that deal with the future and involve a great deal of uncertainty, are dependent on a good sample size. In the case of inferential analytics, combining prescriptive and predictive analytics reports with statistical significance and p-value calculations helps to derive better insights. The figure below explains the relationship between statistical significance and different types of analytics.

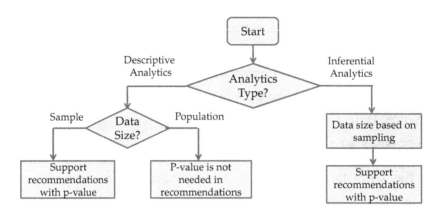

The importance of P-value to different analytics

The key element in the above picture is sampling. Data sampling is using a representative subset of data to identify patterns in the large data set being examined. As discussed above, sampling is a key factor in inferential analytics, as it is used to make inferences about the population. However, sampling strength is based on two main elements: the sample size and the randomization in the selected sample.

Sample size describes the number of observations included in a statistical test. The sample size is dependent on three important factors:

- **Population size.** The approximate total size of the population.
- **Margin of error** or **confidence interval**. Determines how much higher or lower than the population means you are willing to let your sample mean fall. The most common confidence interval is 5%. Margin of error is inversely proportional to sample size.
- **Confidence level**. Describes how confident you are that the actual mean falls within your confidence interval. The most common confidence levels are 90%, 95%, or 99% confident. Confidence level is directly proportional to sample size.

Once the sample size is determined, the other important aspect is the selection of data in such a way that proper randomization is achieved. Basically, randomization ensures that the sample obtained is a representative of the entire population intended to be analyzed, and is not biased in a systematic manner. The three most common sampling designs are:

- **Simple random sampling.** Here the sample is chosen entirely by chance, and each member of the population has an equal chance of being included in the sample.
- **Stratified random sampling.** A stratified random sample is obtained by taking samples from each stratum or sub-group of a population.
- **Multistage random sampling**. The sampling is carried out in stages using smaller and smaller sampling units at each stage.

How does sampling actually work in business inferential analytics? For example, let us presume that a telecom enterprise wants to perform predictive analytics on the average invoice value it can expect to receive from its consumers for 12 months into the future. Let us take the approximate population of invoices (based on the current year numbers) as 20,000,000, the desired margin of error as 5%, and the confidence level as 95%. The appropriate sample size calculated using various tools (including the online tool from www.surveymonkey.com, which is pictured below) is 385.

Calculate Your Sample Size:

			Sample Size
Population Size:	20000000		
Confidence Level (%):	95	⌄	**385**
Margin of Error (%):	5		

Sample size calculation

Once you determine the number of sample invoice data records needed, the next step is to select the sample data records in such a way that proper randomization is achieved. This is where the three most common sampling designs (i.e. simple random sampling, stratified random sampling, and multistage random sampling) come into the picture. But how do we apply these sampling designs? One effective strategy for proper randomization is leveraging the business data types — reference data and master data to select the random invoices (transactional data). The reference data elements could be business categories such as regions, sales persons, invoice category, invoice type, invoice creation date, and so on. The master data elements could be business entities such as customer number, product code, and others. This means when selecting the invoices, have invoices coming from different reference data elements such as regions, sales persons, invoice category and so on, and even different master data elements such as customer number, product code, and others.

SMALL DATA, BIG DATA AND HADOOP

Today, any discussion on data management — especially for deriving insights — includes mention of "big data." According to Doug Laney of Gartner, big data represents the data assets characterized by high volume (with zettabytes of data), velocity (with batch and streaming data), and variety (with structured and unstructured data) — commonly known as the 3V Model [Laney, 2001]. A common misconception is that big data necessarily involves petabytes (1 petabyte is 1 followed by 15 zeros) or zettabytes (1 zettabyte is 1 followed by 21 zeros) of data. In fact, any combination of velocity, variety, or volume may be an indicator of big data. So if there is big data, is there small data?

The term "small data" can be used to describe low-volume (Kilobytes to Terabytes) structured data sets with very specific attributes. If deriving information with smaller, homogenous and curated data sets (i.e. small data) is difficult, deriving timely and accurate information when working with larger, heterogeneous, un-curated data sets (i.e. big data) will definitely be more challenging. For example, even today most organizations which rely on small data figure out their profitability weeks after period closing; moving from the "Daily operating and monthly reporting" cycle to "Daily operating and Daily reporting" cycle is still a challenge for them. How can these organizations benefit from big data? Business management involves striking a balance between different dimensions — inventory versus response time, volume versus quality, focus versus scale, and so on — and managing these trade-offs can be done with small data itself. So how does small data differ from big data?

- **Small data is more personalized than big data.** Big data typically gets the data feed automatically (from machines, social media, and so on) unlike small data, which is typically generated by people. According to Allen Bonde, who defined the term "small data," "Small data connects people with timely, meaningful insights, organized and packaged — often visually — to be accessible, understandable, and actionable for everyday tasks" [Hopfgartner, 2015].

- **Information derived from small data is more certain than big data.** Big data includes a combination of high volume, real time, structured and unstructured data that is captured from a variety of sources. The large and diverse un-curated data brings uncertainty in the correlations and complexity in data analysis. In contrast, small data is specific, targeted, and concrete.

- **Decision making with small data is faster than with big data.** In big data, converting large data sets into insights by identifying hidden patterns and analyzing meaningful correlations is typically done by the data scientist and then communicated to the decision maker. In small data, the conversion of data into information is done directly by the decision maker, resulting in faster decision making.

- **Small data = content + context; big data = content.** Big data encompasses unstructured information records including textual information. While the big data text analytics tools are used to analyze the content, the context is typically missed. For instance the word "bearing" can be a noun (e.g. SKF-30206 bearing) or a verb (e.g. vibration has a bearing on the spindle RPM). If information and knowledge has to be derived from data, it is the context that holds the key; and small data helps provide the context as data typically created by people is comprehensible. Though big data might provide highly correlated associations, the information (or even causation) might be meaningless due to missing context.

- **Small data applies to LoB while big data is at the enterprise level.** The dataset in big data typically belongs to various functional domains; these data objects are owned by different LoBs within the enterprise. Hence taking decisions and implementing them (from the information derived from big data) requires collaboration between different LoBs and business functions within the organization. In addition, big data must involve data scientists in the decision processes within the enterprise. This will require collaborative decision making where the experienced decision makers work together with the data scientists.

- **Most business processes are asynchronous with little dependency on real time data.** While big data is typically generated synchronously in real-time (the velocity dimension), most common business process are asynchronous and do not depend on real-time data feed. For example, abnormal bearing noise in a turbine might create real time notification/alerts (the big data) in the SCADA plant systems (Level 2 as per ANSI/ISA 95), but converting that notification into a work order (the small data) in the ERP systems for the plant technician will have a timeframe of hours or even days. It is the asynchronous business processes (management of the work order) that are consuming more business resources (people, materials, time, and money, among others) than the real time feeds from plant systems (notifications and alerts). In a line, there is very little value for the business in analyzing real time alerts when the real value is in analyzing the work orders.

- **Generating insights from big data is more expensive than small data.** Deriving information from big data which is typically predictive analytics requires a different breed of technologies to efficiently store, index, and compute large volumes of data. However, predictive analytics are not applicable just to big data, but can even be performed on small data. Hence most businesses can perform meaningful business analytics with small data itself (with existing tools).

- **Statistics cannot replace experience.** Imagine a situation where the data scientist looks at numerous sensor data points on numerous SKF-30206 bearings (such as load, RPM, temperature, vibration, friction, and other variables) to come up with a finding that 90% of the SKF-30206 bearings will fail within 10,000 operating hours. While this information might be a great finding for the data scientist, it is already known information for the turbine technician, as he knows from the SKF-30206 bearing specification the operating life of the SKF-30206 bearings.

Fundamentally both big data and small data have specific use cases and benefits. Organizations have to carefully evaluate their needs and make the right choice. However more important than data quantity (big or small) are quality, decision making skills, and the organizational response mechanism to implement the decision successfully.

Let us now look at big data in detail. Generally, big data is associated with digital assets that require new forms of processing for decision-making, insight discovery, and process optimization. The term "big data" can be used to describe any data set that is too big and complex to be processed on one server, too fast-moving to be requested from a data warehouse, and too unstructured to fit in a conventional database. The infographic below, based on the work of Diya Soubra, illustrates the increasing expansion of the 3Vs [Soubra, 2012].

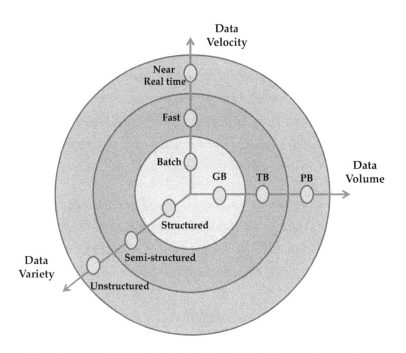

Recently veracity or trustworthiness of data has found its place as the fourth V, because having data in different volumes coming in at high speeds is worthless if that data is incorrect. Furthermore, IDC analyst Benjamin Woo has added a fifth V to the big data definition: value. He says that because big data is about supporting decisions, there is a need to act on the data and derive business value [Maar, 2015]. However, the traditional 3V model of big data is very common even today. But how does big data get generated in the first place? Specifically, big data in enterprises comes from the following data sources:

- Traditional enterprise data from ERP, CRM, SCM (supply chain management), PLM (product lifecycle management) applications, and so on. The data in these applications is normally in structured databases
- Machine-generated sensor data including data from smart meters, equipment logs, trading systems and others. Though the data generated from machines is structured, it is usually in binary format. In other words,

most machine generated data is from machines which are in ISA 95 levels 1, 2, and 3.

- Data from social media such as Twitter, Facebook, and LinkedIn. The data type here is mostly unstructured data.

Even though there exist a great deal of data that is created from business operations, a significant percentage of data is the byproduct of primary business events such as social media interaction, online purchases, financial transactions, among others. Technically known as "data shadows," these data byproducts refer to the sum of all small traces of data left behind after the primary or the main business activity is completed. It is a minute piece of data created when updating a social media profile, swiping a credit card, using an ATM and so on.

Given the amount of volume, variety and velocity involved in big data, what special technical capabilities are required for managing it? This is where big data technologies such as Apache's open-source software framework Hadoop come into the picture. Hadoop's purpose is to store data, process data, and manage compute resources. To address these purposes, the Apache Hadoop framework is composed of the three main modules:

- **Hadoop Distributed File System (HDFS).** HDFS is used to store data that is in SQL and NoSQL data repositories. HDFS is a distributed file system that stores data on low-cost servers called nodes, with very high bandwidth across the cluster of nodes to support large-scale computation.
- **Hadoop Yet Another Resource Negotiator (YARN).** YARN helps in the management of computational resources. YARN is a resource-management platform for scheduling and handling resource requests from the distributed servers that are in HDFS.
- **Hadoop MapReduce (M/R).** MapReduce is a software programming model for simultaneously processing large scale data that is in HDFS. The term "MapReduce" actually refers to two separate and distinct tasks that Hadoop programs perform. The first is the map job, which takes the data

set and breaks it down into tuples known as key-value pairs. The reduce job takes the output from a map as input and combines those data tuples into a smaller set of tuples.

Apache's Hadoop is commercially distributed by companies like Cloudera and Hortonworks, and utilized by companies such as Barclays, Facebook, eBay, and more for very large scale data analytics. But critics say Hadoop is not well-suited to smaller jobs, and is overly complex. So are there any simpler alternatives to Hadoop? Apache itself has come up with Apache Spark, which is increasingly being considered the future of Hadoop. Apart from these two big data solutions from Apache, other options for business enterprises include Pachyderm, Google BigQuery, Facebook Presto, and Oracle Hydra.

TRANSFORMING DATA INTO INSIGHT

In Chapter 6, we used the GQM model to identify data elements that need to be profiled, managed, and governed in order to achieve the specific business goal. While the GQM model helps in selective and proactive management and governance of data elements, given the amount of unplanned and unwarranted data that is captured today, there could be more business opportunities to derive business insights from the available data.

This means that goals don't have to be always formulated top-down by the business; with the colossal amount of data available, there is a bottom-up opportunity to formulate or even validate business goals using data. Data could even provide opportunities to formulate appropriate business goals in anticipation of the need. Henry Ford was fabled to have said, "If I had asked people what they wanted, they would have said faster horses [Vlaskovits, 2011]" illustrating the fact that he formulated the goal in anticipation of the need. Steve Jobs, Apple's founder, said "Get so close to your customer that you tell them what they need well before they realize it themselves" [Isaacson, 2013].

So how can companies proactively develop novel, breakthrough, and actionable business insights — both descriptive and inferential — using the available data sets? The following section talks about the ten-step procedure, again based on the GQM, to derive business insights which are a combination of analyzing, synthesizing and visualizing data. The figure below illustrates the difference in the applications of the GQM models in Chapter 6 and this chapter.

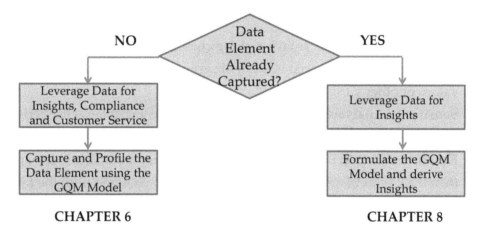

Application of the GQM models in Chapters 6 and 8

However, most of the steps that were used in deriving the GQM model in Chapter 6 are still applicable in this chapter for developing actionable business insights as well.

IDENTIFY THE PROBLEM DOMAIN AND DEFINE THE GOAL

Many analytics programs have a poor track record of delivering value to the business. One key reason is because many teams that embark on analytics programs invest less time in stakeholder analysis. A well-known quote on the impact of stakeholder analysis in the field of Data Analytics is that "one person's data is another person's noise." Hence the four-step "**Identify-Categorize-Assess-Engage**" process can help in identifying the stakeholders and help in formulating a better goal. Chapter 6 explained these four steps in detail.

Once the stakeholders who are serious about deriving insights are identified, the next step is formulating the goal statement. As mentioned in Chapter 6, the goal statement has five key dimensions: object, purpose, focus, viewpoint, and environment. The goal statement can be further bolstered using the SMART criteria. Naturally, the goal statement related to deriving insights will be dependent on the scope of the analytics program. From the insights perspective, businesses mainly look at four main types of goals:

- **What-if Analysis**. This entails making changes to variables, or relationships among variables, and observing the resulting changes in the values of other variables.
- **Sensitivity Analysis**. Here the value of only one variable is changed repeatedly, and the resulting changes in other variables are observed.
- **Result Seeking**. In this scenario, a target value for a variable is set, and then the values of other variables are repeatedly changed until the target value or result is achieved.
- **Optimization**. Here the goal is to find the optimum value. One or more other variables are changed repeatedly until the best values for the target variables are discovered.

FORMULATE QUESTIONS AND HYPOTHESES

Now that the stakeholders and their goals are identified, the next step is to derive specific questions, the answers to which are needed to achieve those goals. A question identifies the phenomenon to be studied. As discussed in Chapter 6, once the "yes-no" dichotomous questions are answered, it is prudent to proceed through the 3-dimensional question framework on "who," "where," "when," "what," "how," and "why." The first four types of questions are classified as informational, since these questions generally gather facts. The last two questions require a higher level of thinking and a deeper understanding of the concept. The questions derived at this point can be further refined using the 4-block question types.

Fundamentally, formulating questions requires deeper thinking; a well-thought-out and focused question can lead directly into the hypotheses. Also, creating a hypothesis means posing a tentative answer to the question to help in the derivation of the attributes pertaining to the goal statement. In essence, hypothesis is a statement that expresses probable relationship between variables that determines the goal.

DERIVE KPIS

This step includes identifying the key metrics or key performance indicators (KPIs) pertaining to the attributes in the hypothesis. Metrics are selected using the attributes in the questions, the answers to these questions, or the variables in the hypothesis. According to Bernard Marr, an expert in analytics and performance management, "KPIs help to measure how well companies, business units, projects or individuals are performing compared to their strategic goals and objectives. Well-designed KPIs provide the vital navigation instruments that give us a clear understanding of current levels of performance" [Marr, 2015].

While defining KPIs or metrics is important, managing behaviors and actions are in fact more important. So KPIs selected should be practical and realistic. According to Jeff Bladt and Bob Filbin, authors of the HBR article *Know the Difference between Your Data and Your Metrics*, "Metrics are only valuable if you can manage to them" [Bladt and Filbin, 2013]. So as mentioned in Chapter 6, any metric "M" is a three-tuple M = (a, b, c) where, "a" is the attribute to be measured, "b" is the measurement scale, and "c" is the unit of measure (UoM).

IDENTIFY AND PROFILE DATA ELEMENTS

Based on the metrics or KPIs, it's now time to select or identify data elements from appropriate data sources — OLTP, OLAP, and integration systems. It is important to know how the data was collected so that proper profiling may be performed. As mentioned in Chapter 6, data profiling entails assessing the data elements against the data quality dimensions to get a better perspective on how the data elements are used in business operations. Data profiling also ensures that the stakeholders identified in the first step are the actual users of these data elements. Along with identifying the data elements, the process of data collection is also important. Typical information gathered during the data collection process include source of data, time horizon, unit of measure, frequency of capture, method of capture, among others.

When profiling data elements, ideally the reference data and master data should come from the SoR. If multiple systems and LoBs are managing the reference data and master data, then the success of the analytics program is at a big risk. Sometimes all the data from the systems might not be sufficient to derive insights. In that situation, a systems-driven data model would need to be complemented by data created manually from surveys and interviews; it could also be supplemented with external data or by using statistical tools such as the Bayesian inference.

COLLECT AND NORMALIZE THE DATA

When many enterprises start with a new analytics initiative, they tend to look for people with skills such as R programming, SQL, Hadoop, statistical modeling, server clustering and the like. While these skills are definitely important, they really come at a later stage. The first prerequisite for any analytics program is good quality data.

According to researchers Andrew McAfee and Erik Brynjolfsson of MIT, the most important analytics skills are cleaning and organizing large data sets [McAfee, and Brynjolfsson, 2012]. DJ Patil, the Chief Data Scientist of the White House in the US, summarizes the data problem well: "You have to start with a very basic idea. Data is super messy, and data cleanup will always be literally 80 percent of the work. In other words, data is the problem" [Levy, 2015]. According to CrowdFlower, a crowdsourcing company that surveyed data scientists with varying levels of experience, about 60 percent of the time spent by data scientists is on cleaning data and preparing it for analysis.

Even though integrating data from different sources is complex and time consuming, this step is required for good and holistic insights. This step, commonly known as data engineering, involves collecting the data, cleansing it, integrating it, and consolidating it so that insights can be derived. According to Forrester's Anjali Lai, "multiple data sources which are the ingredients for well-rounded insight need to be blended correctly for a comprehensive solution" [Lai, 2014].

The challenge with data blended from different systems comes when the data has different formats, types, taxonomies, descriptions, units of measure (UoM), and so on. For example, let's say some sales invoices are in five different systems in different formats, and the insight requirement pertains to improving the daily sales outstanding (DSO) KPI. Integrating all the different data sources into one unified view will surely take significant time and effort in the realm of stakeholder alignment, data dictionary rationalization, and data and business rules transformation.

Basically, without quality data (including a mechanism to ensure consistent data quality) it is impossible for an enterprise to get good insights. The problem becomes more amplified when enterprises own vast quantities of poor data quality. Fundamentally, data quality means ensuring that the data elements adhere to the relevant data quality dimensions explained in Chapter 5.

Along with data quality dimensions, companies must take special consideration while dealing with personal and sensitive data. In these cases, the data at rest protection mechanisms discussed in Chapter 3 should be factored in before the data is fed into the analytics data model. Overall, the data quality and security difficulties in accessing data present a great challenge for companies wanting to systematically utilize their data assets for insights.

VISUALIZE THE DATA

Before working on analytical models, always visualize the data to see if any answer to the questions or the hypotheses can be derived. This is because certain insights are much easier to spot visually than they are to spot numerically with analytic models. Data visualization (DV) can expose patterns in data from OLTP and BI systems by utilizing infographics, dials, gauges, geographic maps, sparklines, heat maps, and charts. Some DV software includes interactive capabilities, enabling users to manipulate data or "drill into" the data for querying and analysis.

Basically, DV presents data in a pictorial or graphical format, allowing the user to clearly see what data is relevant, assess key patterns, grasp complex concepts, and even derive inferences. Many interesting patterns and outliers in the data would remain hidden in the rows and columns of data tables without the help of DV tools. Key tools for data visualization include Tableau, Spotfire, and Qlik.

ANALYZE THE DATASET

Deriving insights involves a combination of visualizing, analyzing, and synthesizing data. Analyzing is the process of decomposing complex data sets into smaller, more manageable components, in order to gain a better understanding of the dataset (which can include both structured and unstructured data).

The outcome of this process is an analytical model, which is basically a mathematical equation that describes relationships among variables or attributes in the data set. The analytical model normally includes descriptive reports; inferential reports are covered in the next step (synthesizing).

Descriptive reports or analytical models can address univariate or multivariate variables. Univariate analysis involves the examination of one variable at a time, and univariate descriptive reports usually present the following details:

- Central tendency such as mean, median, and mode

- Dispersion such as range and quantiles of the dataset
- Measures of spread such as the variance and standard deviation

On the other hand, multivariate analysis (MVA) deals with observations made on many variables. The main objective of MVA is to study how the variables are related to one another. Key techniques in MVA include:

- **Multiple Regression Analysis** — This examines the relationship between a single dependent variable and two or more metric-independent variables, and is often used in forecasting.
- **Discriminant Analysis** — The purpose of discriminant analysis is to classify observations into distinct groups.
- **Multivariate Analysis of Variance (MANOVA)** — This technique examines the relationship between several independent variables and two or more dependent variables.
- **Factor Analysis** — When there are many variables in research design, factor analysis helps to narrow down the variables to a smaller set of factors or variables.
- **Cluster Analysis** — The purpose of cluster analysis is to reduce a large data set to meaningful subgroups of individuals or objects. Outliers are a problem with this technique, often caused by too many irrelevant variables.

Currently, in many enterprises, most of the insights derived are from structured data that mainly comes from OLTP systems. But as discussed earlier, many business scenarios today deal with unstructured data such as images, text, voice, and video. Businesses are keen to extract value from these unstructured datasets. For example, text analytics can provide valuable business insights from social media interactions, sales and purchase contracts, email analysis, medical records, warranty claims, and inspection logs that businesses capture. Leading software vendors such as SAS, IBM, and Microsoft have tools for text analytics, with capabilities such as natural language processing (NLP), ontology and taxonomy modeling, rule-based classification, and sentiment analysis.

Speech or voice analytics can be very valuable to businesses, as they can provide insights on customer interactions and expose subtle details and emotions buried in customer interactions. An important point to be noted here is that the analysis of unstructured data requires a significant amount of structuring. For example, text analytics involves structuring the input text by parsing, categorizing clustering, lexical analysis, deriving relations within the structured format, and finally analyzing the output.

SYNTHESIZE THE DATASET

While analysis dealt with descriptive reports, synthesis is all about inferential reports. Synthesis entails combining the constituent elements into a single unified entity in order to find patterns. Within analytics, inferential reports are closely associated with pattern recognition or machine learning (ML), which is a field within artificial intelligence (AI). Though there are many ML techniques or algorithms, Foster Provost and Tom Fawcett in their book *Data Science for Business* emphasize that all ML algorithms fundamentally address ten main tasks. These are summarized in the table below [Provost and Fawcett, 2013].

#	Task Name	Description	Example Question
1	Classification	Classification helps to identify a set of categories to which the specific element belongs.	Of all the customers of Nordstrom, which ones are likely to respond to a given offer?
2	Scoring (class probability estimation)	A scoring model uses a probability score to determine how likely it is that a specific element belongs in a given class.	What is the probability score when credit risk needs to be forecasted before granting a loan?

#	Task Name	Description	Example Question
3	Regression	Regression analysis is for assessing the relationships between a dependent variable and one or more independent variables. Regression and classification are related. While classification will determine whether something will happen, regression predicts to what degree something will happen.	If a new service is introduced, what would be the level of adoption by the customers?
4	Similarity matching	Similarity matching attempts to identify similar individuals based on the data known about them.	Which customers are most similar to my best customers, so that the sales force can focus on these potential opportunities?
5	Clustering or cohort analysis	Clustering helps to find subgroups that are similar to each other.	Do our customers form natural groups or segments?
6	Co-occurrence grouping	Co-occurrence grouping attempts to find associations between entities based on transactions they're involved in. While clustering looks at similarity between objects, co-occurrence grouping considers similarities of objects based on their appearance together in transactions.	Which items are most commonly purchased together?
7	Profiling	Profiling, also known as behavior description, attempts to characterize the typical behavior of an individual, group, or population.	What is the typical spend amount for this supplier segment?
8	Link prediction	Link prediction attempts to predict connections between data items, usually by suggesting that a link should exist, and possibly suggesting the strength of the link.	Since you and Tom share ten friends, maybe you would like to be Tom's friend? Since every pump downtime resulted in a bearing replacement, maybe you would like to stock bearings?

#	Task Name	Description	Example Question
9	Data reduction	Data reduction attempts to take a large set of data and replace it with a smaller dataset that contains much of the important information found in the larger data set. While this might result in the potential loss of insights, the smaller dataset will likely be easier to manage and process.	A massive dataset on consumer grocery preferences, when reduced to a smaller dataset, may reveal insightful customer buying habits.
10	Causal modeling	Causal modeling attempts to help us understand what events or actions actually influence others.	Did extreme cold weather in Midwest affect retail sales?

The above algorithms can be supported by using appropriate statistical tests such as ANOVA, Kruskal-Wallis, Chi-squared, and other tests based on the data type (numerical or ratio, ordinal, interval, and nominal), sample size, and p-value. The important tools for these statistical tests (i.e. for both analyzing and synthesizing data) are R and Python. While Python is a general purpose language with syntax that is easy to understand, R's functionality is developed with statisticians in mind. Ultimately it is up to the data scientist to pick the programming language that best fits their specific needs. For example, if an enterprise already uses Tableau as a DV tool, then R is usually considered a better choice, as it is generally considered a better fit to Tableau over Python.

INTERPRET AND VALIDATE INSIGHTS

Once relevant insights are identified using visualization, analysis, and synthesis techniques, the next step is combining these individual insights to draw holistic conclusions. These insights are derived by the business user (i.e. the consumer of data) and are very contextual depending on the data captured.

Chapter 6 discussed the importance of context and goals in the way that data elements are captured. In addition, businesses today are increasingly looking at the concept of self-service analytics to allow users to spot business opportunities without having to rely on IT staff or data scientists to create analytics reports.

Below is a simple "Home Energy Report" that was presented by ENMAX, a utilities company based in Alberta, Canada, to its consumers. This simple but effective infographic report helps the consumers understand their home's energy use. The data for the report was captured by ENMAX from consumers. While this report doesn't talk about recommendations to save energy, it potentially helps the consumers to set up appropriate goals, ask relevant questions, and formulate KPIs to get to the next level.

Home energy report of an ENMAX consumer

Another example of analytics is found in a financial services institution, which might desire insights on customer segmentation, customer lifetime value analysis, or market entry, to name a few. But the important point to remember is that all insights depend on the data captured. According to Doug Laney of Gartner, who coined the term "big data," "a bank that does not capture customer milestones such as moving homes, kids entering college and other milestones should not be investing in analytics [Laney, 2016]".

But even after insights are derived, transforming them into actions requires proper evaluation. According to Thomas Davenport, managers have a critical role to play in framing the right questions and analyzing the insights derived. He lists six questions that managers should ask about insights [Davenport, 2016]:

1. What was the source of the data?
2. How well does the sample data represent the population?
3. Does the data distribution include outliers? How did these outliers affect the results?
4. What assumptions are behind the analysis? What are the conditions that render the assumptions and model invalid?
5. Why did you decide on that particular analytical approach? What alternatives did you consider?
6. How likely is it that the independent variables are actually causing the changes in the dependent variable? Might other analyses establish causality more clearly?

COMMUNICATE INSIGHTS (DATA STORYTELLING)

The final step entails mapping these results back to the stakeholders' value propositions, which were covered in Step 1. All the hard work of deriving insights will only make sense if these insights are communicated in an appropriate manner to the stakeholders. This step brings data science and decision science together.

Technically, decision science is a field within operations research. It deals with the selection of a course of action among several alternative possibilities, within the capabilities and the limitations of an enterprise. At the core, decision science fosters an understanding of:

- The cognitive, emotional, social, and institutional factors that influence judgment and choice
- The formal models of rational inference and choice

- Ways to improve how well judgments and decisions are made by individuals, teams, and enterprises

Unless the insights are communicated and presented to the right people at the right time in the right format, the sophistication of the analytics tools and the complexity of statistical analysis doesn't really matter. Therefore, if the insights gleaned from data could help in improving business performance, then those insights must be presented appropriately. "Numbers have no way of speaking for themselves. We speak for them. We imbue them with meaning," noted statistician Nate Silver [Silver, 2013].

So what are strategies for communicating these insights? Before communicating the insights, first check with the stakeholders if they are clear about the problems being discussed. What other insights do these stakeholders lack? Do the stakeholders have the necessary background and knowledge to understand the insights? What will they do with the insights? What can be done to turn insights into decisions and actions?

Communication essentially is telling the story of the data. Fundamentally data storytelling is much more than just creating visually-appealing data charts. Data storytelling is a structured approach for communicating data insights. According to data visualization expert Stephen Few, storytelling involves a combination of three key elements: data, visuals, and narrative. Stephen Few believes, "when narrative is coupled with data, it helps to **explain** to the audience what is happening in the data and why a particular insight is important. When visuals are applied to data, they can **enlighten** the audience to insights that they would not see without charts or graphs. Finally, when narrative and visuals are merged together, they can **engage** the audience. When you combine the right visuals and narrative with the right data, you have a data story that can influence and drive **change**" [Anderson, 2015].

Furthermore, there might be instances where interesting insights might be derived by the data science team, but those insights might have nothing to do with answering the strategic questions or achieving the business goals at hand. In that case, it is better to have a process to share those insights with the relevant stakeholders in a different forum.

Finally, communication of insights is not the end of the insights process. New problems or even opportunities might surface based on the insights presented, or the business situation might change, kick-starting the process at Step 1 once again.

The application of the 10 steps in the derivation of insights based on the GQM framework is illustrated in the figure below.

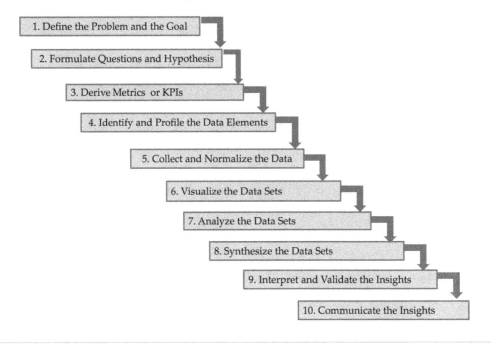

GQM for deriving insights

ANALYTICS IN THE REAL WORLD

While the ten steps described above require significant amounts of statistics and operations research, in reality, most descriptive and inferential analytics can be derived with simple tools, such as Microsoft Excel with the analysis toolpak add-in. But, according to Noah Lorang, a data scientist for leading project management company Basecamp, "Mostly what I do is write SQL queries to get data, perform basic arithmetic on that data (computing differences, percentiles, and other basic statistics), graph the results, and write paragraphs of explanation or recommendation" [Asay, 2016].

According to business analytics experts Piyanka Jain and Puneet Sharma, 80 percent of the analytics reports used in enterprises are descriptive in nature and don't require advanced data analysis [Jain and Sharma, 2014]. According to Gartner, just 13 percent of organizations are using predictive and 3 percent are using prescriptive reports; just 16 percent of the reports used in business pertain to inferential analytics [Williamson, 2015]. Matt Assay, veteran technology columnist, believes that "businesses need accurate and actionable information to help them make decisions about how they spend their time and resources. There is a very small subset of business problems that are best solved by machine learning; most of them just need good data and an understanding of what it means that is best gained using simple methods" [Asay, 2016].

The following is a practical example from a leading global engineering conglomerate where simple insights (i.e. descriptive and inferential) pertaining to IT support were presented to management. The data, which included the IT support tickets, came from different data sources or systems: Remedy (a tool to log support tickets), direct emails from the business users, and phone calls forwarded from the helpdesk.

Because data came from a variety of sources, the first step was normalization of different data formats and content into one unified format with some calculations in Microsoft Excel. The below descriptive and inferential reports based on four simple key metrics (i.e. KPIs) helped senior management to better understand how the IT team serves the business, manages the work load, and manages IT vendor support contracts.

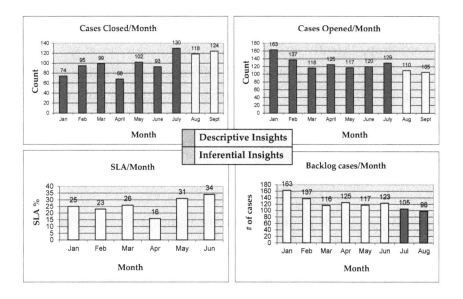

IT support analytics

CONCLUSION

Realizing the value of data involves deriving business insights, complying with industry standards and government regulations, and providing the desired level of services for internal and external stakeholders. While using data to meet compliance and customer service levels is relatively straightforward, deriving insights is complex, difficult, and resource-intensive. According to Bain consulting, only four percent of companies have the right people, tools, data, and intent to draw meaningful insights from that data — and to act on them [Wegener and Sinha, 2013].

The ten-step GQM-based model for deriving insights encompasses both descriptive and inferential analytics, with the core steps involving visualization, analysis, and synthesis. However, all the hard work of deriving insights will only make sense if the insights help the stakeholders to make decisions and take suitable actions. As Thomas Edison once said, "the value of an idea lies in the using of it."

Chapter 9: Managing Change

It is not the strongest or the most intelligent who will survive but those who can best manage change.

Charles Darwin
English Naturalist and Geologist

In the previous chapters, we discussed how systems and GQM processes can play important roles in data management. However, transforming the data into an enterprise asset by leveraging systems and processes is only possible with the active and full participation of people. While only a few companies have the luxury of building new systems and processes, most data management initiatives involve significant change not only to existing systems and processes, but also in the way people behave and perform.

In this regard, most data management or digital transformation initiatives are unsuccessful, as they focus mainly on the systems and processes without giving much attention to the people. When people adapt to change, the task of transforming data into an enterprise asset is much more effective. This chapter is all about the human changes pertaining to leveraging data for business performance.

STAKEHOLDERS IN THE DATA LIFECYCLE

In Chapter 3 we discussed the ten data lifecycle functions, with different activities being performed to manage the data and information in the enterprise. But who performs these functions? There are different stakeholders who play roles in the data lifecycle. Specifically, there are four key roles at the enterprise level:

1. **Data producers**. These are stakeholders from the business who are accountable for the generation, capture, validation, and consolidation of data. The important responsibilities of the data producers are:
   o   Ensure the data is captured in the right format in the right system
   o   Validate the data quality against the respective data quality dimension
   o   If needed, consolidate the data from different systems into one common data format

2. **Data custodians**. Data custodians usually have IT backgrounds. They are responsible for data processing, distribution, storage and security. Some of the important responsibilities of data custodians are:
   o   Implement data transformations, resolve data quality issues, and collaborate with relevant stakeholders on system changes
   o   Perform data validation and reconciliation processes following data integration and distribution
   o   Provide source data or give access to source data to appropriate users and systems
   o   Define, capture, and maintain metadata

3. **Data stewards.** A data steward is the person from the business who is responsible for implementing the data policies and practices in the enterprise. Specifically, at the enterprise level, data stewards own the reference data and master data. A data steward normally acts as a liaison between the IT department and the business consumers in the organization. The key responsibilities of data stewards are:
   o   Define appropriate data quality dimensions
   o   Perform data validation and data quality monitoring
   o   Develop new policies or standards for ensuring appropriate data management
   o   Define data quality checks to be conducted by the data custodians

4. **Data consumers**. Data consumers come from the business world. They are the ones who can recognize the potential of data to carry out its three main business roles. The key responsibilities of data consumers are:

   o   Ensure that data is appropriately consumed according to the business needs
   o   Identify appropriate strategies for archiving and purging of data
   o   Manage transactional data

The mapping of these four roles to the ten functions of the data lifecycle is shown in the figure below.

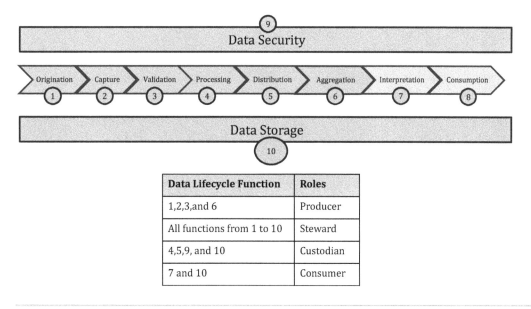

Data Lifecycle Function	Roles
1,2,3,and 6	Producer
All functions from 1 to 10	Steward
4,5,9, and 10	Custodian
7 and 10	Consumer

Mapping of roles to the data lifecycle functions

MANAGING CHANGE

Now that we have the list of key stakeholders or practitioners, how do we manage change so that these individual stakeholders are effectively engaged in the data management change process? Generally, individuals fear change and will resist it.

They may fear losing their status, privilege, or position of power, which are often rooted in the data lifecycle and the organization structure of the enterprise.

How can we ensure that changes pertaining to data management are thoroughly and smoothly implemented, and that the lasting benefits of change are achieved? How do we ensure that digital transformation initiatives are not disjointed and independent efforts? How do we build change progresses holistically in a unified manner?

When seeking to answer these questions, change at the enterprise level can be implemented in two main ways:

- By aligning LoB leadership to the enterprise
- By addressing performance of individual stakeholders (i.e. the practitioners) in the team

Managing change at these levels involves alignment of the company's culture, organization structure, values, people, and behaviors to achieve the desired results. However, proper change management that includes effective communication, sponsorship, coaching, training, and resistance management can help in effectively transitioning the enterprise from the current state toward their desired state. At the same time, change management demands two-way communication where the practitioners and senior management must not only be clear in their communications, but must also listen to employees to understand their concerns and suggestions. The following sections look at different aspects in managing change in these two levels.

ALIGNING LoB LEADERSHIP TO THE ENTERPRISE

Ineffective change sponsorship from senior leaders is often cited as a primary obstacle to the success of many transformation projects, including data management initiatives. When sponsors are inactive or invisible, not at the right level, not aligning with other leaders, or wavering in support, the result is often more resistance and slow progress.

According to Leadership coach Ron Carucci, "Leaders should start a transformational journey accepting that the organization will have to transform them as much as they will have to transform it. The more a leader knows how they will react during change, the better equipped they'll be to foster real change in themselves, others, and the organization" [Carucci, 2016]. Here are some of the ways senior leaders can be influential in managing data as an enterprise asset.

- Senior leaders themselves must be the first ones to lead and embrace change. They must model the desired behaviors and speak with one voice about:

    o Why the change is necessary
    o The risk of not changing
    o How the change aligns with the organization's vision and business direction

- Senior leaders have to understand that all data cannot be managed at the LoB level, and LoBs have to give up some control. Specifically, LoB leaders should understand the fact that reference and master data are enterprise assets critical to the effectiveness of the SoR, so they must be shared between different LoBs and OLTP systems.

- Today many enterprises still think that managing data is the responsibility of the IT department. If data has to be managed as an enterprise business asset, the data management initiatives should be designed and run by the business and supported by IT functions.

- Senior leaders need to develop and enforce the principles for successfully managing data and information on an enterprise-wide scale, so that appropriate patterns and standards can be formulated.

MANAGING CHANGE IN INDIVIDUALS AND TEAMS

How do we effectively manage change at the individual stakeholder level? How do we address the specific concerns and needs of the data producers, data custodians, data stewards, and data consumers? For most individual practitioners, change creates anxiety and fear. In addition, the current status quo will normally have tremendous holding power, which can potentially create resistance to change. Managing individual stakeholder for change involves four key steps.

UNDERSTANDING THE KEY DELIVERABLES OF THE STAKEHOLDERS

Understanding the key deliverables of the four stakeholders types (i.e. data producers, data custodians, data stewards and data consumers) are very important to understand the current situation. Deliverables describe the tangible products that are being built by the stakeholders for specific customers. Deliverables are important because they focus on outcomes and objectives; they express clearly who the customers of these deliverables are and what these customers want. On the contrary, if there is an objective without a deliverable, you need to evaluate whether the objective is really important.

IDENTIFYING THE ELEMENTS THAT PERTAIN TO THE BEHAVIOR OF THE INDIVIDUAL

Once the deliverables of the four types of stakeholders are understood well, the next step is to understand how the impending change could result in changed behaviors. The "ABC" or "Antecedent-Behavior-Consequence" model is an effective way to understand the cause of a behavior. Antecedents are events or environments that trigger behaviors; they can occur immediately before a behavior or can be an accumulation of previous events. A behavior is an action that is both observable and measurable. Finally, the consequence is the outcome; it is how people in the environment react to the behavior. The ABC model helps to see what is going on in the environment before the behavior that might trigger it, and the consequences from the behavior.

UNDERSTANDING THE CHANGE PROCESS

Once the individual is aware of some of the consequence of change, understanding the stages of personal transition is very useful. The Kubler-Ross "5 stages of grief" change curve helps in understanding how people will respond to change. The five stages are as shown below [Kubler-Ross and Kessler, 2005].

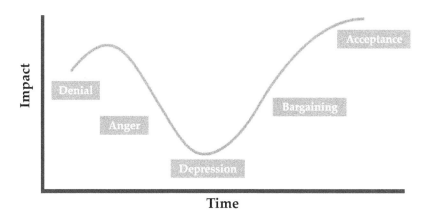

Kubler-Ross "5 stages of grief" change curve

According to Kubler-Ross "5 stages of grief" change curve, it is essential to understand that individuals do not move along the stages in a linear direction or step by step. A person tends to move into stages in a random order and may sometimes even return back to a previous stage after a certain point in time. Each stage can last for a different time period, and it is possible for a person to get stuck in a particular stage and not move on from there. The following are brief descriptions of each of the five stages of grief:

- **Denial**: The stage of shock or denial is usually the first stage and is mostly short-lived. This is a phase during which one puts on a temporary defense mechanism and takes time to process certain disturbing news or reality. One may not want to believe what is happening and that it is happening to him or her. It can bring about a dip in productivity and the ability to think and act.

- **Anger**: When the realization hits, and one understands the gravity of the situation, the individual may become angry. The anger can be manifested in many ways. While some take out the anger on themselves, others may direct it towards others around them.

- **Bargaining**: When the stage of anger passes away, one may start thinking about ways to postpone the inevitable and try to find the best things left in the situation.

- **Depression**: Depression is a stage in which the person tends to feel sadness, fear, regret, guilt, and other negative emotions. The individual may display signs or indifference, reclusiveness, and little engagement at work.

- **Acceptance**: When people realize that fighting the change that is coming is not going to make the grief go away, they resign to the situation and accept it. The resigned attitude may not be a happy space but is one in which the person may stop resisting change and move ahead with it.

TRANSITIONING TO THE DESIRED STATE

Once the individual has accepted the change, the next step is to provide the individual with the right support to move ahead and manage the change. The Prosci® ADKAR®[1] model, which is a goal-oriented change management model, is

---

[1] Prosci, ADKAR, and Awareness Desire Knowledge Ability Reinforcement are registered and unregistered trademarks of Prosci, Inc., used with permission.

frequently used. It is practical, simple, and focuses on the actions and outcomes required for change at the individual and team levels.

ADKAR is an acronym that represents the five milestones or outcomes necessary for change to be successful: **a**wareness, **d**esire, **k**nowledge, **a**bility, and **r**einforcement. The ADKAR model is illustrated in the figure below, where the people side of change is mapped to the data management project phases. At a high level, the data management project phases include five main phases:

- **Initiating**. A data initiative is found feasible based on the business case. The business case is developed based on stakeholder analysis.
- **Planning**. This phase covers how the data initiative project should be delivered based on different components of the project.
- **Executing**. Once the work is planned, the project team completes the work. This phase is where the GQM model is developed with the data elements and data values captured to realize the goals of the stakeholders.
- **Controlling**. This phase ensures that the work is done according to project plan.
- **Closing**. Here the project work is completed and the deliverables are verified and closed.

Phases of the Data Management Project

As the graphic indicates, the process is sequential; each step must be completed before moving on to the next. The details of the five sequential steps or actions are:

1. **Awareness of the need for change.** Understanding why change is necessary is the first key aspect of successful change. This step explains the reasoning and thought that underlies a required change. When this step is successfully completed, the team is expected to fully understand why change is necessary.

2. **Desire to participate in and support the change.** In this step, the individuals in the team reach a point where they make personal decisions to support and participate in the change. Naturally, a desire to support and be part of the change can only happen after the need for change is established. Creating a desire for change is difficult because it is ultimately a personal decision. However, building desire can be accomplished by addressing incentives for the individual, strong senior management support, proactive management of resistance, and more.

3. **Knowledge about how to change.** The third building block of the ADKAR model is providing knowledge about the change. Two types of knowledge need to be addressed here. The first type is knowledge on how to change — what to do during the transition. The second type of knowledge involves how to perform once the change is implemented.

4. **Ability to implement required skills and behavior.** Ability is the means or skill to achieve the desired outcome. This phase can take some time and can be achieved through practice, coaching, and feedback.

5. **Reinforcement to sustain the change.** In this final stage of the model, efforts to sustain the change are emphasized. This step is to make sure that changes stay in place, and teams do not revert to old ways of working. One important approach for reinforcement is regular communication. Regular communication is needed because many senior leaders make the mistake

of believing that others understand the need to change as clearly as they do. The best change programs reinforce core messages that are regular, realistic, and timely. Other strategies to reinforce this change can be achieved through positive feedback, rewards, recognition, measuring performance, and taking corrective actions.

CONCLUSION

Implementation of data management initiatives invariably involves many changes in business processes, system configurations, data models, functions performed by business stakeholders, and so on. But an incredibly high percentage of these initiatives do not reach their full potential and do not produce the intended benefits. The implementation of changes often fails not for technical reasons, but for human reasons. These reasons include leadership alignment, hierarchy, poor organizational structure, team performance, or even individuals being resistant to change. This is where change management comes into the picture. The change management strategy and approach must reflect the needs of the situation, and should be flexible to adjust to the evolving situation.

Chapter 10: Summary

Many concepts have been covered in this book, and this section of the book attempts to summarize them.

Phase 1 of data management — define — was about characterizing and explaining the key elements behind the transformation of data into an enterprise asset.

Chapter 1 started the discussion with the three main purposes of data: deriving business insights, adhering to compliance, and providing the desired level of customer service. It also covered basic terminologies and how enterprises across different industry sectors are leveraging data for business performance and competitive advantage.

Chapter 2 defined and discussed business data. It also explored different types of business data and the role of the stakeholder in determining the value of business data.

Chapter 3 looked at four different types of IT systems used to manage data and information, as per the ten different functions in the data lifecycle. Business operations are captured, validated, and processed in Online Transactional processing (OLTP) systems, they are integrated and aggregated using integration systems, and finally reports are drawn in the business intelligence or online analytical processing (OLAP) systems. If the business needs predictive and prescriptive reports, analytics systems with data visualization capabilities are normally used.

After establishing the necessary background information required to transform business data to an enterprise asset, the second phase analyzed the key factors that help unlock the value of business data.

Chapter 4 looked at different limitations of business data. At this point, the reader is expected to have a balanced approach i.e. opportunities and challenges so as to leverage the value from quality business data. But how does an enterprise derive quality data? Hence the next natural step was to analyze the different dimensions of data quality that matter to business enterprises.

Chapter 5 listed the 12 different data quality dimensions that are relevant for an enterprise. It was noted that because realizing these 12 data quality dimensions takes significant time and effort, the dimensions should map to specific business needs if any initiatives are taken to improve the data quality.

The low cost of storage and increased computational processing capabilities enable enterprises to capture and process both structured and unstructured data. However, most of the data that is captured by a business goes unused.

Chapter 6 discussed the Goal-Question-Metric (GQM) framework. Ten steps were derived as a GQM model to identify key data elements that matter in accomplishing the business goals. This GQM model considered the value propositions of the stakeholders before formulating goals, relevant questions, hypotheses, and KPIs.

While it is important to define and analyze, what really matters is Phase 3: implementation, or actively transforming the business data into an enterprise asset. Essentially, Phase 3 looks at managing data elements that are identified, captured, and managed in the business enterprise.

Chapter 7 introduced the concept of reference architectures and their three components (i.e. principles, patterns, and standards) that facilitate effective data management in the enterprise.

Chapter 8 was about realizing the three purposes of data (i.e. business insights, compliance, and improving customer service). Compliance includes government regulations, standards, and security policies. Improving customer service levels is usually dependent on specific business needs. While accomplishing these two purposes is relatively straightforward, deriving business insights is complex and time consuming — especially considering the tremendous volume, variety, and velocity of data.

To figure out how to derive insights, Chapter 8 again looked at the GQM framework — this time from the viewpoint of analysis and insight. Another ten-step GQM model was created specifically to derive business insights; both descriptive and inferential analytics utilized the data elements that were already captured. The image below shows the key aspects involved to enable business performance from data.

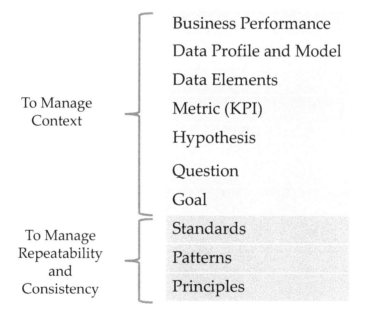

Key business performance elements

Finally, focusing data management initiatives solely on the technology and business processes without giving much attention to people might jeopardize the success of the initiative. This is because it is through people's engagement that businesses can really derive value from data. Hence Chapter 9 looked at different change management models for leadership alignment, and enabling individuals address the ten functions in the data lifecycle.

Many models are presented in this book. Some are novel, some are adapted or changed to suit data management initiatives, and some are in their original form. All these frameworks and models are validated in real world projects and presented to primarily guide the team to successfully derive value from data. These models by any means are not fixed, one-size-fits-all models. The general strategies and approaches in the implementation of these models, however, must always reflect the needs of the situation, and should be flexible to adapt to the evolving and changing business needs. Finally, while the concepts mentioned in the book are applicable to every stakeholder who seeks to improve the value of business data, the implementation of the concepts should be based on a strong business case and senior management support.

Appendix A: Interviews

As mentioned before, business and IT leaders from leading organizations have shared their experiences on the value of data in the book. To provide balanced perspectives, the interviewees included thought leaders, business leaders, and IT leaders. The professionals who gave interviews for the book include:

1. Mario Faria, Managing Vice President, Gartner, US (Thought Leader)
2. Dr. Brandon Rohrer, Data Science Researcher and Author, US (Thought Leader)
3. Bob Pollock, CIO, Cenovus Energy, Canada (IT Leader)
4. Rohit Girdhar, VP, Infineon Technologies, Singapore (Business Leader)
5. Ram Kumar, SVP, QBE Insurance, Australia (IT Leader)
6. Tobias Eckert, CIO, Leapple AG, Germany (IT Leader)
7. Melanie Mecca, Director, CMMI Institute, Carnegie Melon University, US (Thought Leader)
8. Paul Zikopoulos, Vice President, Big Data and Analytics, IBM, Canada (IT Leader)
9. Vibhav Agarwal, SVP, Reliance Power, India (Business Leader).

The following section details the interviews of each of the above professionals.

1. MARIO FARIA, MANAGING VICE PRESIDENT, GARTNER, US

Mario Faria is a Managing Vice President, leading the office of the CDO in Gartner. Mr. Faria helps clients define data and analytics roles, staffing requirements, and organizational design and structures. He is also responsible for developing enterprise data and analytics strategies, data monetization, data brokers, and customer analytics research.

How does data governance play a role in data quality?

Data governance plays a key role in data quality, and data quality initiatives cannot be successful without effective data governance. There has to be a strong synergy between the two initiatives and functions. However, for both data governance and data quality initiatives have to be successful, the performance of these initiatives should be tied to the financial goals and metrics of the enterprise. Only by doing that will data leaders be able to prove why business should invest in both data governance and data quality programs.

How different is data governance when managing data at enterprise level versus managing data quality at the line of business (LoB) level?

Technically, there is no difference in data governance when managed at an enterprise level or at line of business level. However, the effectiveness of the data governance program is higher and better when managed at the enterprise level and all lines of business align with the policies and procedures developed by the enterprise data governance team. After all, data hardly ever is confined to one LoB. It tends to be used outside the LoBs it was created and reside.

How do you measure the success of data governance teams? Do you have any standard KPIs?

The office of the CDO exists for 3 main purposes: (a) to increase revenue and add value, (b) to reduce costs, and increase efficiency and profitability, and (c) to manage business risk. So the KPIs for the success of data governance teams should directly be related to those aspects that impact business performance.

Every data initiative and activity should be associated with business goals and metrics. For example, if the business goal of a media company is to increase the subscription by 50% in 2 years, then the CDOs should be leveraging the data assets to contribute to this goal. If a transportation company wants to reduce the fuel costs by 5% in one year, then the data governance and any other data initiatives undertaken should be towards that business goal. In a line, whatever are the KPIs of the company, those KPIs are relevant for the CDOs to create his or her goals.

What are the differences in data governance practices between and structured and unstructured data (text, voice, and video)?

Data governance practices of unstructured data (like text, voice, and video) should be based on some logic or structure, and this structure comes from the metadata. So while the data governance practices for the structured data is mainly on the data elements — i.e. reference data, master data and transactional data — the data governance practices for unstructured data is on metadata that is based on semantics. For example, today many data lake initiatives that bring structured and unstructured data together are carried without data governance procedures. Ultimately what the companies will end up is not a data lake but a data swamp. And the processes to extract data insights will be so costly that the initiative might fail to deliver value.

Any other thoughts for the readers of this book?

Today companies are increasingly leveraging data for business performance and competitive advantage. The CDO's office has now more gained importance than ever before. In a recent Gartner CDO survey, 38% of the CDOs now report to the CEOs, 51% report of LoB heads and just 11% report to the CIOs. Data is not a technology; it is a business asset that uses technology. Also the CDO function is a support function in a company and exists to serve the business functions. However CDOs can only be effective when there a commitment from the organization including executive support from the senior management.

2. DR. BRANDON ROHRER, DATA SCIENCE RESEARCHER AND AUTHOR, US

Dr. Brandon Rohrer is a practitioner, researcher, and author in the field of data science. He has worked in numerous analytics engagements for Microsoft and Sandia National Laboratories. He holds a PhD from Massachusetts Institute of Technology (MIT) and he is based in Boston, USA.

What is your definition of analytics? For example, analytics for SAP is different from that of SAS.

Analytics is answering the questions we have in order to make decisions. The scope of analytics includes formulating the right questions, massaging the data, answering the questions using appropriate models, deriving insights, and finally facilitating decision making. Massaging of data is sometimes neglected in favor of more glamorous areas such as modeling, but modeling is useless if the data is not curated.

How often do you supplement data from systems (OLTP, BI, and others) with "manual" data for deriving insights?

Often data in analytics programs is supplemented from different data sources and not just from internal enterprise systems. Which external data mainly depends on the question asked. Supplementing with data from diverse data sources gives the data scientist the ability to exercise creativity and leverage his or her domain knowledge. When it comes to getting data from unconventional sources, domain knowledge of the data scientist is critical.

IEEE identified 10 top machine learning models. In actual projects, which are the commonly used ML techniques?

Today, data scientists have a tendency to use deep learning algorithms just for the sake of it. However in most cases simple algorithms do a fantastic job. For example when it comes to predicting customer churn, two-class classification algorithms such as logistic regression can be very useful.

Any examples where you have unstructured data analytics (text, voice and others) in real projects?

Images, text, audio, and voice are commonly used in analytics. I have done imagery analysis on overhead satellite images to measure the health of corn crops. A lot of businesses are starting to pay attention to text analytics. When working with text, the feature engineering methods you use have a big impact on the quality of your results.

As a data scientist how important is storytelling? Any tips or advice?

Storytelling is very important in analytics, but easy to ignore. Since it is normally the last step, it's tempting to drop the ball here. Data scientists have to understand that communicating the insights to the business stakeholders in business language is the key. Sometimes, the stakeholders don't care much on what data science tools are used or the details of the methods. Rather, the stakeholders are looking for a crystal clear answer to the questions they have.

According to Gartner, just 13 percent of organizations are using predictive and 3 percent are using prescriptive reports. Why is the engagement low for these types of Analytics?

There are two main reasons behind the poor application of predictive and prescriptive reports in business:

1. In many cases, good descriptive analytics provide good insights that matter to the business.
2. Predictive and prescriptive analytics is complex, takes lot of hard work, seeks considerable investment, and demands lot of patience. Also the results are also not guaranteed. So companies see risk in pursuing predictive and prescriptive analytics.

What is the recipe for analytics programs to be successful?

Learning data science and business analytics or building a data science team is tough and takes lot of hard work, but it is achievable. If businesses are ready to invest time and money, stay focused, and show patience, they stand to get benefits from their analytics initiatives.

3. ROHIT GIRDHAR, VP, INFINEON TECHNOLOGIES, SINGAPORE

Rohit Girdhar is a Vice President Strategy and Market Development at Infineon Technologies. Prior to joining Infineon, he worked for General Electric (GE) and Teradyne. He is currently based in Singapore.

How has investments in digital helped your enterprise drive business growth and a stronger P&L?

Analytics in the domain of sales has enabled us to identify areas of growth more effectively. In the domain of strategy, it has enabled us to identify leading indicators for the business. This then allows us to react ahead of an upturn or downturn in demand, optimizing our investments.

Is data seen an asset for your enterprise? If so, how are you using it? If not, why is data NOT seen as an asset in your company? What are the challenges?

Data is seen as an asset. Accurate data goes as input into various tools across the organization. Dirty data leads to meaningless results.

How do you build a data-driven culture in an enterprise? What are the core building blocks of a well-defined information strategy?

By demonstrating the value that accrues by use of the data into better business decision making and eventually superior results. The demonstration takes time and requires the build of multiple proofs of concept or pilot models.

How do you identify the right business domain when you try to pursue an analytics project?

Ideally you start with those business domains where traditional models already exist. Then you build analytics models to complement these models. If models exist, then probably accurate data does exist. Secondly, you identify business domains where good business intuition exists based on a long history. This helps to validate early results from analytics models.

How do you translate insights into actions?

By getting buy-in from management and the broader organization that will use the insights as you build the models.

What are your thoughts on metrics/KPIs based initiatives, both pros and cons?

Metrics and KPI-based initiatives can create obstacles in the beginning as you build analytics capability. In the early days, multiple experiments need to be run and capability building needs to be the focus. As the team and capabilities mature, setting metrics and KPIs is necessary to keep a focus on delivery.

4. Ram Kumar Venkatachalam, SVP, QBE Insurance, Hong Kong

Ram Kumar Venkatachalam is the Senior Vice President of QBE Insurance in Australia. He has successfully implemented business solutions of varying program and project sizes, scales, and complexities, for different business environments around the world.

Is data seen an asset for your enterprise? If so, how are you using it? If not, why is data not seen as an asset in your company? What are the challenges?

The culture of seeing data as a strategic asset of an enterprise does not exist at QBE yet. However, this is where QBE wants to be going forward. Data and analytics have now been introduced as one of the key strategic pillars for the organization in May 2016 resulting in the formation of a global data and analytics function in May. So, at the group level (under group data and analytics), we have commenced to define our information strategy.

Traditionally, like other insurers, QBE's focus has been on products, services to customers, processes, people, and technology. Though data is the lifeblood of insurance business, QBE never understood it, and took data for granted with the assumption that data by itself has no value. The challenge is to change the mindset — it is a cultural issue. But with the advent of true data-driven companies that are building products that are specific to customer and partner needs, using data-driven insights through internal and external data, and delivering them through the right technology and processes, traditional insurers like QBE have now started to realize that their strategy and approach needs to change if you want to compete in this data-driven market. The challenge is they do not know how and where to start, as it is a cultural transformation issue and is not just a technology, people, or process issue. QBE has grown purely through mergers and acquisitions in the last 15 years. In the last 10 years, QBE would have acquired some 125+ companies. So, the challenge in bringing all these silo operating businesses under one cohesive strategy is not easy, but QBE has already commenced this transformation process.

Data has a value only if its value is valued. So, to help QBE understand that data-driven culture will bring business benefits in terms of profitable growth and operational efficiency, needs to be shown through data-driven initiatives (like fraud analytics) that bring immediate financial business benefits.

How do you build a data-driven culture in an enterprise?

Building a data-driven culture in an enterprise is not a project or a program, but a journey. This cultural journey must be driven from the top (right at the board level) if an organization truly understands and treats data as a key corporate strategic and competitive asset. Investing into this culture must not be seen as a cost, but must be seen as enabling, nurturing, enriching — protecting and governing the key asset to generate sustainable value. The senior executives must take accountability (and not sponsoring) of managing this asset. They should lead from the front and by example to drive this culture across the organization.

I like the following quote, and this is how an organization must think if it wants to build a data-driven culture:

Someday, on the corporate balance sheet, there will be an entry that reads, "information"; for in most cases, the information is more valuable than the hardware and software that processes it.

— Admiral Grace Murray Hopper (Inventor of COBOL), 1965

Data-related KPI should be a core component of the corporate balance scorecard if the organization is serious about data-driven culture. If such measurable KPIs are in the corporate balance scorecard, they will then be rolled out to all staff across the organization irrespective of their positions or hierarchy. While culture is one thing, you need supporting technologies, and processes to help your staff to timely, accurate, relevant, and trusted information that would help create data-driven insights and that in turn would help staff to make business decisions to generate sustainable benefits to the business, stakeholders, partners and most importantly, customers.

How do you identify the right business domain when you try to pursue an analytics project?

Identifying business opportunities (through pain points and challenges) where there is a quick win in terms of financial business benefits by using data-driven analytical insights is where an analytics project should commence. Big bang will not work. For example, fraud analytics is an area that will provide claims costs savings which in turn will improve the underwriting result for an organization.

How significant is human intuition in data-driven decision making?

Human intuition is extremely critical in data-driven decision making, as it brings years of experiences that cannot be obtained purely through data-driven decisions. The power of decisions is significant when human intuition coupled with data-driven insights support each other in making the decision. For example, providing personalized product to a customer based on data (using internal and external data) may not be the right decision, as the ethical component and the emotional outcomes of that individual cannot be captured completely. This requires human to identify and understand them.

What does data quality mean for your business?

No matter how efficient and smart your business processes are, how smart and capable your people are, how savvy and state of the art your technologies are, and how smartly your analytical insights have been generated, if the underlying data that is used by people, processes, technology, and analytical models to run the business is poor in terms of its quality and integrity, the outcome will be poor. Data is the common denominator here as it touches all these.

There is no silver bullet solution to fix bad data. It requires the right culture across the organization for everyone to treat data as a core strategic asset (as it is the lifeblood of our business) like any other asset, to manage it efficiently and effectively in order to create appreciable value. Any investment into addressing this bad data must be seen as an investment to maximize benefits from the strategic asset, and not as a cost.

For insurance businesses, it is all about pricing the risk accurately and providing the right tailored insurance risk product to the customers; fundamental to this is quality data. If you price the risk accurately, customers will be protected and served well during crisis and customers will get positive experiences, and thereby their loyalty with the organization improves.

Data quality is a business problem and not a process or technology problem. Data quality problems were created by humans as part of defining processes and technologies that did not consider data quality in the first place. Fixing the processes and technologies are the easy bits as they were created by humans. But the culture of understanding data quality is the difficult bit. If the culture is right, a data quality by design culture will ensure that data quality is considered during planning stages and supporting processes and technologies are implemented as part of an initiative design and implementation.

How much of unstructured data (text, voice, and video) do you use in your business? How are you currently using unstructured data?
We have not even started to tap into the value our structured data brings to the business yet. So, use of unstructured data is not something that we want to focus now.

What are your thoughts on metrics/KPIs based initiatives, both pros and cons?

To me any initiative, be it transformation, data-driven, business, or technology, should have measurable business KPIs or metrics, and must be tied to the organization strategy, such as profitable growth, operational efficiency, customer retention, etc. If there is no value to the business, that initiative should not commence. However, some of the core foundational components cannot be measured through KPIs, as they are enablers. One example is data lifecycle governance. This is where educating the business on the foundational components and how it enables value creation is critical. Developing estimated business benefits through KPIs for any initiative is one thing, but then regularly tracking and monitoring the actual business benefits is another thing. It is important to track and monitor and publish the actual business benefits achieved as this will help drive the culture as business generally tend to understand the value the initiatives such as data-driven decision making brings to them when they see financial benefits.

Do you want to share any interesting thoughts in the book?

Data is now seen as the new oil in industry. My view is that data has always been the oil of an organization, except that organizations never realized the value data brings to them. More importance was given to people, process, products, customers, and technology over data — despite data touching all these. But with the advent of the big data revolution, this has changed the mindset.

I often use the analogy of data to blood in your body. All your components of your body may be working fine (like the processes of legs, hands, etc.), the front end looks stunning (e.g. your skin), and your technology is supporting the body (e.g. heart and brain). But when there is a problem with your body, first thing your doctor asks you to do is "blood test." This is where you start realizing the importance of the quality of blood to your body. Until then, you would not have thought about your blood, as you normally would have taken blood for granted, as it is not something that you touch or feel or see on a day-to-day basis; blood works behind the scene. Data is exactly like blood in your body, as you take data for granted, as data works behind the scene. But it is critical to how the process, technology, and people work. This is why data is called the lifeblood of a business.

Big data and analytics to me is nothing new, and for those who see it as new, it is not. My first big data project was in 1992 where I used a large data set (structured, semi-structured, unstructured and sensor) provided by bureau of Meteorology Melbourne (30 year dataset with daily weather pattern) to build advanced predictive analytical models using machine learning algorithms to predict the weather for Melbourne and its suburbs. We used several machine learning algorithms that are used now in the big data world to build the models. The only change I see after 24 years is that machines are much faster, more data sets are available, and machine learning algorithms are now readily available through open source tools. From a machine learning algorithms perspective, introduction of deep learning is new. More than volume, velocity, variety and veracity, the "value" that data or big data brings is critical.

Information/data lifecycle management and governance is fundamental to implementing a successful information strategy of an organization. The concept of information management is not new in industry. This concept has existed for decades, but was never given the attention it deserved as organizations never saw data as a strategic asset. Processes, technologies, et cetera, were introduced to solve some fundamental data management related problems without addressing the actual fundamental problem.

But thanks to the big data revolution, information management is now a key agenda item on tables of executives and therefore, it has started to get the right attention it deserves! The concept of Chief Data Officer is also not new. For decades, many organizations had roles such as information managers or information librarians who were performing the job of managing the lifecycle of data (not sitting under IT) to help business have access to the data and use them. But their role was never visible at the organization level, as they were seen as purely operational, because organizations never saw data as a strategic asset.

These people were fighting the hard and losing battle of pushing data governance to the top.

But now with the emergence of big data, the role of Chief Data Officer has popped up, which is great, as data governance will get the special attention it deserves at the C-level table. The conflict between CIO and CDO will continue for a while (as we are seeing now) as CIOs are now trying to re-invent themselves as a data person who also is a technology person!

My view is the title "CIO" has always been misleading. CIOs should have actually been called CITO (Chief Information Technology Officer), as they were doing everything other than the "I" that is in their title. The reason "I" exists is because they are the bridge between business and technology, and "information" (data) is the common denominator between business and technology. But they were doing everything else other than Information. They were focused on technology dev and management, technology operations management, et cetera. But they never focused on the business side of data — data governance, data lifecycle management, et cetera. This is why the role CDO was created to oversee the data asset. If data is viewed as a key strategic asset of an organization, then the role of CDIO or CDAO is critical. Chief Digital Officers must work closely with CIOs and CDAOs if they want to build a digital organization as at the end of the day, my view is that Data is still the lifeblood of digital!

5. BOB POLLOCK, CIO, CENOVUS ENERGY, CANADA

Bob Pollock is a Senior Vice President and CIO at Cenovus Energy, Canada. His role is supporting the achievement of business results with quality, secure, and compliant information systems, by leading the selection, design, delivery, and support of enterprise information technologies and services. He is based in Canada.

What are the primary business drivers for Cenovus from the information management perspective?

The SAGD (Steam Assisted Gravity Drainage) processes in oil sands are in a very formative stage. Though there is lot of data that is available around this technology, decision making today is primarily based on intuition. So Cenovus is making investments information management to better understand this "new" processes. This could help in productivity improvements and reduce oil production cost/barrel by targeting areas such as water and steam consumption, geological and geophysical (G&G), construction, drilling, production, among others.

In your view, what are the limitations of data?

Data, technology, process, and people are like the 4 legs of a stool in business operations. Timeliness and relevancy of data is very important. One of the many challenges Cenovus has is data collection at the source, and this delay in data capture affects timeliness and relevancy of data.

Should data management happen at the enterprise level? If so, why?

Data management should happen at the enterprise level as it helps to optimize the entire value chain end-to-end. For example, the data originated by the drilling function can be potentially used by the production department in their operations. However, managing data at an enterprise level might be expensive and this cost and time can be better managed by having solid enterprise goals and governance processes.

6. Tobias Eckert, CIO, Leapple AG, Germany

Tobias Eckert is the CIO of Laepple AG. He has managed various areas of IT in multinational corporations such as P&G, Adidas and Burger King. He is based in Stuttgart, Germany.

Is data seen an asset for your enterprise? If so, how are you using it? If not, why is data NOT seen as an asset in your company? What are the challenges?

In the classical administrative departments like finance, sales, procurement, data is clearly seen as an asset and also utilized in a number of ways. In our mechanical engineering projects, we have successfully started to use digital processes in commissioning new production lines. The data gathered during those commissioning processes helps us greatly in improving our time to market in this field. In manufacturing, we have identified numerous opportunities to gather data from our production machinery, and analyze this to improve machine-availability rates, analyze causes for defects and more. This is a pretty new field, where standard technologies are just emerging. We are in research and development mode in this area, but see great opportunities in this field.

How do you build a data-driven culture in an enterprise? What are the core building blocks of a well-defined Information strategy?

I believe a core building block in the corporation needs to be a strong process culture. Only with well-defined processes can I gather meaningful data that allow me to improve my business figures. Obviously this needs to go alongside a well-structured IT application architecture, so that the data can be physically gathered with a reasonable amount of effort.

How do you identify the right business domain when you try to pursue an analytics project?

It's a matter of balancing the extent of the opportunity vs. the chance to succeed. In a field where processes and data structures are well defined, the chances to succeed with a data analysis project are greatest. However, those are also the areas where the processes tend to be most streamlined, and therefore the opportunities to improve, say, process efficiency via data analysis are comparatively small. Areas that are more unstructured provide typically bigger opportunities, but yield the more risky projects to run.

How significant is human intuition in data-driven decision making?

I think human intuition comes mostly into play during the first phases of an analysis project. Choosing what data to look for, having the right hunch about how different elements play together, is where human intuition and human experience have their prime role. Once it is decided what to analyze, routine comes into play in executing the gathering and analysis process.

What does data quality mean for your business?

Good data quality means that we can run efficient business processes. We can reduce inventories, plan projects more tightly, and can generally be more accurate about our calculations as we can be more certain that the numbers are correct. This leads to better prices and conditions we can offer to our customers, shorter reaction times on customer requests, and faster project delivery.

How much of unstructured data (text, voice, and video) do you use in your business? How do you currently use unstructured data?

Most of the data is gathered in a classical automated way. Unstructured data is only used in a small number of areas.

What are your thoughts on metrics or KPIs based initiatives, both pros and cons?

It's an old truth that you can't manage what you can't measure. It's important, though, to set the KPIs on the adequate level of detail. Defining the KPIs too broadly will create difficulties in identifying what action triggered which change in the measured KPIs. Defining the KPIs too narrowly will typically yield unwanted incentives, where people sacrifice common sense goals for achieving ill-defined KPIs — a behavior which will ultimately hurt the business.

What are the different compliance standards you follow in your company?

We adhere to all legal and regulatory standards of the communities we operate in. We follow all compliance standards that are requested from us by our customers. We have a defined set of values and are in the process of publishing our own code of conduct.

7. MELANIE MECCA, DIRECTOR, CMMI INSTITUTE, US

Melanie Mecca is the Director, Data Management Products and Services at CMMI Institute. She brings over 30 years of planning, building and sustaining enterprise-level programs and organization-wide solutions in: Enterprise Data Architecture; Enterprise Data Management; Enterprise Architecture; Master Data Management; and Business Process Reengineering. She is the managing author of the Data Management Maturity Model, a comprehensive reference model for evaluating data management maturity. She is based in Washington DC, USA.

What are the key deliverables pertaining to each of the 5 levels in Data Management Maturity Model (that gives the score)?

There are 596 example work products and they are distributed by capability level within the 25 process areas. The Data Management Maturity (DMM) model is scored by performance with these specific process areas, and work products are corroborating evidence that the practices are being performed.

How do you associate DMM maturity level to business benefits?

DMM focuses on influencing behavior with regards to data and information management. When DMM-based process improvements are implemented, organizations can realize significant benefits, such as controlling costs through the use of reliable and accurate data, mitigating risk, and increasing transparency and data access for more strategic and informed business decisions. The DMM model's successive capability levels provide a clear path for improvement in 25 process areas reflecting fundamental disciplines of data management.

By providing a standard, structured framework of best practices, DMM helps organizations become more proficient in their management of critical data assets, supports trusted data for tactical and strategic initiatives, and provides a consistent and comparable benchmark to gauge progress over time. The DMM model allows an organization to evaluate the current state of its practices with respect to capability and maturity.

Its application is similar to an executive physical. The patient reports in the morning, submits to a battery of sophisticated diagnostic tests, and consults with multiple medical specialists. At the end of the day, the physician team reports on problems, recommends treatments, and provides customized healthy lifestyle guidelines. So the patient knows exactly what health issues pertain, how they will be medically treated, and how overall physical health can be improved. The DMM, by enabling the rapid discovery of gaps and strengths, quickly leads to formulation of initiatives to advance the organization's data management program and gain business value in the areas of highest priority, based on the business strategy and objectives.

What types of organizations should use DMM?

DMM was initially developed as the joint collaboration of the Software Engineering Institute, which spun out of the CMMI Institute, with corporate sponsors Booz Allen Hamilton, Lockheed Martin, and Microsoft. But today, hundreds of companies have employed the DMM to evaluate their capabilities and build improved data management capabilities. The companies that are already using the DMM are wide-ranging — including those from the IT, aerospace, financial, healthcare, and government sectors. However, all industries, types, and sizes of organizations can benefit from the DMM. All organizations that seek to realize more value from their data assets can benefit from its application, and those which are launching or enhancing and organization-wide data management program can follow the built-in path to strengthening capabilities.

How does DMM work?

Organizations that are keen to leverage data for business performance should conduct a DMM Assessment. The assessment is facilitated with representatives from all of the primary business lines within scope, as well as enterprise-focused groups such as enterprise architecture, risk, internal audit, business architecture, and information technology.

The outcome of this assessment is a report on the current state on the 25 process areas, observations, findings (gaps), strengths (accomplishments) and work product reviews (identifying work products which can be leveraged across the organization). The report includes improvement opportunities, which are initiatives (projects) that align with the organization's business objectives while building data management capabilities. These initiatives, both short-term tactical and long-term strategic in scope, are totally customized for the organization based on the bi-directional exchange of information in the assessment, so each organization that uses the DMM will have a unique set of recommendations based on its own priorities.

From this it is a small step to developing a roadmap with a sequence plan of appropriate data management strategies and projects. Typically, since a broad range of business representatives are involved, the slate of initiatives is already socialized and therefore is more likely to be funded.

8. Paul Zikopoulos, VP, Big Data and Analytics, IBM, Canada

Paul Zikopoulos is the Vice President, Big-Data and Analytics at IBM Canada. He is an award winning international speaker and author (19 published books including Hadoop for Dummies, Big Data Beyond the Hype, among others). He is based in Toronto, Canada.

What are the core building blocks of a well-defined Information management strategy?

The 3 main building blocks of a well-defined information management strategy are: business strategy, data-driven organizational culture, and finally technological capabilities. Specifically the key elements in these three areas include: mission driven by the C-suite, the goal statement i.e. specific aim that an individual or team works towards, collaboration between individuals and teams, governance, and finally the deployment technology.

What is your definition of analytics? For example, definition of analytics for SAP is different from that of SAS.

In my personal view, analytics is using data to lead or assist business operations and decisions. Analytics could encompass tools and processes that pertain to data science, decision science, artificial intelligence, natural language processing, machine learning, and cognitive learning. Hence the scope of the analytics varies depending on the portfolio of solutions these IT vendors offer. For example, IBM's Watson is a technology platform that uses natural language processing and machine learning to reveal insights from large amounts of data.

According to Gartner, just 13 percent of organizations are using predictive and 3 percent are using prescriptive reports. Why is the engagement low for these types of analytics?

There are many reasons, such as governance, data quality, and the like. However, one of the key causes is the challenge resulting from over-selling self-serve analytics tools. This has resulted in having an expectation in many organizations that the business users will draw predictive and prescriptive reports. But that is not so simple because technical, procedural, training, and cultural issues can cause significant challenges in the adoption of predictive and prescriptive reports.

How do you ensure that the risks of poor data/information projects are not blamed on technology? What are the common reasons for the failure of data/information/analytics projects?

This is going back to the first question. Technology should be the last design aspect when an organization is working on a data-driven initiative. Unfortunately in most cases, technology is often the first element that is discussed, and as a result most data-driven initiatives end up failing, as there is no solid business strategy and culture for data-driven business operations. Hence data-driven initiatives should be supported by a strong business case, and technology implementations should directly support the business case. If the business case is not strong and if the data-driven culture in the company is very nascent, pursuing technology solutions is risky.

How significant is human intuition in data-driven decision making? Is human intuition a challenge to the technology tools used in decision making?

Human intuition causes bias and bias results in false validation of the results. Data analysis with the right amount of statistical significance helps to reduce bias in the human intuition to a large extent. While human intuition is definitely helpful in decision-making, data when combined with human intuition can significantly improve decision-making.

Are in-memory databases (ex: SAP HANA) and big-data technologies (ex: Hadoop/Spark) complementary or competing solutions?

Today if any organization believes that one tool or technology can address all their informational needs, it is committing a grave mistake. The information management landscape will typically include a mixture of tools and technologies. For example an organization can bring its huge data sets into Hadoop HDFS and if it needs highly performance reports, it can draw it from a system that runs on SAP HANA or Amazon Redshift.

Do you want to share any interesting thoughts in the book?

The current analytics landscape is still maturing and evolving. Technologies such as IoT and Blockchain will significantly alter the information management landscape of the organization in the coming years. Hence enterprises have to build a strong talent pool and a data-driven culture to support these new technologies, and to survive and thrive in the market.

9. VIBHAV AGARWAL, SVP, RELIANCE POWER, INDIA

Vibhav Agarwal is Sr Vice President & Business Head at Reliance Power Limited. He worked in developing and operating the business of Power, Oil & Gas and Infrastructure. He is based in Mumbai, India.

How has investment in digital helped your enterprise drive business growth and a stronger P&L?

We are a utility involved in the business of power generation in India. This kind of business in India has a very unique B2B model where one doesn't have too many customers and has to operate under heavily regulated and compliance oriented regime. Almost the entire value chain of energy and electricity business in India is regulated and operates on either extremely thin margins or on regulated 'return on equity' principles.

Hence, extreme caution is required to be taken in every aspect of business associated with the energy value chain to protect the returns which are highly susceptible to political and regulatory interference and litigations due to public or media outcry.

Investment in digital has indeed helped the business in terms of the following:

- Real time update on happening of all remote location operations
- Efficient real time scan of competition
- Real time monitoring and fulfillment of compliances
- Access of all above information to all concerned on real time basis

To put a number to growth and impact on P&L due to digital may be really difficult but digital has indeed reduced the level of risks which has the potential of disrupting the operations and business to a significant extent as it has shifted the management style of being reactive to pre-emptive to mitigate risks.

Is data seen an asset for your enterprise? If so, how are you using it? If not, why is data NOT seen as an asset in your company? What are the challenges?
Data is certainly as asset which is used very effectively to improve the operating performance whether technical or commercial, in future as well as to minimize the risks. Digital platform of managing data indeed helps to remain updated at all times and also in synch when it comes to its sharing with multiple outside agencies or compliance authorities.

How do you build a data-driven culture in an enterprise? What are the core building blocks of a well-defined Information strategy?

In utility businesses there is always an overload of information flowing in, including (a) technical, which contains plant operations, efficiency, fuel inventory, quality, (b) commercial and financial, which contains sales, purchases, cash inflows, cash outflow and (c) policy and regulatory, which contains information published by various regulatory and statutory instrumentalities which directly affect the business viability, and its competitiveness.

It is important to understand that all three blocks of information referred above are inter-linked to each other and their processing and application must be ensured in a manner which gives meaningful outcome and facilitate perfect decision making. Therefore, the building blocks for defining the information strategy work on following principles:

- Establishing the ownership of 3 blocks mentioned above. This is the most critical aspect of driving an information / data-oriented culture in the enterprise.
- Capturing of information / data by respective owners.
- Processing of information / data and its sharing among all owners jointly.
- Collation of data, analysis, and its conversion into decision-making tools, which requires the investment of time by most senior management or business leadership.
- Execution of action plan.

How do you identify the right business domain when you try to pursue an analytics project?

Business decisions are driven purely on risk and return play. Every dollar proposed to be spent must bring in an acceptable return, or in other words should convert into a positive NPV. This applies in every aspect of business domain where it is to do with human resource, operations, financing, procurement, or staying put in business or divest.

How do you translate insights into actions?

I would say that insight into actions is very instinctive, and one learns this art over a period of time with experience. In organizations like Reliance, what one learns (which is never taught in any B-School) is spotting the opportunities. Opportunity spotting is a habit which comes naturally with experience and observing others. This habit only propels individuals to process the data, store in sub-conscious minds which flashes as insights and turns into action at the right time.

What are your thoughts on metrics/KPIs based initiatives — pros and cons?

Enterprises are driven by profits and commercial gains. Hence, any initiative by enterprises ought to have measurable performance indicators for them to decide their course of action. KPIs based initiatives works very well when enterprises operating with simple business models deals with less no of variables, risks and uncertainties.

However, in case of enterprises with complex business models, such as operating in a heavily regulated environment, KPI-based initiatives would tend to fail if one has to necessarily deliver within a given timeframe. In such a situation, the performance must be replaced with efforts. Measurable performance in such complex businesses is often driven from the actions of a third person, outside agency, or bureaucracy beyond the control of the enterprise.

Appendix B: References

1. Ackoff, Russell, "From Data to Wisdom," Journal of Applied Systems Analysis, 1989

2. American National Standards Institute, ANSI/X3/SPARC Study Group on Data Base Management Systems; Interim Report. FDT (Bulletin of ACM SIGMOD), 1975

3. Anderson, Carl, "Creating a Data-Driven Organization: Practical Advice from the Trenches", O'Reilly Media, 2015

4. Asay, Matt, "Why data science is just grade school math and writing," http://tek.io/1RMGmSm, March 2016

5. Ayers, James, "Supply Chain Project Management: A Structured Collaborative and Measurable Approach", CRC Press, 2003

6. Balsillie, Jim, "For Canadian innovators, will TPP mean protection or colonialism?," The Globe and Mail, January, 2016

7. Basili, Victor; Gianluigi Caldiera; H. Dieter Rombach, "The Goal Question Metric Approach," 1994

8. BBC, "Colgate warned over '80%' boast", http://news.bbc.co.uk/2/hi/uk_news/6269521.stm, 2007

9. Bean, Randy, "How Time-to-Insight Is Driving Big Data Business Investment," MIT Sloan Management Review, January 26, 2016

10. Behmen, Adnan, "P&G Minimizes Operational Risk through Master Data Governance" http://www.ssonetwork.com/data-management-analytics/podcasts/p-d-minimizes-operational-risk-through-master-data, 2016

11. Bellinger, Gene; Castro, Durval; Mills, Anthony, "Data, Information, Knowledge, and Wisdom," http://bit.ly/2i1Y9Za

12. Bird, Jane and Swabey, Pete, "Decisive action: How businesses make decisions and how they could do it better," Economist, June, 2014

13. Bladt, Jeff and Filbin, Bob , "Know the Difference Between Your Data and Your Metrics", Harvard Business Review, March, 2013

14. Bloom, B.S, Engelhart, M.D, Furst, E.J, Hill, W., Krathwohl, D.R, "Taxonomy of Educational Objectives, Handbook I: The Cognitive Domain," David McKay Co Inc, 1956

15. Carucci, Ron, "Organizations Can't Change If Leaders Can't Change with Them", Harvard Business Review, October 2016

16. Chatter, Rohit, "Star schema vs. snowflake schema: Which is better?," http://bit.ly/2hGXbk5, July 2012

17. CMMI, "Data Management Maturity (DMM) Model", CMMI Institute, 2014

18. Crosby, Philip, "Quality is Free", McGraw-Hill, 1979

19. Crowdflower, "2016 Data Science Report", www.Crowdflower.com, 2016

20. Curran, Chris and Antao, Rohit "The New IT Platform: Bridging the Gap Between Business and IT", 2015

21. Davis, Jessica, "Big Data, Analytics Sales Will Reach $187 Billion By 2019", http://ubm.io/1sO2zIH, May 2016

22. DAMA, "The Six Primary Dimensions of Data Quality Assessment," 2003

23. Davenport, Thomas, "Competing on Analytics", Harvard Business Review, Jan 2006

24. Davenport, Thomas, "Keep Up with Your Quants", Harvard Business Review, August 2013

25. Davenport, Thomas, "Big Data and the Role of Intuition", Harvard Business Review, December 2013

26. Davenport, Thomas and Harris, Jeanne, "Competing on Analytics: The New Science of Winning". Boston: Harvard Business School Press, 2007.

27. Davenport, Tom, "7 Ways to Introduce AI into Your Organization", Harvard Business Review, October 2016

28. Decelles, Germain, "Change Your Future, Now!", Webtech Management and Publishing, November, 2013

29. Desfray, Philippe and Raymond, Gilbert, "Modeling Enterprise Architecture with TOGAF", Morgan Kaufmann ,May 2014

30. Deutsch, Randy, "Data-Driven Design and Construction: 25 Strategies for Capturing, Analyzing and Applying Building Data", John Wiley & Sons, 2015

31. Dobbs Richard, Koller Tim, Ramaswamy Sree, Woetzel Jonathan, Manyika James, Krishnan Rohit, and Andreula Nicolo, "The new global competition for corporate profits," Mckinsey Global Institute, September 2015

32. DoDCIO, "Reference Architecture Description", http://bit.ly/2lawQRJ, 2010

33. Doran, George, "There's a S.M.A.R.T. way to write management's goals and objectives", Management Review. AMA FORUM. **70** (11): 35–36, 1981.

34. Dravis, Frank, "Data Quality Strategy: A step-by-step Approach," Proceeding of the 9th International Conference on Information Quality, 2004

35. Dyer Jeff; Gregersen, Hal; Christensen Clay, "The Innovator's DNA: Mastering the Five Skills of Disruptive Innovators Audible – Unabridged", Harvard Business Review, 2011

36. Dykes, Brent, "Data Storytelling: The Essential Data Science Skill Everyone Needs," http://bit.ly/2iAewA0, March 2016

37. Eckerson, Wayne, "Data Quality and the Bottom Line", TDWI, 2002

38. Fanelli, Daniele, "How Many Scientists Fabricate and Falsify Research? A Systematic Review and Meta-Analysis of Survey Data", PLoS ONE, 2009

39. Fehrenbacher, Katie, "GE's CEO Reveals How To Transform Into A Digital Company", http://fortune.com/2016/11/15/ges-ceo-digital-remake/, November 2016

40. Feldman, Martha and March, James, "Information in Organization as Signal and Symbol," Administrative Science Quarterly, June 1981

41. Feravich, Stuart **"Ensuring Protection for Sensitive Test Data", http://bit.ly/2kJCgIL,** December 2011

42. Fox, Mark and Gruninger, Michael, "Enterprise Modeling," American Association for Artificial Intelligence, 1998

43. Frick, Walter, "Nate Silver on Finding a Mentor, Teaching Yourself Statistics, and Not Settling in Your Career", Harvard Business Review, September 2013

44. Friedman, Ted and Smith, Michael "Measuring the Business Value of Data Quality", Gartner, 2011

45. Gartner, "Gartner Says Worldwide Enterprise IT Spending to Reach $2.7 Trillion in 2012", http://www.gartner.com/newsroom/id/1824919, October 2011

46. Gartner, "Gartner Says Adopting a Pace-Layered Application Strategy Can Accelerate Innovation" http://gtnr.it/1ChFEnn, 2012

47. Gartner Glossary, "Master Data Management", http://www.gartner.com/it-glossary/master-data-management-mdm/, 2016

48. Gartner, "Gartner Estimates That 90 Percent of Large Organizations Will Have a Chief Data Officer by 2019", http://www.gartner.com/newsroom/id/3190117, Jan 2016

49. Gelb, Michael J, "Innovate Like Edison: The Five-Step System for Breakthrough Business Success", Plume; Reprint edition, 2008

50. Godbout, Alain, "Filtering Knowledge: Changing Information into Knowledge Assets," Journal of Systemic Knowledge Management, January 1999

51. Greefhorst, Danny and Proper, Erik "Architecture Principles: The Cornerstones of Enterprise Architecture", Springer, 2011

52. Guardian, http://bit.ly/2hJHJav, 2013

53. Henderson, James, "INSIGHT: Why only half of CDOs are poised for success", http://www.computerworld.co.nz/article/597948/insight-why-only-half-cdos-poised-success/, April, 2016

54. Henschen, Doug, "3 Trends Driving Big Data Breakthroughs: A CIO's View", Information Week, July, 2014

55. Henschen, Doug, "5 Priorities For Chief Data Officers," http://ubm.io/1skKZcf, August 2014

56. Hey, Jonathan, "The Data, Information, Knowledge, Wisdom Chain: The Metaphorical link," http://bit.ly/R1tDAz, 2014

57. Hopfgartner, Frank "Smart Information Systems: Computational Intelligence for Real-Life Applications", Springer, 2015

58. Howson, Cindi, "Successful Business Intelligence: Secrets to Making BI a Killer App," McGraw-Hill, 2007

59. Hubbard, Douglas W, "How to Measure Anything: Finding the Value of Intangibles in Business," Wiley, 2014

60. Hubbard, Douglas W, "Everything Is Measurable," http://bit.ly/1UjhuQw, May, 2007

61. Hauser, John and Katz, Gerald, "Metrics: You Are What You Measure!", ICRMOT and CIPD, 1998

62. Hurwitz, Judith; Nugent, Alan; Halper, Fern; Kaufman, Marcia, "Big Data for Dummies", Wiley, 2013

63. Inmon, William H, "Advanced Topics in Information Engineering", QED Information Sciences, January 1989

64. Irfan, Kamal, "Metrics Are Easy; Insight Is Hard," Harvard Business Review, September 24, 2012

65. Isaacson, Walter, "Steve Jobs", Simon & Schuster, 2013

66. Jain, Piyanka and Sharma, Puneet "Behind Every Good Decision: How Anyone Can Use Business Analytics to Turn Data into Profitable Insights", AMACOM, 2014

67. Jeston, John and Nelis, Johan "Business Process Management", Routledge, 2008

68. Johnston, Norm "Adaptive Marketing: Leveraging Real-Time Data to Become a More Competitive and Successful Company", Palgrave Macmillan, 2015

69. Jugulum, Rajesh, "Competing with High Quality Data", Wiley, March 2014

70. Kahneman, Daniel, "Thinking, Fast and Slow", Farrar, Straus and Giroux ,April 2013

71. Keen, Andrew, "Digital Vertigo: How Today's Online Social Revolution Is Dividing, Diminishing, and Disorienting Us," St. Martin's Griffin, 2013

72. Kimball, Ralph; Ross, Margy ; Thornthwaite, Warren; Mundy, Joy ; Becker, Bob, "The Data Warehouse Lifecycle Toolkit", Wiley, 2011

73. Kotter, John, "Leading Change: Why Transformation Efforts Fail," Harvard Business Review, January 2007

74. Kubler-Ross, Elisabeth and David Kessler, "On Grief and Grieving: Finding the Meaning of Grief Through the Five Stages of Loss", Scribner's & Company, 2005

75. Lai, Anajali, "Synthesis Is In", http://blogs.forrester.com/anjali_lai/14-12-16-synthesis_is_in, December 2014

76. Lake, Peter and Drake, Robert, "Information Systems Management in the Big Data Era", Springer, 2015

77. Laney, Doug, "3D Management: Controlling Data Volume, Velocity and Variety", Meta Group, February 2001

78. Laney, Doug, "Failing to Monetize Data? You Can Bank on It.", http://blogs.gartner.com/doug-laney/failing-to-monetize-data-you-can-bank-on-it/, November 2016

79. Latham, Gary P, Budworth, Marie-Helene , "The study of work motivation in the 20th century", Series in Applied Psychology, 2007

80. Lee, Lara and Sobol, Daniel, "What Data Can't Tell You About Customers," Harvard Business Review, August 27, 2012

81. Levy, Jeremy, "Enterprises Don't Have Big Data, They Just Have Bad Data," http://tcrn.ch/2iWcfM5, July 2015

82. Loshin, David, "Evaluating the business impacts of Poor Data Quality", 2010

83. Luellig, Lorrie and Frazier, Jake, " COBIT Approach to Regulatory Compliance and Defensible Disposal," http://bit.ly/2hGUajT,2013

84. Kalakota, Ravi and Robinson, Marcia, "E-Business: Roadmap for Success", Addison-Wesley, 1999

85. Maar, Bernard, "Big Data: Using SMART Big Data, Analytics and Metrics To Make Better Decisions and Improve Performance", Wiley, 2015

86. McAfee, Andrew and Brynjolfsson, Erik, "Big Data: The Management Revolution", Harvard Business Review, October 2012

87. Magnone, Paul, "Big Data: The Goldilocks Paradox," http://bit.ly/2hGSU0j, 2013

88. Maydanchik, Arkady, "Data Quality Assessment," Technics Publications, May 2007

89. Manyika, James; Chui, Michael; Brown, Brad; Bughin, Jacques; Dobbs, Richard; Roxburgh, Charles; Hung Byers; Angela, "Big data: The next frontier for innovation, competition, and productivity," McKinsey Global Institute (MGI),May 2011

90. McKenna , Brian, "Jeanne Harris: Successful business analytics combines data and intuition," http://bit.ly/1ma5bvt, September 2014

91. Mildeberger, Hubertus, "Business Integration", IBM, 2013

92.

93. Noyes, Katherine, "Hottest job? Data scientists say they're still mostly digital 'janitors'," http://bit.ly/25nw6Ye, March 2016

94. Olavsrud, Thor , "Even Data-Driven Businesses Should Cultivate Intuition," http://bit.ly/1ns0rzo, June, 2014

95. Olavsurd, Thor, "IDC says big data spending to hit $49.6 billion," http://bit.ly/1iVzy7N, 2015

96. Pohlmann, Tom and Thomas, Mary, "Relearning the Art of Asking Questions," Harvard Business Review, March 2015

97. Porter, Michael and Miller, Victor, "How Information Gives You Competitive Advantage," Harvard Business Review, August 1985

98. Porter, Michael, "Competitive Advantage: Creating and Sustaining Superior Performance," Free Press, 1998

99. Prosci, "Seven Principles of Effective Change Management," http://bit.ly/2iGSUz6

100.Provost, Foster and Tom Fawcett, "Data Science for Business: What You Need to Know about Data Mining and Data-Analytic Thinking," O'Reilly Media, 2013

101.Redman, Thomas, "Data Driven: Profiting from Your Most Important Business," Harvard Business Review Press, August 2008

102.Redman, Tom, "Data Quality Should Be Everyone's Job," Harvard Business Review, May 2016

103.Ries, Eric, "The Lean Startup: How Today's Entrepreneurs Use Continuous Innovation to Create Radically Successful Businesses", Crown Business,2011

104.   Robertson, Susan, "Clover Leaf website will let consumers track the source of their fish", The Globe and Mail ,October 2016

105.Ross, Judith, "How to Ask Better Questions," Harvard Business Review, May 2009

106.Rubin, Howard, "Technology Economics: The Cost of Data," http://ubm.io/2iZjgPZ, August 2011

107.Office of the CIO, "Reference Architecture — Department of Defense," June 2010

108.Saran, Cliff, "Companies must rethink data sharing, says GE CEO Jeff Immelt," http://bit.ly/1lk4OXK, 2013

109.Saves Antony, "Firms need data stewards to optimise business initiatives", http://bit.ly/2lffAqm, January 2008

110.Savitz, Eric," Defensible Disposal: You Can't Keep All Your Data Forever", http://bit.ly/2kyGsTp, July 2012

111.Schein, Edgar, "Organizational Culture and Leadership", Jossey-Bass, 2004

112.Sheina, Madan. "Best practices for evaluating data quality tools." Ovum, August 2010.

113.Smith, Howard and Fingar, Peter, "Business Process Management — the third wave," Meghan Kiffer, 2006

114.Silver, Nate, "The Signal and the Noise: Why So Many Predictions Fail-but Some Don't", Penguin Press, 2013

115.Solis, Brain, "Who Owns Digital Transformation? According To A New Survey, It's Not The CIO", http://www.forbes.com/sites/briansolis/2016/10/17/who-owns-digital-transformation-according-to-a-new-survey-its-the-cmo/#277d741e5a0c,Oct 2016

116.Soubra, Diya, "The 3Vs that define Big Data", http://bit.ly/1izIQzk, July 2012

117.Southekal, Prashanth, "Implementing the Stakeholder based Goal-Question-Metric (GQM) Measurement Model for Software Projects," Trafford Publications, 2014

*118.*Stevens, Stanley, "On the Theory of Scales of Measurement." Science, 1946.

119.Strassmann, Paul A, "What is Alignment? Alignment is The Delivery of the Required Results," Cutter IT Journal, August 1998

120.Terpeluk, Larissa ; Majid, Moss; Sid Adelman, Abai, "How to Improve Data Quality," InformIT, July 22, 2005

121.TOGAF, "Architecture Principles," http://bit.ly/2iH0jOX

122.Tonidandel, Scott; King, Eden; Cortina, Jose, "Big Data at Work: The Data Science Revolution and Organizational Psychology," Routledge Publications, 2015

123.Troster, Heiko, "Misleading Statistics — The Potential for Statistical Misuse of Data in the Digital Age" http://bit.ly/2hJWg5J, August 2016

124.Vijayan, Jaikumar, "Solving the Unstructured Data Challenge", http://www.cio.com/article/2941015/big-data/solving-the-unstructured-data-challenge.html, June 2015

125.Vlaskovits, Patrick, "Henry Ford, Innovation, and That "Faster Horse" Quote", Harvard Business Review, August 2011

126.Vogt, Eric, "The Art of Asking Powerful Questions," http://bit.ly/2hGTv29, 2016

127.Wang, Richard; Kon, Henry; Madnick, Stuart, "Data Quality Requirement Analysis and Modelling," TDQM, 1992

128.Wegener, Rasmus and Sinha, Velu, "The value of Big Data: How analytics differentiates winners," Bain & Company, 2013

129.Weinberger, Mark , "Cutting through the noise: how can leaders combat short-termism today?", https://go.ey.com/2bsi166, Oct 2016

130.West, Matthew, "Developing High Quality Data Models," Morgan Kaufmann, 2011

131.Whitehorn, Mark, and Marklyn, Bill, "Inside Relational Databases," Springer Verlag, 2001

132.Williamson, Jason "Getting a Big Data Job For Dummies", Wiley, 2015

133.Woodie, Alex, "How Do You Value Information?", http://bit.ly/2kixtXW, September 2016

134. "Information Systems Used", http://bit.ly/2iW4lCb

Appendix C: Abbreviations

- ABC - Antecedent, Behavior, Consequence
- ABAC - Attribute Based Access Control
- ACID - Atomicity, Consistency, Isolation, Durability
- ADKAR - Awareness, Desire, Knowledge, Ability, Reinforcement
- AIDC - Automatic Identification and Data Capture
- ANSI - American National Standards Institute
- API - Application Programming Interface
- ARTS - Association for Retail Technology Standards
- B2B - Business to Business
- BA - Business Analytics
- BI - Business Intelligence
- CDO - Chief Data Officer
- CIO - Chief Information Officer
- CMMI - Capability Maturity Model Integration
- COBIT - Control Objectives for Information and Related Technologies
- COTS - Commercial-off-the-shelf
- CRM - Customer Relationship Management
- CRUD - Create, Read, Update and Delete
- DAMA - Data Management Association
- DBMS - Database Management System
- DIKW - Data, Information, Knowledge, and Wisdom
- DLP - Data Loss Prevention
- DMBOK - Data Management Body of Knowledge
- DMMM - Data Management Maturity Model
- DR - Disaster Recovery
- DV - Data Visualization

- EAI - Enterprise Application Integration
- EAV - Entity Attribute Model
- EDGB - Enterprise Data Governance Board
- EDI - Electronic Data Interchange
- ERP - Enterprise Resource Planning
- ETL - Extract, Transform, and Load (ETL)
- GQM - Goal Question Metric
- GTIN - Global Trade Item Number
- HDFS - Hadoop Distributed File System
- HIPAA - Health Insurance Portability and Accountability Act
- ISO - International Organization for Standardization
- IT - Information Technology
- ITIL - IT Infrastructure Library
- IoT - Internet of Things
- KDD - Knowledge Discovery in Databases
- KPI - Key Performance Indicator
- LoB - Line of Business
- MDC - Manual Data Capture
- MDM - Master Data Management
- ML - Machine Learning
- NIST - National Institute of Standards and Technology
- NLP - Natural Language Processing
- OLTP - Online Transaction Processing
- OLAP - Online Analytical Processing
- PCI DSS - Payment Card Industry Data Security Standard
- PIDX - Petroleum Industry Data Exchange
- PIPEDA - Personal Information Protection and Electronic Documents Act of Canada
- PDPA - Personal Data Protection Act of Singapore
- PoS - Point of Sale
- RA - Reference Architecture

- RBAC - Role Based Access Control
- ROI - Return on Investment
- SaaS - Software as a Service
- SCADA - Supervisory Control And Data Acquisition
- SIN - Social Insurance Number
- SLA - Service Level Agreement
- SMAC - Social media, Mobile, Analytics and Cloud
- SOC - Service Organization Controls
- SoD - System of Differentiation
- SoE - System of Engagement
- SoI - System of Innovation
- SoR - System of Record
- SOX – Sarbanes -Oxley Act
- SPOF - Single Point of Failure
- SQL - Structured Query Language
- SSAE - Statement on Standards for Attestation Engagements
- TCO - Total Cost of Ownership
- TDWI - The Data Warehousing Institute
- TOGAF - The Open Group Architecture Framework
- UNSPSC - United Nations Standard Products and Services Code
- UoM - Unit of Measure
- VSM - Value Stream Mapping
- YARN - Yet Another Resource Negotiator

Appendix D: Glossary

ACID model. A model applied to data for atomicity, consistency, isolation, and durability.

Aggregation. Collecting data from various databases for the purpose of data processing or analysis.

Algorithm. A mathematical formula placed in software that performs analysis on a set of data.

Analytics. Use of software-based algorithms and statistics to derive insights from data.

API (Application Program Interface). A set of programming standards and instructions for accessing or building web-based software applications.

Automatic identification and capture (AIDC). A method of automatically identifying and collecting data on items, and then storing the data in a computer system. For example, a scanner might collect data about a product being shipped via an RFID chip.

Big data. A term for data sets that is so large or complex that traditional data processing applications are inadequate to deal with them.

Business intelligence (BI). The general term used for the identification, extraction, and analysis of data.

Cassandra. A popular choice of columnar database for use in big data applications. It is an open source database managed by The Apache Software Foundation.

CDO. The Chief Data Officer is the senior executive who bears responsibility for the firm's enterprise-wide data and information strategy, governance, control, policy development, and effective exploitation. The CDO's role will combine accountability and responsibility for information protection and privacy, information governance, data quality and data lifecycle management, along with the exploitation of data assets to create business value.

Cloud computing. A broad term that refers to any Internet-based application or service that is hosted remotely.

Cube. A data structure in OLAP systems. It is a method of storing data in a multidimensional form, generally for reporting purposes. In OLAP cubes, data (measures) are categorized by dimensions. OLAP cubes are often pre-summarized across dimensions to drastically improve query time over relational databases.

Dashboard. A graphical reporting of data visually at a high level, to give managers a quick report on status or performance.

Data. A set of values of qualitative or quantitative variables.

Data analytics. The application of software to derive information or meaning from data. The end result might be a report, an indication of status, or an action taken automatically based on the information received.

Data broker. A business that aggregates information from a variety of sources; processes it to enrich, cleanse or analyze it; and licenses it to other organizations as data products.

Data custodian. The person responsible for the database structure and the technical environment, including the storage of data.

Data democratization. The notion of making data available directly to workers throughout an organization, as opposed to having that data delivered to them by another party, often IT, within the organization.

Data governance. A set of processes or rules that ensure the integrity of the data and that data management best practice are met.

Data element. Any data structure that can organize and hold data. It can be a database, tables, or fields.

Data lake. A storage repository that holds a vast amount of raw data in its native format, including structured and unstructured data. The data structure and requirements are not defined until the data is needed.

Data integration. It is the process of combining data from different sources and presenting it in a single view.

Data integrity. The measure of trust an organization has in the accuracy, completeness, timeliness, and validity of the data.

Data mart. The access layer of a data warehouse used to provide data to users.

Data mining. The process of deriving patterns or knowledge from large data sets.

Data model. Defines the structure of the data for the purpose of communicating between functional and technical people, to show data needed for business processes, or for communicating a plan to develop how data is stored and accessed among application development team members.

Data profiling. Data profiling is the process of collecting statistics and information about data in an existing data repository.

Data quality. The measure of data to determine its worthiness for decision making, planning, or operations.

Data science. A discipline that incorporates statistics, data visualization, computer programming, data mining, machine learning, and database engineering to solve complex problems.

Data security. The practice of protecting data from destruction or unauthorized access.

Data steward. A person who is responsible for the management and oversight of an organization's data assets, and providing business users with high-quality data that is easily accessible in a consistent manner.

Data visualization. A software tool that provides visual abstraction of data for deriving meaning or communicating information more effectively.

Data virtualization. A term used to describe any approach to data management that allows an application to retrieve and manipulate data without requiring technical details about the data, such as how it is formatted or where it is physically located.

Data warehouse (DWH). A database that stores data for the purpose of reporting and analysis.

Database. A digital collection of data and the structure around which the data is organized. The data is typically entered into and accessed via a database management system (DBMS).

Database management system (DBMS). Software that collects and provides access to data in a structured format.

Enterprise resource planning (ERP). ERP is a software system that allows an organization to coordinate and manage all its resources, information, and business functions.

Entropy. A process in which order or quality deteriorates with the passage of time.

Exploratory data analysis. An approach to data analysis focused on identifying general patterns in data, including outliers and features of the data that are not anticipated by the experimenter's current knowledge or preconceptions. EDA aims to uncover underlying structure, test assumptions, detect mistakes, and understand relationships between variables.

Extract, transform, and load (ETL). A process used in data warehousing to prepare data for use in reporting or analytics.

Gartner. A multinational research and advisory firm providing information technology related insight for IT and other business leaders.

GQM (Goal - Question - Metric). A performance management framework. In GQM, you first identify a goal that you would like to achieve, formulate a set of questions whose answers are pertinent to achieving that goal, and then devise a set of metric(s) to help answer each question and accomplish the goal.

Hadoop. An open-source software framework administered by the Apache Software Foundation to facilitate distributed processing of large data sets across clusters of computers.

Infographic. A visual representation of data or information intended to present details quickly and clearly. Infographics improve cognition by utilizing graphics to enhance the human visual system's ability to see patterns and trends.

Internet of Things (IoT). The network of physical objects or "things" embedded with electronics, software, sensors, and connectivity. These "things" deliver greater value and service by exchanging data with the manufacturer, operator, and other connected devices. Each thing is uniquely identifiable through its embedded computing system but is able to interoperate within the existing internet infrastructure.

Machine learning. The use of algorithms to allow a computer to analyze data for the purpose of "learning" what action to take when a specific pattern or event occurs.

Master data management (MDM). Master data is any non-transactional data that is critical to the operation of a business — for example, customer or supplier data, product information, or employee data. MDM is the process of managing that data to ensure consistency, quality, and availability.

Metadata. Any data used to describe other data — for example, a data file's size or date of creation.

Namespace. Namespace uniquely identifies a set of names so that there is no ambiguity when technical objects (programs, data elements, and so on) having different origins but the same names are mixed together.

Natural language processing (NLP). The ability of a computer program or system to understand human language. Applications of natural language processing include enabling humans to interact with computers using speech, automated language translation, and deriving meaning from unstructured data such as text or speech data.

NoSQL. A class of database management system that do not use the relational model. NoSQL is designed to handle large data volumes that do not follow a fixed schema and this is usually unstructured data. The most popular NoSQL database is Apache Cassandra.

Online analytical processing (OLAP). The process of analyzing multidimensional data using three operations: consolidation (the aggregation of available), drill-down (the ability for users to see the underlying details), and slice and dice (the ability for users to select subsets and view them from different perspectives).

Online transactional processing (OLTP). The process of providing users with access to large amounts of transactional data in a way that they can derive meaning from it.

Pattern recognition. Classification or labeling of an identified pattern in the machine learning process.

Performance management. The process of monitoring system or business performance against predefined goals to identify areas that need attention.

Predictive analytics. Using statistical functions on one or more datasets to predict trends or future events.

Privacy. The need and/or requirement to control access to and dissemination of sensitive, personal, and personally identifiable information in an organization's data stores.

Reference data. Data that reflects the business categorization.

Report. The presentation of information derived from a query against a dataset, usually in a predetermined format.

Schema. The structure that defines the organization of data in a database system.

Statistically significant. The likelihood that a relationship between two or more variables is caused by something other than random chance.

Structured data. Data that is organized by a predetermined structure.

Structured query language (SQL). A programming language designed specifically to manage and retrieve data from a relational database system.

System of record (SoR). The authoritative data source for a given data element. To ensure data integrity in the enterprise, there must be one — and only one — system of record for a given data element.

Taxonomy. The science of naming, describing, and classifying according to a pre-determined system — normally into hierarchical relationships. The resulting catalog is used to provide a conceptual framework for discussion, analysis, or information retrieval.

Text analytics. The application of statistical, linguistic, and machine learning techniques on text-based sources to derive meaning or insight.

Transactional data. Data describing a business event; usually described with verbs. Transaction data always has a time dimension. Examples include accounts payable and receivable data, or data about product shipments.

Unstructured Data. Data that has no identifiable structure.

Index